CALIFORNIA'S

Best

CALIFORNIA'S

Best

TWO CENTURIES OF
GREAT WRITING FROM
THE GOLDEN STATE

FARCOUNTRY
PRESS

HELENA, MONTANA

PETER FISH

edited by

The author would like to thank Jessica Solberg, Eric Hanson,
Theresa Rush, Caroline Patterson, and Kathy Springmeyer
of Farcountry Press for their enthusiasm, expertise, and patience
in shepherding this book from dream to reality.

ISBN 10: 1-56037-494-2
ISBN 13: 978-1-56037-494-7

© 2009 Farcountry Press

See a complete list of reprint credits on page 339.

Adair, Virginia Hamilton. "Mojave Evening." *Ants on the Melon.* Copyright 1996 by Virginia Hamilton Adair. Used by permission of Random House, Inc.

Caen, Herb. *Only in San Francisco.* Copyright 1960 by Herb Caen. Used by permission of Doubleday, a division of Random House, Inc.

Doerr, Harriet. "Low Tide at Four." *The Tiger in the Grass.* Copyright 1995 by Harriet Doerr. Used by permission of Viking Penguin, a division of Penguin Group (USA) Inc.

Miller, Max. *I Cover the Waterfront.* Copyright 1932 by E. P. Dutton and Company, Inc. Used by permission of Dutton, a division of Penguin Group (USA) Inc.

Mosley, Walter. *Devil in a Blue Dress.* Copyright 1990 by Walter Mosley. Used by permission of W. W. Norton and Company, Inc.

Stegner, Wallace. *Angle of Repose.* Copyright 1971 by Wallace Stegner. Used by permission of Doubleday, a division of Random House, Inc.

Steinbeck, John. *The Grapes of Wrath.* Copyright 1939, renewed 1967 by John Steinbeck. Used by permission of Viking Penguin, a division of Penguin Group (USA) Inc.

Wolff, Tobias. "Desert Breakdown, 1968." *Our Story Begins: New and Selected Stories.* Copyright 2008 by Tobias Wolff. Used by permission of Alfred A. Knopf, a division of Random House. Inc.

For more information on our books, write Farcountry Press,
P.O. Box 5630, Helena, MT 59604; call (800) 821-3874;
or visit www.farcountrypress.com.

Library of Congress Cataloging-in-Publication Data

California's best : two centuries of great writing from the Golden State / edited by Peter Fish.
    p. cm.
  Includes bibliographical references.
  ISBN 978-1-56037-494-7
  1. American literature--California. 2. California--Literary collections. I. Fish, Peter, 1954-
  PS571.C2C273 2009
  810.8'09794--dc22

                        2009015123

Created, produced, and designed in the United States.
Printed in United States.

15   14   13   12   11   10   09   1   2   3   4   5   6   7

*For Nancy, an immigrant to California,
and for Joseph, a native*

CONTENTS

Introduction x

THE PACIFIC

Richard Henry Dana Jr.
  Selection from *Two Years Before the Mast* 3
Jack London
  Selection from *The Sea Wolf* 11
J. Smeaton Chase
  "The Malibu: No Trespassing," from *California Coast Trails:
  A Horseback Ride from Mexico to Oregon* 19
Robinson Jeffers
  "November Surf," from *The Selected Poetry of Robinson Jeffers*. . 24
  "Point Joe," from *The Selected Poetry of Robinson Jeffers* 25
Max Miller
  Selection from *I Cover the Waterfront* 27
Harriet Doerr
  "Low Tide at Four," from *The Tiger in the Grass* 30
Dana Gioia
  "Cruising with the Beachboys," from *Daily Horoscope* 33
Daniel Duane
  Selection from *Caught Inside: A Surfer's
  Year on the California Coast* 35

THE MOUNTAINS

Louise Amelia Knapp Smith Clapp (Dame Shirley)
  "Letter Tenth, A Trip into the Mines," from *The Shirley Letters:
  From the California Mines, 1851–1852* 47
Joaquin Miller
  "The Gold that Grew by Shasta Town," from
  The Complete Poetical Works of Joaquin Miller 54

CONTENTS

Clarence King
"Mount Whitney 1871," from
Mountaineering in the Sierra Nevada 59

John Muir
"The Sequoia and General Grant National Parks," from
Our National Parks 73

Judy Van der Veer
Selection from *November Grass* 81

Wallace Stegner
Selection from *Angle of Repose* 85

Gary Snyder
"John Muir on Mt. Ritter," from *The Gary Snyder Reader* 96
"Hay for the Horses," from *The Gary Snyder Reader* 97
"Mid-August at Sourdough Mountain Lookout," from
The Gary Snyder Reader 98

THE VALLEYS

William Lewis Manly
Selection from *Death Valley in '49* 103

Robert Louis Stevenson
"Napa Wine," from *The Silverado Squatters* 108

Frank Norris
Selection from *The Octopus* 113

Mary Austin
Selection from *The Land of Little Rain* 129

John Steinbeck
Selection from *The Grapes of Wrath* 136

Wilma McDaniel
"1939 in California," from *The Last Dust Storm* 147
"Valley Fog," from *Sister Vayda's Song* 149
"The Long Wait," from *A Primer for Buford* 150
"Watching Truck Drivers at Pancake House," from
A Primer for Buford 151

CONTENTS

Joan Didion
   "Notes from a Native Daughter," from
   Slouching Toward Bethlehem 153
Gary Soto
   "The Elements of San Joaquin," from
   Gary Soto: New and Selected Poems 165

SAN FRANCISCO BAY

Mark Twain
   "Early Rising, As Regards Excursions to the Cliff House" 173
Bret Harte
   "San Francisco (From the Sea)," from
   The Poetical Works of Bret Harte 180
Ina Coolbrith
   "Copa de Oro, " from *Songs from the Golden Gate* 183
   "From Russian Hill" 184
Mary Edith Griswold
   "Three Days Adrift" 187
George Sterling
   "The Cool, Grey City of Love" 195
Gertrude Atherton
   Selection from *Adventures of a Novelist* 198
Herb Caen
   "Miracle in October," from *Only in San Francisco* 206
Anne Lamott
   "The Town Where I Live," from *Hard Laughter* 210
Amy Tan
   "Rules of the Game," from *The Joy Luck Club*.............. 222
Ron Hansen
   "My Communist" 235
Robert Hass
   "After the Winds," from *Time and Materials* 242

CONTENTS

SOUTHERN CALIFORNIA

Helen Hunt Jackson
  Selection from *Ramona* 247
Charles Nordhoff
  Selection from *California: For Health, Pleasure,*
  and Residence—A Book for Travellers and Settlers 259
Walter Mosley
  Selection from *Devil in a Blue Dress* 264
Tobias Wolff
  "Desert Breakdown, 1968," from
  Our Story Begins: New and Selected Stories 273
Virginia Hamilton Adair
  "Mojave Evening," from *Ants on the Melon* 299
Tom McNeal
  "Winter in Los Angeles" 301
Jenny Price
  Selection from "Thirteen Ways of Seeing Nature in L.A." 325

Bibliography and Reprint Credits 339

◟ *Peter Fish*

INTRODUCTION

THIS IS A BOOK OF CALIFORNIA LITERATURE, but let's start with a scene from California, the physical place. Say you've taken a day trip out to Santa Cruz Island, off the Southern California coast. After a few hours of looking for elephant seals, you head back toward Santa Barbara Harbor. From the boat's deck you see the Santa Barbara Channel, always choppier than you expect, and the spidery forms of the channel's offshore oilrigs. Ahead of you runs the white strip of sand that marks the shoreline, then the red roofs of Santa Barbara and the wall of mountains rising behind the city.

Much about the view is modern: the oil platforms, the Hobie Cat sailboats cutting across the waves in front of you, the buzz of traffic on US 101 as you near shore. But something essential is timeless: ocean, land, sky, sun. The sense, very strong here, of being someplace set apart. "It was a beautiful day, and so warm that we wore straw hats, duck trousers, and all the summer gear," Richard Henry Dana Jr. wrote when he arrived in January of 1835.

Dana had sailed here from Boston, a Harvard boy attempting to gain health and a little adventure by signing on as a common seaman aboard the brig *Pilgrim*. At times during the six-month voyage around Cape Horn, he must have thought he'd made a mistake. He was an ill-prepared sailor, and *Pilgrim*'s captain was brutal. There were floggings, and one man fell overboard and drowned. Now, at last, after 150 days at sea, the *Pilgrim*'s sailors made their first California landfall. As they did, Dana admired the beauty of Santa Barbara's natural setting: "The town is certainly finely situated, with a bay in front, and an amphitheater of hills behind." He marked this new world's distance from the world he knew. "Well, Dana," the second mate called to him, "this does not look much like Harvard college, does it?" It did not.

Dana returned to Boston and in 1840 published his *Two Years Before the Mast,* which became for most Americans a first introduction to the distant, Mexican-ruled land that was California. Dana went on to become an expert in maritime law and a diplomat. Yet at the end of his life he was said to regret that his youthful memoir of a voyage to California outshone all his other accomplishments. His regrets, too, hit on something essential about California: it has a way of putting other places in its shadow.

In these pages you will find forty-one writers, starting with Dana in mid-nineteenth-century California and ending with Jenny Price in modern-day Los Angeles. They include poets and novelists and journalists. All but Dana were or are residents. One writer (Joaquin Miller) was convicted of being a horse thief. One was a Nobel laureate (John Steinbeck). Many are well known, and some are not but should be.

The anthology is organized by region. California's regions exert unusual power, which is why at various times citizens have tried to break up the state into smaller pieces: north and south, coast and inland. You can consider these movements hare-brained without denying that they've hit on an underlying truth. The California you experience in Laguna Beach is a world away from the one you see in Lone Pine. Berkeley exists in a different universe from Alturas. The writing from each place is different, too.

So we start with the Pacific, following Dana to the Santa Barbara coast and Jack London across San Francisco Bay, riding with the indefatigable British traveler J. Smeaton Chase up through the Malibu that existed long before beach hotties and gazillion-dollar homes. Then the mountains: the Sierra Nevada, limned in poetry by Gary Snyder; the Cascades, serenaded by Joaquin Miller; and San Diego County's Cuyamacas, painted by rancher and writer Judy Van der Veer. The valleys: Sacramento, San Joaquin, Owens, and Death. We finish with California's two larger-than-life metropolitan areas: San Francisco and the Bay Area—from Bret Harte's ode to a San Francisco "indifferent to fate" to contemporary poet Robert Hass's subtly uneasy Berkeley—and Los Angeles and Southern California.

It is a lot of territory to cover—a lot of people, a lot of years. Any anthology is subjective. You want to include everything but end up choosing what you most love. Some of this book's selections were chosen both because I thought they were great writing and because they reminded me with such pleasurable power of my own personal California. Take Mark Twain's carriage ride out to San Francisco's Cliff House, where the fog was so thick that all he could see were the horses' ears. I live now down the hill from the Cliff House and can report that the neighborhood's fogs remain as thick, although now people steer their cars through the murk by keeping an eye on the taillights ahead of them. Harriet Doerr's luminous recollection of afternoons on an Orange County beach make me remember my childhood afternoons, Dana Gioia's "Cruising with the Beachboys" my own teenage driving, fast and with the radio on.

Still. As I scattered pages across the dining room table, something unexpected happened. I realized I was compiling an informal portrait of California: a mosaic, in words, of a complicated state.

What do you notice when you read a century-and-a-half worth of California writers? The initial impression is that, unlike other parts of the West, the essential California story is not one of deprivation but one of plenty. This is not to say that life here cannot exact a brutal toll. William Manly's memoir of his passage across Death Valley in 1849 is harrowing. So is Mary Edith Griswold's account of her flight from earthquake-stricken San Francisco in 1906.

But what strikes you most is that California is beautiful, and California is bountiful. John Muir and Clarence King explored the Sierra Nevada with an almost adolescent sense of glee; nobody had ever seen anything like these big mountains, like these big trees. Ina Coolbrith on the California poppy, George Sterling on San Francisco, his "Cool, Grey City of Love"—these are love poems to a place. So is Herb Caen's evocation of the joys of October in San Francisco—which, again speaking from personal experience, does go far in making up for its foggy Augusts. California's beauty can be primal, as with Robinson Jeffers's "November Surf." It can be austere, as with Mary Austin's "The Land of Little Rain", and Virginia Hamilton Adair's "Mojave Evening." But it is beautiful.

It is also rich. Between 1849 and 1869, miners withdrew an estimated $250,000,000 worth of gold from the Sierra Nevada foothills. Mining booms gave California a weakness for get-rich-quick schemes, but also a looseness, a humor that bubbles up in Louise Clapp's account of a Feather River gold camp. A century-plus later, Wallace Stegner looks at a quicksilver mining town in the Santa Cruz Mountains with the long view of both a novelist and a historian, pondering the process by which Easterners become Californians.

California farmland proved the equal of California mines. Robert Louis Stevenson followed a woman to California, married her, and honeymooned in the Napa Valley. In *The Silverado Squatters,* he shares a charming account of early California wine-making; today the state's vineyards support an $18 billion industry. So seductive was California's agrarian wealth that it could derail writers' attempts at social criticism. Helen Hunt Jackson intended her novel *Ramona* to be a blistering criticism of the mistreatment of Southern California's Mission Indians. Instead, people across the country read her accounts of life on a sun-kissed rancho and thought, I want to move there. They did, first by the thousands, then by the millions.

That's the other thing these writers make you see. With its wealth and beauty, California became the place where America, indeed the world, came to find their dreams. One could argue that all of the West is like that. But no place drew as many dreamers as fast and for so long as the Golden State. They came to recover from illness, as you see in Charles Nordhoff's boosterish *California: For Health, Pleasure, and Residence.* They came from the South to work in Los Angeles's defense plants, as does Walter Mosley's private detective, Easy Rawlins. They came because California is where stars are made: Tobias Wolff's Mark drives across the desert to become a comedian, and Tom McNeal's Marcy hopes for a job with Steven Spielberg. They came—and they come, still—from China, as do the families in Amy Tan's *The Joy Luck Club*; from Mexico, as does the family in Gary Soto's "The Elements of San Joaquin"; and from Poland, as does Ron Hansen's sweet, befuddled Catholic priest.

So many people—36 million now—and so many dreams, all in one state. That's the true California story. How can one place accommodate so many hopes, and what happens when they collide? Frank Norris's San Joaquin Valley is fertile, but also bitterly contested; *The Octopus* climaxes with a murderous battle between wheat farmers and the forces of the Southern Pacific Railroad. Decades later, John Steinbeck came to the same San

Joaquin Valley to research and write *The Grapes of Wrath,* which memorably damns the state for turning its back on newcomers who want to share in its abundance. Population growth turns small towns, nostalgically recalled, into faceless suburbs; Joan Didion writes of her Sacramento Valley: "All that is constant about the California of my childhood is the rate at which it disappears." In "Thirteen Ways of Seeing Nature in L.A.," Jenny Price notes that the city has turned its namesake river into a concrete-lined highway for toxins. Sometimes, glorious California mocks the fallen human beings who live here. In *Hard Laughter,* Anne Lamott writes of her Marin County home: "In this town of almost unspeakable physical beauty, our boredom and conceit has bred the worst sort of self-righteous paranoia."

But that's on a bad day. The title of Lamott's novel is, after all, *Hard Laughter,* and along with the paranoia she shows us the sheer joy of being here. It's never wise to be too gloomy about California; the state always retains the ability to surprise. Poet Wilma McDaniel endured the hardscrabble farm life Steinbeck wrote about in *The Grapes of Wrath.* Yet poems like "Watching Truck Drivers at Pancake House" make you laugh out loud. So does Max Miller's account of grunion, those small, shining, and outlandish fish, splashing up on the beach in San Diego. And some dreams come true. Gertrude Atherton survives a disrupted childhood to become a famous novelist. Daniel Duane becomes a surfer.

I finished compiling this book while visiting my father in the house I grew up in. The house sits near the ocean about thirty miles south of where Richard Henry Dana Jr. first landed. When I walked down to the beach, I couldn't quite see Dana's landing spot—it's blocked by the mountains above Rincon Point—but I could see the Pacific that brought him here. It was, in fact, January, and although I didn't have Dana's straw hat and duck trousers—think t-shirt and shorts—it was as fine a winter day as he encountered. On a warm January day, California still feels special—a place that contains so many dreams and so many possibilities, and so many good stories waiting for you to read them.

Peter Fish was born in Santa Barbara, California, and grew up in Ventura. He received a B.A. in history from Yale University, where he focused on the history of the American West. He was a Mirrielees Fellow in creative writing at Stanford University and a Hoyns Fellow in fiction at the University of Virginia. He has written and edited for Sunset Magazine *for many years and is currently* Sunset's *editor-at-large. He lives in San Francisco with his wife, Nancy, and son, Joseph.*

THE PACIFIC

❧ *Richard Henry Dana Jr.*

Selection from *Two Years Before the Mast*

C ALIFORNIA EXTENDS ALONG NEARLY the whole of the western coast of Mexico, between the Gulf of California in the south and the Bay of San Francisco on the north, or between the 22d and 38th degrees of north latitude. It is subdivided into two provinces,—Lower or Old California, lying between the gulf and the 32d degree of latitude, or near it (the division line running, I believe, between the bay of Todos Santos and the port of San Diego), and New or Upper California, the southernmost port of which is San Diego, in lat. 32° 39', and the northernmost, San Francisco, situated in the large bay discovered by Sir Francis Drake, in lat. 37° 58', and now known as the Bay of San Francisco, so named, I suppose, by Franciscan missionaries. Upper California has the seat of its government at Monterey, where is also the custom-house, the only one on the coast, and at which every vessel intending to trade on the coast must enter its cargo before it can begin its traffic. We were to trade upon this coast exclusively, and therefore expected to go first to Monterey, but the captain's orders from home were to put in at Santa Barbara, which is the central port of the coast, and wait there for the agent, who transacts all the business for the firm to which our vessel belonged.

The bay, or, as it was commonly called, the *canal* of Santa Barbara, is very large, being formed by the main land on one side (between Point Conception on the north and Point Santa Buenaventura on the south), which here bends in like a crescent, and by three large islands opposite to it and at the distance of some twenty miles. These points are just sufficient to give it the name of a bay, while at the same time it is so large and so much exposed to the southeast and northwest winds, that it is little better than an open roadstead; and the whole swell of the Pacific Ocean rolls in here before a southeaster, and breaks with so heavy a surf in the shallow waters, that it is highly dangerous to lie near in to the shore during the southeaster season, that is, between the months of November and April.

This wind (the southeaster) is the bane of the coast of California. Between the months of November and April (including a part of each), which is the rainy season in this latitude, you are never safe from it; and accordingly, in the ports which are open to it, vessels are obliged, during these months, to lie at anchor at a distance of three miles from the shore, with slip-ropes on their cables, ready to slip and go to sea at a moment's warning. The only ports which are safe from this wind are San Francisco and Monterey in the north, and San Diego in the south.

As it was January when we arrived, and the middle of the southeaster season, we came to anchor at the distance of three miles from the shore, in eleven fathoms water, and bent a slip-rope and buoys to our cables, cast off the yard-arm gaskets from the sails, and stopped them all with rope-yarns. After we had done this, the boat went ashore with the captain, and returned with orders to the mate to send a boat ashore for him at sundown. I did not go in the first boat, and was glad to find that there was another going before night; for after so long a voyage as ours had been, a few hours seem a long time to be in sight and out of reach of land. We spent the day on board in the usual duties; but as this was the first time we had been without the captain, we felt a little more freedom, and looked about us to see what sort of a country we had got into, and were to pass a year or two of our lives in.

It was a beautiful day, and so warm that we wore straw hats, duck trousers, and all the summer gear. As this was midwinter, it spoke well for the climate; and we afterwards found that the thermometer never fell to the freezing point throughout the winter, and that there was very little difference between the seasons, except that during a long period of rainy and southeasterly weather, thick clothes were not uncomfortable.

The large bay lay about us, nearly smooth, as there was hardly a breath of wind stirring, though the boat's crew who went ashore told us that the long ground-swell broke into a heavy surf on the beach. There was only one vessel in the port—a long, sharp brig of about three hundred tons, with raking masts, and very square yards, and English colors at her peak.

We afterwards learned that she was built at Guayaquil, and named the Ayacucho, after the place where the battle was fought that gave Peru her independence, and was now owned by a Scotchman named Wilson, who commanded her, and was engaged in the trade between Callao and other parts of South America and California. She was a fast sailer, as we frequently afterwards saw, and had a crew of Sandwich-Islanders on board. Beside this vessel, there was no object to break the surface of the bay. Two points ran out as the horns of the crescent, one of which—the one to the westward— was low and sandy, and is that to which vessels are obliged to give a wide berth when running out for a southeaster; the other is high, bold, and well wooded, and has a mission upon it, called Santa Buenaventura, from which the point is named. In the middle of this crescent, directly opposite the anchoring ground, lie the Mission and town of Santa Barbara, on a low plain, but little above the level of the sea, covered with grass, though entirely without trees, and surrounded on three sides by an amphitheatre of mountains, which slant off to the distance of fifteen or twenty miles. The Mission stands a little back of the town, and is a large building, or rather collection of buildings, in the centre of which is a high tower, with a belfry of five bells. The whole, being plastered, makes quite a show at a distance, and is the mark by which vessels come to anchor. The town lies a little nearer to the beach,—about half a mile from it,—and is composed of one-story houses built of sun-baked clay, or *adobe,* some of them white-washed, with red tiles on the roofs. I should judge that there were about a hundred of them; and in the midst of them stands the Presidio, or fort, built of the same materials, and apparently but little stronger. The town is finely situated, with a bay in front, and an amphitheatre of hills behind. The only thing which diminishes its beauty is, that the hills have no large trees upon them, they having been all burnt by a great fire which swept them off about a dozen years ago, and they had not yet grown again. The fire was described to me by an inhabitant, as having been a very terrible and magnificent sight. The air of the whole valley was so heated that the people were obliged to leave the town and take up their quarters for several days upon the beach.

Just before sundown, the mate ordered a boat's crew ashore, and I went as one of the number. We passed under the stern of the English brig, and had a long pull ashore. I shall never forget the impression which our first landing on the beach of California made upon me. The sun had just gone down; it was getting dusky; the damp night-wind was beginning to blow, and the heavy swell of the Pacific was setting in, and breaking in loud and high "combers" upon the beach. We lay on our oars in the swell, just outside of the surf, waiting for a good chance to run in, when a boat, which had put off from the Ayacucho, came alongside of us, with a crew of dusky Sandwich-Islanders, talking and hallooing in their outlandish tongue. They knew that we were novices in this kind of boating, and waited to see us go in. The second mate, however, who steered our boat, determined to have the advantage of their experience, and would not go in first. Finding, at length, how matters stood, they gave a shout, and taking advantage of a great comber which came swelling in, rearing its head, and lifting up the sterns of our boats nearly perpendicular, and again dropping them in the trough, they gave three or four long and strong pulls, and went in on top of the great wave, throwing their oars overboard, and as far from the boat as they could throw them, and, jumping out the instant the boat touched the beach, they seized hold of her by the gunwale, on each side, and ran her up high and dry upon the sand. We saw, at once, how the thing was to be done, and also the necessity of keeping the boat stern out to the sea; for the instant the sea should strike upon her broadside or quarter, she would be driven up broadside on, and capsized. We pulled strongly in, and as soon as we felt that the sea had got hold of us, and was carrying us in with the speed of a race-horse, we threw the oars as far from the boat as we could, and took hold of the gunwales, ready to spring out and seize her when she struck, the officer using his utmost strength, with his steering-oar, to keep her stern out. We were shot up upon the beach, and, seizing the boat, ran her up high and dry, and, picking up our oars, stood by her, ready for the captain to come down.

Finding that the captain did not come immediately, we put our oars in the boat, and, leaving one to watch it, walked about the beach to see what we could of the place. The beach is nearly a mile in length between the two points, and of smooth sand. We had taken the only good landing-place, which is in the middle, it being more stony toward the ends. It is about twenty yards in width from high-water mark to a slight bank at which the soil begins, and so hard that it is a favorite place for running horses. It was growing dark, so that we could just distinguish the dim outlines of the two vessels in the offing; and the great seas were rolling in in regular lines, growing larger and larger as they approached the shore, and hanging over the beach upon which they were to break, when their tops would curl over and turn white with foam, and, beginning at one extreme of the line, break rapidly to the other, as a child's long card house falls when a card is knocked down at one end. The Sandwich-Islanders, in the mean time, had turned their boat round, and run her down into the water, and were loading her with hides and tallow. As this was the work in which we were soon to be engaged, we looked on with some curiosity. They ran the boat so far into the water that every large sea might float her, and two of them, with their trousers rolled up, stood by the bows, one on each side, keeping her in her right position. This was hard work; for beside the force they had to use upon the boat, the large seas nearly took them off their legs. The others were running from the boat to the bank, upon which, out of the reach of the water, was a pile of dry bullocks' hides, doubled lengthwise in the middle, and nearly as stiff as boards. These they took upon their heads, one or two at a time, and carried down to the boat, in which one of their number stowed them away. They were obliged to carry them on their heads, to keep them out of the water and we observed that they had on thick woollen caps. "Look here, Bill, and see what you're coming to!" said one of our men to another who stood by the boat. "Well, Dana," said the second mate to me, "this does not look much like Harvard College, does it? But it is what I call *'head work.'*" To tell the truth, it did not look very encouraging.

After they had got through with the hides, the Kanakas laid hold of the bags of tallow (the bags are made of hide, and are about the size of a common meal-bag), and lifted each upon the shoulders of two men, one at each end, who walked off with them to the boat, when all prepared to go aboard. Here, too, was something for us to learn. The man who steered shipped his oar and stood up in the stern, and those that pulled the two after oars sat upon their benches, with their oars shipped, ready to strike out as soon as she was afloat. The two men remained standing at the bows; and when, at length, a large sea came in and floated her, seized hold of the gunwales, and ran out with her till they were up to their armpits, and then tumbled over the gunwales into the bows, dripping with water. The men at the oars struck out, but it wouldn't do; the sea swept back and left them nearly high and dry. The two fellows jumped out again; and the next time they succeeded better, and, with the help of a deal of outlandish hallooing and bawling, got her well off. We watched them till they were out of the breakers, and saw them steering for their vessel, which was now hidden in the darkness.

The sand of the beach began to be cold to our bare feet; the frogs set up their croaking in the marshes, and one solitary owl, from the end of the distant point, gave out his melancholy note, mellowed by the distance, and we began to think that it was high time for "the old man," as a shipmaster is commonly called, to come down. In a few minutes we heard something coming towards us. It was a man on horseback. He came on the full gallop, reined up near us, addressed a few words to us, and, receiving no answer, wheeled round and galloped off again. He was nearly as dark as an Indian, with a large Spanish hat, blanket cloak or serape, and leather leggins, with a long knife stuck in them. "This is the seventh city that ever I was in, and no Christian one neither," said Bill Brown. "Stand by!" said John, "you haven't seen the worst of it yet." In the midst of this conversation the captain appeared; and we winded the boat round, shoved her down, and prepared to go off. The captain, who had been on the coast before, and "knew the ropes," took the steering-oar, and we went off in the same way as the other boat. I, being the youngest, had the pleasure of standing at the bow, and getting wet through. We went off well, though the seas were high. Some of them lifted us up, and, sliding from under us, seemed to let us drop through the air like a flat plank upon the body of the water. In a few minutes we were in the low, regular swell, and pulled for a light, which, as we neared it, we found had been run up to our trysail gaff.

Coming aboard, we hoisted up all the boats, and, diving down into the forecastle, changed our wet clothes, and got our supper. After supper the sailors lighted their pipes (cigars, those of us who had them), and we had to tell all we had seen ashore. Then followed conjectures about the people ashore, the length of the voyage, carrying hides, &c., &c., until eight bells, when all hands were called aft, and the "anchor watch" set. We were to stand two in a watch, and, as the nights were pretty long, two hours were to make a watch. The second mate was to keep the deck until eight o'clock, all hands were to be called at daybreak, and the word was passed to keep a bright lookout, and to call the mate if it should come on to blow from the southeast. We had, also, orders to strike the bells every half-hour through the night, as at sea. My watchmate was John, the Swedish sailor, and we stood from twelve to two, he walking the larboard side and I the starboard. At daylight all hands were called, and we went through the usual process of washing down, swabbing, &c., and got breakfast at eight o'clock. In the course of the forenoon, a boat went aboard of the Ayacucho and brought off a quarter of beef, which made us a fresh bite for dinner. This we were glad enough to have, and the mate told us that we should live upon fresh beef while we were on the coast, as it was cheaper here than the salt. While at dinner, the cook called "Sail ho!" and, coming on deck, we saw two sails bearing round the point. One was a large ship under top-gallant sails, and the other a small hermaphrodite brig. They both backed their topsails and sent boats aboard of us. The ship's colors had puzzled us, and we found that she was from Genoa, with an assorted cargo, and was trading on the coast. She filled away again, and stood out, being bound up the coast to San Francisco. The crew of the brig's boat were Sandwich-Islanders, but one of them, who spoke a little English, told us that she was the Loriotte, Captain Nye, from Oahu, and was engaged in the hide and tallow trade. She was a lump of a thing, what the sailors call a butter-box. This vessel, as well as the Ayacucho, and others which we afterwards saw engaged in the same trade, have English or Americans for officers, and two or three before the mast to do the work upon the rigging, and to be relied upon for seamanship, while the rest of the crew are Sandwich-Islanders, who are active and very useful in boating.

The three captains went ashore after dinner, and came off again at night. When in port, everything is attended to by the chief mate; the captain, unless he is also supercargo, has little to do, and is usually ashore much of his time. This we thought would be pleasanter for us, as the mate was a good-natured man, and not very strict. So it was for a time, but we were worse off in the end; for wherever the captain is a severe, energetic man, and the mate has neither of these qualities, there will always be trouble.

And trouble we had already begun to anticipate. The captain had several times found fault with the mate, in presence of the crew; and hints had been dropped that all was not right between them. When this is the case, and the captain suspects that his chief officer is too easy and familiar with the crew, he begins to interfere in all the duties, and to draw the reins more taut, and the crew have to suffer.

In 1815 Richard Henry Dana Jr. was born into a distinguished Massachusetts family whose members included Dana's grandfather Francis, a delegate to the Continental Congress and later chief justice of the Massachusetts Supreme Court. During his sophomore year at Harvard, Dana contracted a case of measles that seriously damaged his eyesight. Travel was advised, and Dana left college to sign on as a sailor on the brig Pilgrim, *bound for California. The* Pilgrim *sailed from Boston on August 14, 1834; 150 days later, after sailing around Cape Horn, it anchored in Santa Barbara harbor. Other stops were made at Monterey, San Pedro, and San Diego. The trip was a hard one, with the sheltered Dana serving under a captain who was later discharged for brutality. Dana kept a diary, and when he returned to Boston in 1836, it became the inspiration for his book* Two Years Before the Mast *(Harper and Brothers). Published in 1840,* Two Years Before the Mast *was an immediate bestseller, showing readers both the harsh realities of the sailor's life and giving them a vivid portrait of far-off California. Dana returned to Harvard to study law, later becoming an expert on maritime law, an advocate for sailors' rights, and a prominent abolitionist. He died in Rome in 1882.*

Jack London

Selection from *The Sea Wolf*

I SCARCELY KNOW WHERE TO BEGIN, though I sometimes facetiously place the cause of it all to Charley Furuseth's credit. He kept a summer cottage in Mill Valley, under the shadow of Mount Tamalpais, and never occupied it except when he loafed through the winter months and read Nietzsche and Schopenhauer to rest his brain. When summer came on, he elected to sweat out a hot and dusty existence in the city and to toil incessantly. Had it not been my custom to run up to see him every Saturday afternoon and to stop over till Monday morning, this particular January Monday morning would not have found me afloat on San Francisco Bay.

Not but that I was afloat in a safe craft, for the *Martinez* was a new ferry-steamer, making her fourth or fifth trip on the run between Sausalito and San Francisco. The danger lay in the heavy fog which blanketed the bay, and of which, as a landsman, I had little apprehension. In fact, I remember the placid exaltation with which I took up my position on the forward upper deck, directly beneath the pilot-house, and allowed the mystery of the fog to lay hold of my imagination. A fresh breeze was blowing, and for a time I was alone in the moist obscurity—yet not alone, for I was dimly conscious of the presence of the pilot, and of what I took to be the captain, in the glass house above my head.

I remember thinking how comfortable it was, this division of labor which made it unnecessary for me to study fogs, winds, tides, and navigation, in order to visit my friend who lived across an arm of the sea. It was good that men should be specialists, I mused. The peculiar knowledge of the pilot and captain sufficed for many thousands of people who knew no more of the sea and navigation than I knew. On the other hand, instead of having to devote my energy to the learning of a multitude of things, I concentrated it upon a few particular things, such as, for instance, the analysis of Poe's place in American literature—an essay of mine, by the way, in the current *Atlantic*. Coming aboard, as I passed through the cabin, I had noticed with greedy eyes a stout gentleman reading the *Atlantic*, which was open at my very essay. And there it was again, the division of labor, the special knowledge of the pilot and captain which permitted the stout gentleman to read my special knowledge on Poe while they carried him safely from Sausalito to San Francisco.

A red-faced man, slamming the cabin door behind him and stumping out on the deck, interrupted my reflections, though I made a mental note of the topic for use in a projected essay which I had thought of calling "The Necessity for Freedom: A Plea for the Artist." The red-faced man shot a glance up at the pilot-house, gazed around at the fog, stumped across the deck and back (he evidently had artificial legs), and stood still by my side, legs wide apart, and with an expression of keen enjoyment on his face. I was not wrong when I decided that his days had been spent on the sea.

"It's nasty weather like this here that turns heads gray before their time," he said, with a nod toward the pilot-house.

"I had not thought there was any particular strain," I answered. "It seems as simple as A, B, C. They know the direction by compass, the distance, and the speed. I should not call it anything more than mathematical certainty."

"Strain!" he snorted. "Simple as A, B, C! Mathematical certainty!"

He seemed to brace himself up and lean backward against the air as he stared at me. "How about this here tide that's rushin' out through the Golden Gate?" he demanded, or bellowed, rather. "How fast is she ebbin'? What's the drift, eh? Listen to that, will you? A bell-buoy, and we're a-top of it! See 'em alterin' the course!"

From out of the fog came the mournful tolling of a bell, and I could see the pilot turning the wheel with great rapidity. The bell, which had seemed straight ahead, was now sounding from the side. Our own whistle was blowing hoarsely, and from time to time the sound of other whistles came to us from out of the fog.

"That's a ferry-boat of some sort," the newcomer said, indicating a whistle off to the right. "And there! D'ye hear that? Blown by mouth. Some scow schooner, most likely. Better watch out, Mr. Schooner-man. Ah, I thought so. Now hell's a-poppin' for somebody!"

The unseen ferry-boat was blowing blast after blast, and the mouth-blown horn was tooting in terror-stricken fashion.

"And now they're payin' their respects to each other and tryin' to get clear," the red-faced man went on, as the hurried whistling ceased.

His face was shining, his eyes flashing with excitement, as he translated into articulate language the speech of the horns and sirens. "That's a steam siren a-goin' it over there to the left. And you hear that fellow with a frog in his throat—a steam schooner as near as I can judge, crawlin' in from the Heads against the tide."

A shrill little whistle, piping as if gone mad, came from directly ahead and from very near at hand. Gongs sounded on the *Martinez.* Our paddle-wheels stopped, their pulsing beat died away, and then they started again. The shrill little whistle, like the chirping of a cricket amid the cries of great beasts, shot through the fog from more to the side and swiftly grew faint and fainter. I looked to my companion for enlightenment.

"One of them dare-devil launches," he said. "I almost wish we'd sunk him, the little rip! They're the cause of more trouble. And what good are they? Any jackass gets aboard one and runs it from hell to breakfast, blowin' his whistle to beat the band and tellin' the rest of the world to look out for him, because he's comin' and can't look out for himself! Because he's comin'! And you've got to look out, too! Right of way! Common decency! They don't know the meanin' of it!"

I felt quite amused at his unwarranted choler, and while he stumped indignantly up and down I fell to dwelling upon the romance of the fog. And romantic it certainly was—the fog, like the gray shadow of infinite mystery, brooding over the whirling speck of earth; and men, mere motes of light and sparkle, cursed with an insane relish for work, riding their steeds of wood and steel through the heart of the mystery, groping their way blindly through the Unseen, and clamoring and clanging in confident speech the while their hearts are heavy with incertitude and fear.

The voice of my companion brought me back to myself with a laugh. I too had been groping and floundering, the while I thought I rode clear-eyed through the mystery.

"Hello; somebody comin' our way," he was saying. "And d'ye hear that? He's comin' fast. Walking right along. Guess he don't hear us yet. Wind's in wrong direction."

The fresh breeze was blowing right down upon us, and I could hear the whistle plainly, off to one side and a little ahead.

"Ferry-boat?" I asked.

He nodded, then added, "Or he wouldn't be keepin' up such a clip." He gave a short chuckle. "They're gettin' anxious up there."

I glanced up. The captain had thrust his head and shoulders out of the pilot-house, and was staring intently into the fog as though by sheer force of will he could penetrate it. His face was anxious, as was the face of my companion, who had stumped over to the rail and was gazing with a like intentness in the direction of the invisible danger.

Then everything happened, and with inconceivable rapidity. The fog seemed to break away as though split by a wedge, and the bow of a steamboat emerged, trailing fog-wreaths on either side like seaweed on the snout of Leviathan. I could see the pilot-house and a white-bearded man leaning partly out of it, on his elbows. He was clad in a blue uniform, and I remember noting how trim and quiet he was. His quietness, under the circumstances, was terrible. He accepted Destiny, marched hand in hand with it, and coolly measured the stroke. As he leaned there, he ran a calm and speculative eye over us, as though to determine the precise point of the collision, and took no notice whatever when our pilot, white with rage, shouted, "Now you've done it!"

On looking back, I realize that the remark was too obvious to make rejoinder necessary.

"Grab hold of something and hang on," the red-faced man said to me. All his bluster had gone, and he seemed to have caught the contagion of preternatural calm. "And listen to the women scream," he said grimly—almost bitterly, I thought, as though he had been through the experience before.

The vessels came together before I could follow his advice. We must have been struck squarely amidships, for I saw nothing, the strange steamboat having passed beyond my line of vision. The *Martinez* heeled over, sharply, and there was a crashing and rending of timber. I was thrown flat on the wet deck, and before I could scramble to my feet I heard the scream of the women. This it was, I am certain,—the most indescribable of blood-curdling sounds,—that threw me into a panic. I remembered the life-preservers stored in the cabin, but was met at the door and swept backward by a wild rush of men and women. What happened in the next few minutes I do not recollect, though I have a clear remembrance of pulling down life-preservers from the overhead racks, while the red-faced man fastened them about the bodies of an hysterical group of women. This memory is as distinct and sharp as that of any picture I have seen. It is a picture, and I can see it now,—the jagged edges of the hole in the side of the cabin, through which the gray fog swirled and eddied; the empty upholstered seats, littered with all the evidences of sudden flight, such as packages, hand satchels, umbrellas, and wraps; the stout gentleman who had been reading my essay, encased in cork and canvas, the magazine still in his hand, and asking me with monotonous insistence if I thought there was any danger; the red-faced man, stumping gallantly around on his artificial legs and buckling life-preservers on all comers; and finally, the screaming bedlam of women.

This it was, the screaming of the women, that most tried my nerves. It must have tried, too, the nerves of the red-faced man, for I have another picture which will never fade from my mind. The stout gentleman is stuffing the magazine into his overcoat pocket and looking on curiously. A tangled mass of women, with drawn, white faces and open mouths, is shrieking like a chorus of lost souls; and the red-faced man, his face now purplish with wrath, and with arms extended overhead as in the act of hurling thunderbolts, is shouting, "Shut up! Oh, shut up!"

I remember the scene impelled me to sudden laughter, and in the next instant I realized I was becoming hysterical myself; for these were women of my own kind, like my mother and sisters, with the fear of death upon them and unwilling to die. And I remember that the sounds they made reminded me of the squealing of pigs under the knife of the butcher, and I was struck with horror at the vividness of the analogy. These women, capable of the most sublime emotions, of the tenderest sympathies, were open-mouthed and screaming. They wanted to live, they were helpless, like rats in a trap, and they screamed.

The horror of it drove me out on deck. I was feeling sick and squeamish, and sat down on a bench. In a hazy way I saw and heard men rushing and shouting as they strove to lower the boats. It was just as I had read descriptions of such scenes in books. The tackles jammed. Nothing worked. One boat lowered away with the plugs out, filled with women and children and then with water, and capsized. Another boat had been lowered by one end, and still hung in the tackle by the other end, where it had been abandoned. Nothing was to be seen of the strange steamboat which had caused the disaster, though I heard men saying that she would undoubtedly send boats to our assistance.

I descended to the lower deck. The *Martinez* was sinking fast, for the water was very near. Numbers of the passengers were leaping overboard. Others, in the water, were clamoring to be taken aboard again. No one heeded them. A cry arose that we were sinking. I was seized by the consequent panic, and went over the side in a surge of bodies. How I went over I do not know, though I did know, and instantly, why those in the water were so desirous of getting back on the steamer. The water was cold—so cold that it was painful. The pang, as I plunged into it, was as quick and sharp as that of fire. It bit to the marrow. It was like the grip of death. I gasped with the anguish and shock of it, filling my lungs before the life-preserver popped me to the surface. The taste of the salt was strong in my mouth, and I was strangling with the acrid stuff in my throat and lungs.

But it was the cold that was most distressing. I felt that I could survive but a few minutes. People were struggling and floundering in the water about me. I could hear them crying out to one another. And I heard, also, the sound of oars. Evidently the strange steamboat had lowered its boats. As the time went by I marvelled that I was still alive. I had no sensation whatever in my lower limbs, while a chilling numbness was wrapping about my heart and creeping into it. Small waves, with spiteful foaming crests, continually broke over me and into my mouth, sending me off into more strangling paroxysms.

The noises grew indistinct, though I heard a final and despairing chorus of screams in the distance and knew that the *Martinez* had gone down. Later,—how much later I have no knowledge,—I came to myself with a start of fear. I was alone. I could hear no calls or cries—only the sound of the waves, made weirdly hollow and reverberant by the fog. A panic in a crowd, which partakes of a sort of community of interest, is not so terrible as a panic when one is by oneself; and such a panic I now suffered. Whither was I drifting? The red-faced man had said that the tide was ebbing through the Golden Gate. Was I, then, being carried out to sea? And the life-preserver in which I floated? Was it not liable to go to pieces at any moment? I had heard of such things being made of paper and hollow rushes which quickly became saturated and lost all buoyancy. And I could not swim a stroke. And I was alone, floating, apparently, in the midst of a gray primordial vastness. I confess that a madness seized me, that I shrieked aloud as the women had shrieked, and beat the water with my numb hands.

How long this lasted I have no conception, for a blankness intervened, of which I remember no more than one remembers of troubled and painful sleep. When I aroused, it was as after centuries of time; and I saw, almost above me and emerging from the fog, the bow of a vessel, and three triangular sails, each shrewdly lapping the other and filled with wind. Where the bow cut the water there was a great foaming and gurgling, and I seemed directly in its path. I tried to cry out, but was too exhausted. The bow plunged down, just missing me and sending a swash of water clear over my head. Then the long, black side of the vessel began slipping past, so near that I could have touched it with my hands. I tried to reach it, in a mad resolve to claw into the wood with my nails, but my arms were heavy and lifeless. Again I strove to call out, but made no sound.

The stern of the vessel shot by, dropping, as it did so, into a hollow between the waves; and I caught a glimpse of a man standing at the wheel, and of another man who seemed to be doing little else than smoke a cigar. I saw the smoke issuing from his lips as he slowly turned his head and glanced out over the water in my direction. It was a careless, unpremeditated glance, one of those haphazard things men do when they have no immediate call to do anything in particular, but act because they are alive and must do something.

But life and death were in that glance. I could see the vessel being swallowed up in the fog; I saw the back of the man at the wheel, and the head of the other man turning, slowly turning, as his gaze struck the water and casually lifted along it toward me. His face wore an absent expression, as of deep thought, and I became afraid that if his eyes did light upon me he would nevertheless not see me. But his eyes did light upon me, and looked squarely into mine; and he did see me, for he sprang to the wheel, thrusting the other man aside, and whirled it round and round, hand over hand, at the same time shouting orders of some sort. The vessel seemed to go off at a tangent to its former course and leapt almost instantly from view into the fog.

I felt myself slipping into unconsciousness, and tried with all the power of my will to fight above the suffocating blankness and darkness that was rising around me. A little later I heard the stroke of oars, growing nearer and nearer, and the calls of a man. When he was very near I heard him crying, in vexed fashion, "Why in hell don't you sing out?" This meant me, I thought, and then the blankness and darkness rose over me.

Jack London was born in San Francisco in 1876 and grew up in Oakland. His family struggled financially; much of London's schooling took place in public libraries. (Among his librarian mentors was poet Ina Coolbrith.) As an adolescent he took jobs in a cannery and on a sealing ship bound for Japan. He became a fervent Socialist and an aspiring but unsuccessful writer. In the winter of 1897, London traveled north to join the Klondike gold rush. The experience gave him the material that would make him famous: on his return to California he began selling stories to publications including The Overland Monthly *and the* Saturday Evening Post, *the latter of which published* The Call of the Wild *(Grosset and Dunlap) in 1903. The next year, London published* The Sea Wolf *(Macmillan), based in part on his experiences aboard the sealing ship. Later books—he would publish more than fifty—included* White Fang *(Macmillan, 1906) and* Martin Eden *(Macmillan, 1909). In 1910 London and his second wife, Charmian, moved to a ranch in Sonoma County, now set aside as Jack London State Historic Park, where he experimented with sustainable agriculture. In 1916 he died of kidney failure—probably exacerbated by alcoholism.*

J. Smeaton Chase

From *California Coast Trails:
A Horseback Ride from Mexico to Oregon*

THE MALIBU: NO TRESPASSING

I WAS ASTIR BY FIRST DAYLIGHT, and was early on the way to the mouth of the cañon. As I reached the top of a little rise, the roar of the sea close by met me with a sort of boisterous friendliness, like the welcome of some tremendous mastiff. Looking eastward from the cliff on which I stood, I could see the long wharf at Santa Monica, and, beyond, a long curve of shore that ran to the Palos Verdes and the promontory of Point Fermin. Beyond that lay the town of San Pedro, detested of Dana, who in 1835 reported it as being "universally called the hell of California," and who himself wrote of it that "This rascally hole of San Pedro is unsafe in every wind but a southwester, which is seldom known to blow more than once in half a century." Now, three quarters of a century later, the "rascally hole" is in process of becoming a great port, with a much wider range of interests than the shipping of "California bank-notes" (as Dana calls the hides which formed the return cargo of the Pilgrim). Turning to the west, my eye followed the long reaches of broken cliff along which ran my road, until the land view was closed by the low yellow cape of Point Dume.

I lingered here a few minutes while I enjoyed the occasion, for here my northern coast trip was actually to begin. It seemed in a modest way momentous to be turning my face northward and westward; and I surveyed in fancy the long leagues of coast which I was to travel, to where, instead of languid dunes and sunburned brush, I should ride by stalwart cliffs and through stately alleys of forest. There was deep pleasure in the prospect. Thoreau says that the southwest was his point of inclination for travel, and enlarges, in his ingenious way, upon the reasons for his preference. For me it is always the northwest that captures my imagination. "The West is but another name for the Wild," Thoreau remarks; and in the same fanciful way the North seems to me somehow to signify the Noble. Was not the Northwest Passage always a natural goal for enterprise and gallantry? Farewell, then, I said, land of the South and sea of the South; and welcome the ultimate West, and the dark, the gray, the solitary North.

My Chino, meanwhile, free from such unpractical abstractions, was employing his leisure with the cliffside herbage. He is an engaging creature, and we had many sentiments, and even conversations, together, sharing confidences upon the quality of the water, or the state of the roads, and other such matters of mutual interest. Automobiles, naturally, were often a topic, and I may say that Chino's views on that subject, which may easily be guessed, were quite my own.

Turning, then, westward, a few miles of pleasant road brought us to the entrance to the Malibu Ranch, a long strip of land lying between the southward-facing foothills of the Santa Monica Mountains and the shore. At the gate was posted a warning that Trespassing was Strictly Prohibited. I knew that public right of way through the ranch had long been contested by the owners, and I had been warned that I might find my way disputed by their myrmidons with shotguns. But there was nothing except the passive placard to prevent my entering, and I passed in with little doubt of making an equally peaceable exit at the western end.

On a limb of a sycamore that overhung the road a large cross was roughly cut. It marks the place of one of the many commonplace tragedies of early California days. Some horsethief, name now unknown, was hanged there. Perhaps it would be better to say, some alleged horsethief, for mistakes no doubt occurred on occasions when somebody had to hang, and quickly, too; and when Justice, playing a sort of hide-and-seek, might let her sword fall suddenly upon any member of the free-and-easy community, who was so unwise as to get in the way.

The hard sand beach here offered a tempting road along the water's edge, and I turned Chino down to it. He was a little averse at first to facing the burst of the rollers and stepping into the hissing froth, but he soon caught the idea, and with arched neck and gay bearing splashed through the wash of the breakers, and kicked the creamy fans of water into sparkling showers.

I had seen only one or two people on the road that day, and it seemed as if we were quite the only trespassers, until I saw a mass of whitish objects approaching and heard a new sound mingling with the lazy booming of the sea. As we came nearer I saw that it was a band of sheep, which were being driven along the beach by a mounted Mexican, aided by dogs. It seemed odd to see these pastoral creatures marching composedly along on Neptune's frontier, nibbling at seaweed, their voices rising in plaintive *crescendo* above the recitative of the surf.

A splendid ram walked with immense dignity at the head of the flock, his long fleece quivering as he stepped, like that great beard of the Prophet by which good Mussulmans swear. The herder rode behind on a lively broncho. We stopped to pass a few words, and I learned that he and his band had come down the coast over a hundred miles, and were bound for the neighborhood of San Juan Capistrano, nearly as far still to the south. The mention of my own destination excited his pity.

"Ah! it makes much cold there. I have heard that it rains always; is it not true?"

I explained that it was not quite so bad as that; but he still gazed at me with compassion, and rejoined with a shrug,—

"Huy! not to see ever the sun! And the fruits and the good wine do not grow there! Huy! such a country! I should not like it."

His sheep had left him far behind while we talked, and he now said *Adios,* and turned to overtake them. But as he rode away he still shook his head over the thought of a country where it rained always, and the good wine could not grow.

The promontory of Point Dume, like a flattened turret, stands well out to the south about midway of the Malibu. Here the road bent inland for a mile or two, but soon again came down to the shore. Frequent cañons, each of them carrying a small stream of water, broke the seaward slope of the mountains. Evening was drawing near when I found myself at the Trancas Cañon, at the mouth of which lies a small brackish lagoon. Here I found a good camping-place under a great tent-like sycamore. Orioles supplied my supper with music; and a night of balmy airs, with the drowsy rumble of breakers not a hundred yards away, rounded off a highly pleasant day.

The first sound of the morning was the wild cry of gulls as they quarrelled over breakfast. As I ate my solitary flapjacks I was half inclined to wish that it had been possible for me also to quarrel with somebody; but the presence of Chino, grazing hard by, allayed the loneliness for me, as I hope mine did for him. We were early on our march, following the shore under a bright morning sun. I could see, a few miles out, a white steamer making eastward, and waved my good-morning to the passengers who, I took for granted, were gazing toward me, though not exactly at me, from over the side.

The road lay alternately along the beach and the cliff, where yuccas bloomed plentifully among the brush. These white-burnoosed Arabs looked out of place standing here within stone's throw of the ocean, and their exotic scent mingled strangely with the sharp tang of seaweed. Now we pushed through thickets of head-high mustard that dusted us with yellow; next, sunflowers stared at us eye to eye; and again, lavender sage refreshed us with fugitive dashes of perfume. The rattle of machinery came faintly to me, and I could see the mower and his team creeping along high up on the hillside a mile away. It was far too heavenly a day for one to be in a hurry, and I dismounted and removed Chino's bridle, leaving him at liberty to saunter and graze while I sauntered and praised. Only here and there a clump of thorny cactus obtruded a suggestion of evil. I suppose that cactus may have been unknown before the Fall.

One of the compensations to be set against the lack of a companion was that I was free to stop or proceed, hurry or delay, camp here or there, entirely at my own choice (only having regard to my horse's needs as to forage). So when, early in the afternoon, I came to an attractive little stream that ran in a deep cañon filled with sycamores and wind-blown oaks, I paused and considered. The brook chattered happily over the rocks of the beach until it met the sea, like the sudden cutting-off of the life of a child. Close by it was a triangle of clean sand, littered with driftwood; and near at hand there was a space of good fodder. It is not always that things arrange themselves so propitiously: I could make camp not twenty yards from the very verge of the ocean. The opportunity was not to be missed. I got my little tent pitched in spite of a strong breeze which showered me with flying sand; and then spent a lazy afternoon in the society of the gulls, my loquacious little brook, and the indolent roar of breakers.

The wind increased during the evening to a point that made a camp-fire something more than a luxury; so I started a noble blaze and humbly emulated the poet with his "Fire of Driftwood." I found, too, that my little shelter, like his "farmhouse old . . . gave to the sea-breeze, damp and cold, an easy entrance."

Sand makes one of the least desirable of sleeping places, and all night I was consciously or subconsciously aware of the thunder of the waves close by. Once or twice I heard the spray rattling like hail on the tent, or the hiss of the sea-froth as it washed far up on the beach and then sank away into the sand. I had picketed Chino in a more sheltered spot fifty yards away, and, blanketed warmly, I think he passed the night quite as comfortably as his master.

I was up at four o'clock, and broke camp early. The breeze was strong and keen, and an inexhaustible freshness was in the air, as if the world had been created within the week. Gulls and pelicans were fishing busily, and on the horizon two faint smudges marked where steamers were passing. After a few miles more of alternate shore and cliff, we crossed the line into Ventura County, and at the same time bade adieu to the Malibu and its cantankerous but futile placards.

*Born in England in 1865, Joseph Smeaton Chase moved to the United States at age twenty-five and settled in California, living for a time in the Cuyamaca Mountains of San Diego County. He was later employed as a social welfare worker in Los Angeles, but his true passion was the exploration of his adopted state. An excellent horseman, he trekked through California tirelessly, documenting his travels in three books—*Yosemite Trails *(Houghton Mifflin, 1911),* California Desert Trails *(Houghton Mifflin, 1919), and* California Coast Trails *(Houghton Mifflin, 1913)—the last of which tells the story of his epic journey from Southern California to the Oregon border in the company of his horse, Chino. Chase moved to the Palm Springs area in 1915; he died in Banning, California, in 1923.*

Robinson Jeffers

From *The Selected Poetry of Robinson Jeffers*
NOVEMBER SURF

Some lucky day each November great waves awake and are drawn
Like smoking mountains bright from the west
And come and cover the cliff with white violent cleanness: then suddenly
The old granite forgets half a year's filth:
The orange-peel, egg-shells, papers, pieces of clothing, the clots
Of dung in corners of the rock, and used
Sheaths that make light love safe in the evenings: all the droppings of the
　　summer
Idlers washed off in a winter ecstasy:
I think this cumbered continent envies its cliff then. . . . But all seasons
The earth, in her childlike prophetic sleep,
Keeps dreaming of the bath of a storm that prepares up the long coast
Of the future to scour more than her sea-lines:
The cities gone down, the people fewer and the hawks more numerous,
The rivers mouth to source pure; when the two-footed
Mammal, being someways one of the nobler animals, regains
The dignity of room, the value of rareness.

From *The Selected Poetry of Robinson Jeffers*
POINT JOE

Point Joe has teeth and has torn ships; it has fierce and solitary beauty;
Walk there all day you shall see nothing that will not make part of a poem.

I saw the spars and planks of shipwreck on the rocks, and beyond the
    desolate
Sea-meadows rose the warped wind-bitten van of the pines, a fog-bank
    vaulted

Forest and all, the flat sea-meadows at that time of year were plated
Golden with the low flower called footsteps of the spring, millions of
    flowerets,

Whose light suffused upward into the fog flooded its vault, we wandered
Through a weird country where the light beat up from earthward, and was
    golden.

One other moved there, an old Chinaman gathering seaweed from the
    sea-rocks,
He brought it in his basket and spread it flat to dry on the edge of the
    meadow.

Permanent things are what is needful in a poem, things temporally
Of great dimension, things continually renewed or always present.

Grass that is made each year equals the mountains in her past and future;
Fashionable and momentary things we need not see nor speak of.

Man gleaning food between the solemn presences of land and ocean,
On shores where better men have shipwrecked, under fog and among
    flowers,

Equals the mountains in his past and future; that glow from the earth was
    only
A trick of nature's, one must forgive nature a thousand graceful subtleties.

Robinson Jeffers was born near Pittsburgh, Pennsylvania, in 1887, the son of a theology professor. At age sixteen, he moved with his family to Los Angeles and enrolled at Occidental College; he graduated in 1905. Jeffers attempted graduate studies in forestry and medicine before deciding to become a poet; he published his first collection, Flagons and Apples *(Grafton), in 1912. While at the University of Southern California he began an affair with Una Call Kuster, the wife of a local attorney and the woman who would become Jeffers's wife and his muse. In 1914 Jeffers and Kuster moved up the coast to the village of Carmel, on Monterey Bay. Here Jeffers built his stone retreat, Tor House, and began writing poetry inspired by Monterey Bay and the rugged coast of Big Sur. His major collections include* Roan Stallion, Tamar and Other Poems *(Boni and Liveright, 1925),* The Women at Point Sur *(Liveright, 1927),* The Selected Poetry of Robinson Jeffers *(Stanford University Press, 1927),* Cawdor and Other Poems *(Liveright, 1928),* Dear Judas and Other Poems *(Liveright, 1929),* Thurso's Landing *(Liveright, 1932), and* Give Your Heart to the Hawks *(Random House, 1933). His translation of Euripedes's* Medea *played successfully on Broadway in 1947. His final collection,* Hungerfield and Other Poems *(Random House), was published in 1954. Jeffers died in 1962.*

✿ *Max Miller*

Selection from *I Cover the Waterfront*

W E HAVE FISH WHICH COME ASHORE here and can be gathered off the beach for eating. But I hesitate to mention them because such phenomena usually occur in the Southern Hemisphere, in the South Seas, in the interior of Africa, far away where only explorers are allowed to report on them.

Yet I do not recall ever having read of similar fish in those countries, and the schoolboy natives there may be interested in learning what is in my own front yard of an ocean. For all of the ocean as far as I can see is my estate, and the vessels moving along the horizon of the estate belong to me, too. They are moving along out there merely for me to watch them.

This also is true of the fish which come ashore on certain nights. On these nights I am a Biblical character. I am living three thousand years ago. The fish are being sent to me as a demonstration that perhaps, after all, there is some sort of God who wants to convert me into a disciple. But the demonstration is not strong enough, and I remain a doubter. Even when the fish shower into the sand by the thousands I still remain a doubter. For the fish may as well come ashore as remain out where they are, and apparently I am hard to please.

These fish are grunion, built much after the order of fair-sized sardines. Grunion belong to the smelt family, yet grunion and smelt are not the same. Unfortunately for the grunion, their arrivals on the beach can be predicted with the accuracy of a time-table. The spring tides, which accompany the full and dark of the moon, are the time-tables by which the grunion runs can be predicted. And unless the grunion watch out they soon may be exterminated as punishment for their own regularity. Nothing on this earth should be as regular as grunion and still hope to survive.

The grunion arrive on the third or fourth nights following the full of the moon and the dark of the moon. For about an hour after the turn of the tide these little fish flop about on the beach. The female digs tail-first into the sand depositing her eggs, which the male fertilizes as he lies arched around her. To be sure, the female makes an undignified show of herself. She spins about on her tail as though indifferent to what other fish may think of her. This is her night, her big minute away from her home the ocean, and she behaves as if drunk. She behaves this way until the figurative stroke of twelve when another wave carries her and her man back to sea where they belong.

The succeeding tides bury the eggs more deeply into the sand where they lie until dug out two weeks later by the next series of high tides. At this time the eggs hatch and the tiny fish are washed into the ocean. Their life has been going on like this for a good many fish-generations now, and their family tree was blackened by the scandal of many beach parties long before the coming of Cabrillo to this sunny coast. But the grunion never will learn to hunt new shorelines distant from the reach of automobiles of this city, and for this reason the grunion-run has turned into an entertainment which I no longer sit up to watch.

On grunion-run night the beach is not the lonely beach of most nights. Instead, the sands are illuminated by fires each few yards. People by the dozens have arrived to turn the ocean, my ocean, into theatricals. And if I had the power to call out to the grunion not to come ashore on these nights I would do so. I would call as loudly as I could. And on some other night when the people were all gone I would whisper to the grunion: "It's all right now. You may come in."

But of course the grunion do arrive, and they arrive on schedule. First a few arrive, and the people begin to scream in their excitement. They have not had fish come right up to them before like this, and in the heat of the chase the people forget about their shoes and their clothing. They follow the fish back into the surf. They capture the fish with their bare hands and with hand-nets and with common window-screen. They jab the screen down into the sand between the grunion and the sea. The ebbing surf rushes through the screen, but the grunion is caught by it and held for capture.

When the run is over, men walk away with grunion by the buckets. And when too many are caught for eating, the surplus is thrown away.

Being the waterfront reporter my job includes writing the story predicting the next grunion runs. But lately I have been growing mighty careless about this assignment. Mighty, mighty careless. The fish-and-game warden knows of my carelessness, but so far he has not told.

Max Miller was born in Traverse City, Michigan, in 1899. He attended the University of Washington, worked as a reporter for the Everett (WA) Daily News, *and then took a job as the waterfront reporter for the* San Diego Sun. *In 1932 a collection of his newspaper columns was published in the book* I Cover the Waterfront *(E. P. Dutton). It became a bestseller, inspiring a Claudette Colbert film and a hit song recorded by Louis Armstrong and Billie Holiday, among others. Miller went on to publish some twenty additional books, many of them about Southern California. During World War II and the Korean War, he served as a writer for the U.S. Naval Department of Public Information. He died in 1967.*

Harriet Doerr

From *The Tiger in the Grass*
LOW TIDE AT FOUR

WHAT I REMEMBER OF THOSE SUMMERS at the beach is that every afternoon there was a low tide at four.

I am wrong, of course. Memory has outstripped reality. But before me as I write, in all its original colors, is a scene I painted and framed and now, almost fifty years later, bring to light.

HERE, THEN, IS A CALIFORNIA BEACH IN SUMMER, with children, surfers, fishermen, and gulls. The children are seven and three. We are on the sand, a whole family—father, mother, a boy and a girl. The year is 1939. It is noon. There will be a low tide at four.

Days at the beach are all the same. It is hard to tell one from another. We walk down from our house on the side of the hill and stop on the bluff to count the fishermen (five) on the pier and the surfers (three), riding the swells, waiting for their waves. We turn into Mrs. Tustin's pergola restaurant for hamburgers. Though we recognize them as the best in the world, we never eat them under the matted honeysuckle of the pergola. Instead, we carry them, along with towels, buckets, shovels, books, and an umbrella, down the perilous, tilting wooden stairs to the beach. Later we go back to the pergola for chocolate and vanilla cones.

"Ice cream special, cherry mint ripple," says Mrs. Tustin on this particular day, and we watch a fat man lick a scoop of it from his cone. We wait for him to say, "Not bad," or "I'll try anything once," but he has no comment. A long freight train rattles by on the tracks behind the pergola.

As we turn away, Mrs. Tustin says, "The world's in big trouble," and the fat man says, "You can say that again. How about that paperhanger, Adolf?" But it is hard to hear because of the train.

Back on the beach, our heads under the umbrella, we lie at compass points like a four-pointed star. The sun hangs hot and high. Small gusts of wind lift the children's corn-straw hair. We taste salt. Face down, arms wide, we cling to the revolving earth.

Now Mr. Bray, the station agent, a middle-aged Mercury in a shiny suit, crosses the dry sand in his brown oxford shoes. He is delivering a telegram. Everyone listens while I read the message from our best and oldest friends. Sorry, they can't come next weekend after all. Good, we say to ourselves, without shame.

I invite Mr. Bray to join us under the umbrella. "Can't you stay on the beach for a while?" He pauses with sand sifting into his shoes. Oh, no, he has to get back to his trains. He left his wife in charge, and the new diesel streamliner will be coming through.

At this moment a single-seated fighter plane from the navy base north of us bursts into sight along the shore, flying so low it has to climb to miss the pier. The children jump into the air and wave. The pilot, who looks too young for his job, waves back.

"Look at that," says Mr. Bray. "He could get himself killed."

Time and the afternoon are running out. A fisherman reels in a corbina. Three gulls ride the swells under the pier. The children, streaked with wet sand, dig a series of parallel and intersecting trenches into the ebb tide. Their father walks to the end of the pier, dives into a swell, rides in on a wave, and walks out to the end of the pier again. I swim and come back to my towel to read. I swim and read again.

Winesburg, Ohio; Sister Carrie; Absalom, Absalom; Ethan Frome; The Magic Mountain; Studs Lonigan; A Handful of Dust; A Room with a View. There are never books enough or days enough to read them.

I look up from my page. Here is old Mrs. Winfield's car being parked at the top of the bluff. It must be almost four. Her combination driver, gardener, and general manager, Tom Yoshimura, helps her into a canvas chair he has set up in front of the view. His wife, Hatsu, new from Japan, is stringing beans for dinner in Mrs. Winfield's shingled house on the hill.

Hatsu can't speak English. She bows good morning and good afternoon.

Mrs. Winfield has survived everything: her husband's death and the death of a child, earthquakes, floods, and fires, surgical operations and dental work, the accidents and occasional arrests of her grandchildren. All these, as well as intervals of a joy so intense it can no longer be remembered. I watch Tom Yoshimura bring her an ice cream cone from the pergola.

IT IS FOUR O'CLOCK. We are standing in shallow water at low tide. The children dig with their toes and let the waves wash in and out over their feet. They are sinking deeper and deeper. During the summer, their skins have turned every shade of honey: wildflower, orange, buckwheat, clover. Now they are sage. I look into my husband's face. He reaches over their heads to touch my arm.

At this time on this August day in 1939, I call up my interior reserves and gather strength from my blood and bones. Exerting the full force of my will, I command the earth to leave off circling long enough to hold up the sun, hold back the wave. Long enough for me to paint and frame low tide.

Harriet Doerr was born in Pasadena, California, in 1910, the granddaughter of railroad magnate Henry Huntington. She attended Smith College in Massachusetts, but after a year she returned west and enrolled at Stanford University, later explaining that she was homesick and "half in love"—the latter with Stanford engineering student Albert Doerr, whom she left school to marry in 1930. The Doerrs lived in Pasadena for twenty-five years, raising a daughter and a son. In the late 1950s, the couple moved to a village in the Mexican state of Aguascalientes, hoping to revive a copper mine owned by Albert Doerr's family. They remained there until his death in 1972. Doerr later returned to Stanford to finish her B.A. and then studied in the university's graduate creative writing program. It was there that she began the linked stories, based in part on her experiences in Mexico, that became her first book, Stones for Ibarra *(Viking, 1984).* Stones for Ibarra *won the America Book Award, among other honors; it was followed by* Consider This, Señora *(Harcourt Brace, 1993) and* The Tiger in the Grass *(Viking, 1995). Doerr died in Pasadena in 2002.*

✹ *Dana Gioia*

From *Daily Horoscope*
CRUISING WITH THE BEACHBOYS

So strange to hear that song again tonight
Travelling on business in a rented car
Miles from anywhere I've been before.
And now a tune I haven't heard for years
Probably not since it last left the charts
Back in L.A. in 1969.
I can't believe I know the words by heart
And can't think of a girl to blame them on.

Every lovesick summer has its song,
And this one I pretended to despise,
But if I was alone when it came on,
I turned it up full-blast to sing along—
A primal scream in croaky baritone,
The notes all flat, the lyrics mostly slurred.
No wonder I spent so much time alone
Making the rounds in Dad's old Thunderbird.

Some nights I drove down to the beach to park
And walk along the railings of the pier.
The water down below was cold and dark,
The waves monotonous against the shore.
The darkness and the mist, the midnight sea
The flickering lights reflected from the city—
A perfect setting for a boy like me,
The Cecil B. DeMille of my self-pity.

I thought by now I'd left those nights behind,
Lost like the girls that I could never get,
Gone with the years, junked with the old T-Bird.
But one old song, a stretch of empty road,
Can open up a door and let them fall
Tumbling like boxes from a dusty shelf,
Tightening my throat for no reason at all
Bringing on tears shed only for myself.

Dana Gioia was born in Los Angeles in 1950. He earned a B.A. from Stanford University and an M.A. in Comparative Literature from Harvard University before returning to Stanford to earn an M.B.A. Gioia moved to New York and entered the business world, eventually becoming a vice president at General Foods. At the same time, he remained a practicing poet and critic. He published his first volume of poetry, Daily Horoscope *(Graywolf Press), in 1986; it was followed by* The Gods of Winter *(Graywolf Press, 1991) and* Interrogation at Noon *(Graywolf Press, 2001). His collection of essays titled* Can Poetry Matter: Essays on Poetry and American Culture *(Graywolf Press) was published in 1992. From 2003 to 2007 he served as the chairman of the National Endowment for the Arts.*

Daniel Duane

Selection from *Caught Inside: A Surfer's Year
on the California Coast*

UNLESS YOU'RE A STROLLING NATURALIST by nature, or a farmer or commercial fisherman or ranger, you need a medium, a game, a pleasure principle that turns knowing your home into passionate scholarship. City dwellers know nothing about neap tides or the topography of local reefs for the same reason few Americans know a second language: not out of moral or personal weakness but because *it doesn't matter.* I didn't move to the beach to perfect my backside aerial attack (or even just to learn what the hell a backside aerial attack *is*, for that matter); I moved because my need to be in the clear, alive water of my California's Pacific, on a real, honest-to-God surfboard, on a daily basis, had been a source of nagging angst since the first time I'd ridden a wave. And Monterey Bay was all the watery home I could ask for—a big dent in California's coast about seventy miles south of San Francisco Bay. Santa Cruz, an unpretentious college and resort town, crowds the cliffs of its northern lip and ends abruptly at the fields and hills of the open coast. South of Santa Cruz, small towns dot the sheltered bay shore for ten or twelve miles before Salinas Valley farmland stretches clear to the fishing and tourist town of Monterey at the bay's southern lip. As a teaching assistant at the university two days a week, I made enough to rent a room smack in the middle of all that coastline in a two-story shingled house with big gables, green trim, bits of student sculpture strewn among pear and palm trees in the front yard, and a surfboard shed so old it was held together by hand-forged nails. Built as a summer cottage when fields still ran along these cliffs, the house had old-growth redwood interior paneling, making the inside warm and woodsy and pretty off-level here and there. Most of the floors sloped one way or another, none of the doors sat quite right in their jambs, and the whole upstairs swayed gently in high winds. That house could also have used some work: the chimney just a pile of bricks from a recent earthquake, pine floors scuffed bare, black mildew spotting the bathroom ceilings, countless thumbtack holes in the door frames, sluggish drains, no hot water upstairs, and spiders in most of the ceiling corners. But in spite of very low rent, my bedroom had a clear view of the water (the outer bay in one direction, shore break in another) and windows that opened outward like double doors; and with deep reddish-brown walls, floor, ceiling, and even window frames, it felt like a stateroom on an old sailing ship.

I'd lived for the last few years in a town full of familiar faces, near great bookstores, within a few blocks of Thai, Mexican, Tuscan, and Mediterranean restaurants, next door to world-class coffee, and, like I said, in an apartment building also inhabited by eight of my oldest friends. (Nearby ran an interstate commute artery, and in the middle of the night with the city's ambient din quiet the highway made a roaring hiss much like surf.) And those friends mostly nodded with forced enthusiasm when I declared my intention to move to the water; the kind of move everyone will acknowledge *sounds* great, but in a way that lets you know they'd never make such a mistake themselves. But I had no complaints about waking that first Santa Cruz morning on my still-sheetless futon to a fog breeze misting through the curtainless windows, sea lions barking needfully under the municipal pier, and small seas making a soft, light washing sound. Duffel bags of clothes still unpacked, nothing yet hanging on those bedroom walls, licorice herbal tea (I thought it best to quit caffeine at a time of such existential uncertainty) and cereal out on the wooden porch. Green paint all but worn off, floor planks warped and loose, wisteria wrapping up a trellis to the bathroom window—all of a late-summer morning with inland sun just starting to push back the fog. Sat barefoot in the wet grass and read the local paper, even took time out for a front-page story about a PTA meeting. Nodded to an older man—a neighbor I soon got to know better, who had a long blond ponytail and a deeply weathered, handsome face—strolling to the cliff for his daily breath of space. Twenty-seven years old, and I was residing among retirees and the apparently unemployed, without a retail shift or a commute … deep breathing an absolute necessity to ward off vertigo. Exchanged good mornings with a white-haired woman weeding energetically across the street. Emma lived alone, I later learned, and quite happily. She walked on the beach daily at dawn, kept a ferociously tidy garden, drove a cherry-pink '65 Mustang, and entertained regular visits from polite grandchildren.

I flipped over the paper and found, on the weather page, a full-color icon of a surfer next to the words, "Swell small, in the 2–3 foot range at the best spots." But where? Those who know, go; those who don't know, don't go: nobody who knows will tell you where to go, precisely so you won't. And *when* to go, on which tide, which wind and swell direction—well, that's entirely up to you to learn. Every surf town has its obvious breaks, visible from the sidewalk, lined with parking lots, and crowded with thirty lifelong locals during even the faintest hint of surf, but a nonexpert outsider's chances of getting a few are tiny. And greener pastures, less crowded and urban, are hard to find: not on any map, not in any guidebook, and never mentioned in mixed company. Permit a comparison with the other sport I know well: Yosemite's rock climber's campground, six a.m., with sky just lightening behind Half Dome; you're loading the packs while your partner drip-brews a little French Roast and a rail-thin, wild-haired guy in the next tent shoves taped water bottles into a giant canvas haul bag—sure sign of great ambitions. You offer him some coffee, but his thermo-mug is already steaming with Peet's 101 Blend; so you get to chatting, discuss weather predictions, swap anxieties and illegal camping spots, maybe even directions to a secret hot spring. Packs packed, coffee drunk, day not getting any younger, you wish each other good luck and go face your respective makers. Now try somewhere on the Pacific Coast Highway: six a.m. again, damp fog dragging through the redwoods, and you're in line at the AM/PM for lousy coffee and shrink-wrapped cinnamon rolls. You notice a couple of nice-looking guys in uniform: surf-brand sweatpants, fur-lined suede Ugg boots (one of the more distinct surfer fashion items, perfect for cold, damp feet after a long session), Hang Ten revival sweatshirts (produced in the current fetishization of all things early 1960s; "Bitchin' Before You Were Born"), and surf-shop bill caps. New to the area and a little unsure, you ask for suggestions. Do they tell you about the reeling reef across that farm?

Or the secluded beach with a perfect sandbar? Do they warn you about the dangerously shallow water right at the takeoff or tell you the secret is to backdoor the peak before it heaves?

"Nope," the smaller of the two snarls, apparently pained by talking to you, "no idea."

A little surprised, because you *know* you saw the bastard gouging a Fijian reef wave in last month's *Surfer* magazine, you pleasantly ask where they're heading. They barely look at you; the question has stunned them—such presumption! The same guy, whose mother should've taught him better, grumbles sourly, "North." Translation: *If I told you, you might go there, and then I'd have to kill you.* Take photo credits as an index: where climbing, skiing, biking, sailing, diving, and white-water magazines identify every place in every photograph, with detailed travel and camping information, surfing magazines do their level best to disguise them: *Delighted you bought the mag, but please, don't ever come here.* A position I've since learned to appreciate, since good breaks are few and surfers are many, but I could still do without the cannibalism.

Anyway, I diligently washed my plate and cup, loaded my uncle's hand-me-down surfboard and dilapidated wetsuit into the pickup, and headed out for a look. Along eucalyptus-shaded lagoons with rowboats tethered to backyard docks, past funky cottages in big, overgrown lots next to neighborhood beaches, and eventually to a strip of road where small homes with big picture windows faced a mile of bright blue cove. Not much falls in fall in a Mediterranean climate, but this latter part of California's summer, when the inland valleys cool enough for the fog banks to stay at sea and allow the coast a few precious weeks of warm weather, still passes as autumn; the fog now a swirling, blurring cloud far beyond the horde of surfers drifting in the sun. There was a delicious crispness to these mornings, the air cold and bright and briny, the sun low and splashing white off the placid sea as small swell lines rolled under the kelp and left no doubt in any witness's mind that the best things in life are free, or at least don't directly cost money, which is admittedly a little different. And so, apparently, felt the hundred or so idlers along the cliff, neighbors chatting over their late morning coffee on little benches, drunks sobering up with a little Thunderbird, joggers keeping their heads toward the water; and all of them, every single one, watching the slip and glide of those boards along the waves.

A crowd of shirtless teenage boys stood where I'd parked, looking lean and relaxed and very, very healthy. Also a few with shaven heads and mean, beaten-up faces, tattoos, headbands, baggy clothes—*jailin'* with whitey's surfer/skater appropriation of the L.A. Chicano gangster style. Enjoying the abiding pleasure of belonging, jostling, and hooting at passing convertibles, a few smoking cigarettes, others making a show of drinking malt liquor for breakfast. Not the virgin green valley I'd had in mind, all the claims pretty well staked and a few too many improvements for my taste, but I grabbed a pint of orange juice anyway, from a little market/ home of Chinese freeholders in the Western world. Sat on a guardrail and watched two stoned derelicts on the beach below. With a pump-action BB gun, they had cornered a big wharf rat and were flushing him out for the kill, laughing themselves to pieces. While I pulled on my seal costume, a boy in a yellow-and-black wetsuit got out of the water, picked up his board, and waved an anxious hello to the rat hunters. The one with the rifle—a well-built, shirtless tattooed man with small eyes—stared blankly back and chuckled, then looked at his nodding friend and started pumping.

"What you hunting, guys?" asked the boy timorously, as he walked quickly toward the concrete steps. The sidewalk crowd leaned over to watch.

"Oh," said the marksman, "nothing much, Barn," Then he sighted on the boy's retreating ass and fired. The boy yelped, then laughed, then cried a little, then courageously tried to keep on laughing as if the joke were shared.

With an abstracted stare out to sea, I rubbed coconut-scented wax over the deck of my sun-yellowed, six-foot-one-inch twin-finned surfboard. Then I pulled on that rubber superhero outfit (although mine looked less like the latest from Marvel Comics than like an old Captain Nemo deep-sea suit) and scrambled down the foot-worn, makeshift concrete steps with designated handholds and several posted notices advertising surfboard repair. In the open cove below, waves wrapped well around the bay mouth before peeling across these rock reefs—refined, *edited* versions of the Pacific's rough drafts. During the executive hours of ten a.m. to two p.m., most of the kids went to school and the dawn-patrol surf crowd hustled off to work, leaving only the true delinquents loitering on the cliff and a friendly crowd in the water, chatting and splashing, complaining to each other about the crowds. But none of it malicious, which was nice, since I was rusty. Adults, all of them, I noticed: not retirement age, but grown-ups, watching a few pelicans skim the air cushion inches over glassy-smooth, clear water with waist-high walls lifting out of a mirror. "Surfboards, small craft, and animals," writes Willard Bascom, "can take energy out of the waves to propel themselves by sliding down the forward surface of an advancing wave … The trick of surfing, of course, is to get the board moving and the weight properly balanced so that the slope drag can take over the work of propulsion at the moment the wave passes beneath." *Take energy?* But of course. Wave approaching, paddle hard toward its steepest section, turn, and paddle back with it. Feeling the board gliding on its own, hop in one motion from prone to upright, slip down the face, lean to the right, turn up into the wall and laugh out loud at the watery road rising to greet you, step a little forward to speed across the steep spots, drag a finger in the water just to believe it's really happening, and feel the light joy of effortless, combustion-free speed. And then, in the moment of detumescence, flop off the board with—as Bascom would have it—just a little more juice than when you started.

Unless, of course, someone else has jockeyed in front of you and claimed the wave: limited resources, overpopulation, pecking order against you, precisely why honest emigrants took to the Oregon Trail. The tide had dropped enough to lure the hooky-playing teenagers, the boys with grave manhood issues. I'd just ducked out of one's way, and surfaced sneezing water, when I heard a yell aimed at me.

"Hey, kook," said the little blond Apollo, a sharp-nosed and deeply unhappy-looking kid. "Barney … you going to get in the way all day?" (*Kook* being a universal surfing term for the unknown, unimpressive other, and suggesting the ridiculous jerking motions of an incompetent surfer; *Surfer* magazine even runs a regular cartoon about a hapless idiot named Wilbur Kookmeyer. *Barney,* meaning roughly the same thing, seems to derive from Fred Flintstone's little buddy, Barney Rubble.) Apollo was outraged, livid, and, worst of all, he was right. In my time away from the water, I'd forgotten the code, the traffic rules; by my out-of-shape sluggishness, I'd ruined his wave. Nevertheless, his fury struck me as almost comical: aside from the fact that I had about fifty pounds on him, how could he know, in this day and age, that I didn't have a Glock in my car? Something so sweet about the confidence in humanity required to shout at a complete stranger, but before I could suggest that to him, he paddled off shaking his head as though I'd just peed on my own shoes and shouldn't be pitied for it.

In a surf town, nothing makes for a finer proving ground than a good break in broad view of a neighborhood. Apollo performed for the cliff-side audience, attacking waves like an off-road motorcyclist attacks the desert, his eyes full of the rage one associates with schoolyard fistfights. Still, he was beautiful to watch, generating great speed on even the slowest of waves, throwing hard turns with precision. A few of the others were equally agile— including one no more than thirteen who was clearly lost in a Peaceful Warrior fantasy, a look of calm intent in his eyes as he drew out each move with long, stylized arm gestures. A dream sport in any life: venting so much steam, giving shape to every waking moment and partial meaning to the future, coming to understand a specific piece of the earth.

And watching Apollo subdue nature, I got the first hint of caffeine withdrawal, of the faint vise-tightening around the temples (terrifying, if you've never been through it). Out of shape and out of sync, with no chance at a wave, I became a breathing, decomposing buoy. Nearby, a boy no more than eight years old, suit bagging around him as he lay on a huge longboard, took a shove into a wave from his dad and made it successfully to his feet. Suddenly, he found himself zipping sideways through the sunshine, and the shock almost overwhelmed him. He screamed in his shrill little voice, "No way! Wow! Oh, man!" with such unbridled joy—so out of the code of taciturn surfer cool—that every man in the water, tough guys included, smiled magnanimously.

"Well, that's that," said a portly guy on a huge board to the proud father. "You can forget about him ever being President."

A square kelp-harvesting boat floated just outside the crowded lineup of surfers, dragging the long stalks of glistening green weed up a conveyer belt that hung off the bow. I could see the reef and its waving grass beneath my board and saw a silvery darter rise up and break the surface sheen. It floated off gulping and choking at the fish trapped in its long throat, and I tried to forget about surfing for the moment, about the game that narrows one's focus: watched the air and water with all the openness of the fool on the hill, tried to let the sky into my brain, and found, much to my surprise, that this Monday morning in September was the very first morning of mystical sign clouds I had personally ever seen. By which I mean that a diving man with broad ribs and thick out-thrust arms plunged out of wispy raw materials into the river that was the horizon, even as overhead three blown eagle feathers spread with delicate perfection in the late summer's pale-blue sky. I'm not kidding. I don't go around seeing eagle feathers in the sky, but there they were, each spine fine and clear with a long quill trailing behind, all below a sun that brushed barely visible rainbows of green and purple through those downy fibers. And *that,* you see, was enough for one day, a cycle of Platonic cloud forms Rorschaching my soul right back at me, because just then a line of liquid green light came my way with nobody on it. I paddled like hell on my nutty old purple-and-orange board—early eighties vintage with a logo that looked like it belonged on a beer can—felt the wave's lift, then had it. Got to my feet, and as I steered that round blob of fiberglass down the face of the wave among several guys paddling, I noticed the most peculiar thing—no look of terror in their eyes! Didn't they realize I could just screw up and kill them? Apparently not, so, gliding along that lovely undulating wall, up to trim then back to the curl, playing the play and flying along in the morning; pure, quiet pleasure. But paddling back out I managed to get in Apollo's way again: he gouged a turn as I crested his wave and we both went down. He came up furious as we drifted together in the foam and current, reached for our boards.

"You know," he said, almost shaking with rage, "this isn't fucking amateur night or something."

I drifted inside, away from the crowd, unsuccessfully paddled for several little leftovers, and watched the tribe of boys chatter, sneak glances. Spray-painted on the sea wall: "Wave segregation begins with you. Get out or bleed." A swastika rambled across the erratic concrete. Charming.

"Say, Bra," I heard a little green-eyed and aggressive towhead squeak to his eighty-pound friend. "You know that second bowl at inside second peak? The one where it sucks out really quick? I got the raddest floater off it just now." Don't be fooled—this line carries more water knowledge than most of us learn in a lifetime: "second peak" being a shoaling of the reef that produced the lesser of two breaks; "inside," where smaller waves broke closer to shore; "second bowl," a still shallower place where inside second peak waves sucked out and pitched. For a floater, one unweighted as the pitching lip broke, and glided over the back of the falling crest. After a while, I got to chatting with a handsome guy who had short red hair and a pleasant expression and had been getting his share of waves. He turned out to be a skydiving instructor who strapped a board to his feet during jumps: "Air surfing, dude! It's out*rageous!*" From a middle-class family in New Jersey, he said he'd lost touch with his parents, could never quite explain his life to them. (So many of us, after all, living by the same myths!)

Then Apollo paddled past, returning from his fifteenth wave in the time I'd ridden two.

"Hey, grommet," grumbled a potbellied bearded man in an all-black wetsuit, reminding the kid of his age. His face had a heavy-lidded gravitas from years in the sun; he was speaking to Apollo. "We need to talk." The man's yellowed ten-foot board set him apart from the shredders—it might have just marked him an out-of-shape adult, but he had the stature of a legitimate old-timer, soul-surfer. The kid remained defiant but nervous, undisputed best surfer in the water but apparently familiar with the older man and perhaps a hundred pounds lighter. Human awkwardness in water makes surfer fights largely verbal: guys can be six feet apart and completely unable to reach each other, so squabbles often take on the comic futility of shouting matches between potted lemon trees.

"You got some things to learn," said the longboarder, with confident authority. "If you ever want to be truly cool, and actually have people like you, you gotta not be an asshole. As long as you're an asshole, it doesn't matter how good you are. You're still an asshole."

Pith, and it hit the spot. "Fuck you," the kid muttered, paddling off. But the next time he passed me, his lesson in the social contract got the better of him. "Look, dude," he said to me, actually trying to be friendly, "you're over like a deep spot, so waves don't jack here. You're not going to catch anything." It troubled him to condescend, but it was excellent advice and a generous gesture, and he went on, making his first crack at being both a great surfer and a decent guy. "Might as well come out to the peak for a few," he said, and then he snapped. He'd almost done it, almost done a good deed, but as he paddled off, he said over his shoulder, "Least you might get better."

Daniel Duane was born in Berkeley, California, in 1967 and earned his B.A. at Cornell University. Influenced by his father and uncle, both mountaineers, Duane became interested in climbing; his first book, Lighting Out: A Vision of California and the Mountains *(Graywolf Press, 1994), details an ascent up El Capitan. Duane later did graduate work in American literature at the University of California, Santa Cruz. While there, he became interested in surfing and surf culture; these inspired his second book,* Caught Inside: A Surfer's Year on the California Coast *(North Point Press, 1997). In 1998 he published his first novel,* Looking for Mo *(Farrar, Straus and Giroux); his second novel,* A Mouth like Yours *(Farrar, Straus and Giroux), was published in 2005. Duane lives in San Francisco with his wife, writer Elizabeth Weil, and their two daughters.*

THE MOUNTAINS

Louise Amelia Knapp Smith Clapp
(Dame Shirley)

From *The Shirley Letters: From the California Mines, 1851–1852*
LETTER TENTH, A TRIP INTO THE MINES

NOTHING OF IMPORTANCE HAS HAPPENED since I last wrote you, except that I have become a *mineress,* that is, if the having washed a pan of dirt with my own hands, and procured therefrom three dollars and twenty-five cents in gold-dust, which I shall inclose in this letter, will entitle me to the name. I can truly say, with the black-smith's apprentice at the close of his first day's work at the anvil, that I am sorry I learned the trade, for I wet my feet, tore my dress, spoilt a pair of new gloves, nearly froze my fingers, got an awful headache, took cold, and lost a valuable breastpin, in this my labor of love. After such melancholy self-sacrifice on my part, I trust you will duly prize my gift. I can assure you that it is the last golden handiwork you will ever receive from Dame Shirley.

Apropos of lady gold-washers in general, it is a common habit with people residing in towns in the vicinity of the diggings to make up pleasure-parties to those places. Each woman of the company will exhibit, on her return, at least twenty dollars of the oro, which she will gravely inform you she has just panned out from a single basinful of the soil. This, of course, gives strangers a very erroneous idea of the average richness of auriferous dirt. I myself thought (now, don't laugh) that one had but to saunter gracefully along romantic streamlets on sunny afternoons, with a parasol and white kid gloves perhaps, and to stop now and then to admire the scenery, and carelessly rinse out a small panful of yellow sand (without detriment to the white kids, however, so easy did I fancy the whole process to be), in order to fill one's work-bag with the most beautiful and rare specimens of the precious mineral. Since I have been here I have discovered my mistake, and also the secret of the brilliant success of former gold-washeresses.

The miners are in the habit of flattering the vanity of their fair visitors by scattering a handful of "salt" (which, strange to say, is *exactly* the color of gold-dust, and has the remarkable property of often bringing to light very curious lumps of the ore) through the dirt before the dainty fingers touch it, and the dear creatures go home with their treasures, firmly believing that mining is the prettiest pastime in the world.

I had no idea of permitting such a costly joke to be played upon me; so I said but little of my desire to "go through the motions" of gold-washing, until one day, when, as I passed a deep hole in which several men were at work, my companion requested the owner to fill a small pan, which I had in my hand, with dirt from the bed-rock. This request was, of course, granted, and the treasure having been conveyed to the edge of the river, I succeeded, after much awkward maneuvering on my own part, and considerable assistance from friend H., an experienced miner, in gathering together the above-specified sum. All the diggers of our acquaintance say that it is an excellent "prospect" even to come from the bed-rock, where, naturally, the richest dirt is found. To be sure, there are, now and then, "lucky strikes," such, for instance, as that mentioned in a former letter, where a person took out of a single basinful of soil two hundred and fifty-six dollars. But such luck is as rare as the winning of a hundred-thousand-dollar prize in a lottery. We are acquainted with many here whose gains have *never* amounted to much more than wages, that is, from six to eight dollars a day. And a claim which yields a man a steady income of ten dollars *per diem* is considered as very valuable.

I received an immense fright the other morning. I was sitting by the fire, quietly reading "Lewis Arundel," which had just fallen into my hands, when a great shout and trampling of feet outside attracted my attention. Naturally enough, my first impulse was to run to the door, but scarcely had I risen to my feet for that purpose, when a mighty crash against the side of the cabin, shaking it to the foundation, threw me suddenly upon my knees. So violent was the shock that for a moment I thought the staunch old logs, mossed with the pale verdure of ages, were falling in confusion around me. As soon as I could collect my scattered senses, I looked about to see what had happened. Several stones had fallen from the back of the chimney, mortar from the latter covered the hearth, the cloth overhead was twisted into the funniest possible wrinkles, the couch had jumped two feet from the side of the house, the little table lay on its back, holding up *four* legs instead of *one,* the chessmen were rolling merrily about in every direction, the dishes had all left their usual places, the door, which, ever since, has obstinately refused to let itself be shut, was thrown violently open, while an odd-looking pile of articles lay in the middle of the room, which, upon investigation, was found to consist of a pail, a broom, a bell, some candlesticks, a pack of cards, a loaf of bread, a pair of boots, a bunch of cigars, and some clay pipes (the only things, by the way, rendered utterly *hors de combat* in the assault). But one piece of furniture retained its attitude, and that was the elephantine bedstead, which nothing short of an earthquake could move. Almost at the same moment several acquaintances rushed in, begging me not to be alarmed, as the danger was past.

"But what has happened?" I eagerly inquired.

"O, a large tree, which was felled this morning, has rolled down from the brow of the hill." And its having struck a rock a few feet from the house, losing thereby the most of its force, had alone saved us from utter destruction.

I grew sick with terror when I understood the awful fate from which Providence had preserved me, and even now my heart leaps painfully with mingled fear and gratitude when I think how closely that pale death-shadow glided by me, and of the loving care which forbade it to linger upon our threshold.

Every one who saw the forest giant desending the hill with the force of a mighty torrent expected to see the cabin instantly prostrated to the earth. As it was, they all say that it swayed from the perpendicular more than six inches.

Poor W., whom you may remember my having mentioned in a former letter as having had a leg amputated a few weeks ago, and who was visiting us at the time, (he had been brought from the Empire in a rocking-chair,) looked like a marble statue of resignation. He possesses a face of uncommon beauty, and his large, dark eyes have always, I fancy, a sorrowful expression. Although he knew from the first shout what was about to happen, and was sitting on the couch which stood at that side of the cabin where the log must necessarily strike, and in his mutilated condition had, as he has since said, not the faintest hope of escape, yet the rich color for which he is remarkable paled not a shade during the whole affair.

The woodman who came so near causing a catastrophe was, I believe, infinitely more frightened than his might-have-been victims. He is a good-natured, stupid creature, and did not dare to descend the hill until some time after the excitement had subsided. The ludicrous expression of terror which his countenance wore when he came in to see what damage had been done, and to ask pardon for his carelessness, made us all laugh heartily.

W. related the almost miraculous escape of two persons from a similar danger last winter. The cabin, which was on Smith's Bar, was crushed into a mass of ruins almost in an instant, while an old man and his daughter, who were at dinner within its walls, remained sitting in the midst of the fallen logs, entirely unhurt. The father immediately seized a gun and ran after the careless woodman, swearing that he would shoot him. Fortunately for the latter (for there is no doubt that in the first moments of his rage the old man would have slain him), his younger legs enabled him to make his escape, and he did not dare to return to the settlement for some days.

It has heretofore been a source of great interest to me to listen to the ringing sound of the ax, and the solemn crash of those majestic sentinels of the hills as they bow their green foreheads to the dust, but now I fear that I shall always hear them with a feeling of apprehension mingling with my former awe, although every one tells us that there is no danger of a repetition of the accident.

Last week there was a post-mortem examination of two men who died very suddenly in the neighborhood. Perhaps it will sound rather barbarous when I tell you that as there was no building upon the Bar which admitted light enough for the purpose, it was found necessary to conduct the examination in the open air, to the intense interest of the Kanakas, Indians, French, Spanish, English, Irish, and Yankees, who had gathered eagerly about the spot. Paganini Ned, with an anxious desire that Mrs.—— should be *amused* as much as possible in her mountain-home, rushed up from the kitchen, his dusky face radiant with excitement, to inform me that I could see both the bodies by just looking out of the window! I really frightened the poor fellow by the abrupt and vehement manner in which I declined taking advantage of his kindly hint.

One of the deceased was the husband of an American lady lecturess of the most intense description, and a strong-minded bloomer on the broadest principles.

Apropos, how *can* women, many of whom, I am told, are *really* interesting and intelligent,—how *can* they spoil their pretty mouths and ruin their beautiful complexions by demanding with Xanthippian *fervor*, in the presence, often, of a vulgar, irreverent mob, what the gentle creatures are pleased to call their "rights"? How *can* they wish to soil the delicate texture of their airy fancies by pondering over the wearying stupidities of Presidential elections, or the bewildering mystifications of rabid metaphysicians? And, above all, how *can* they so far forget the sweet, shy coquetries of shrinking womanhood as to don those horrid bloomers? As for me, although a *wife,* I never wear the—well, you know what they call them when they wish to quiz henpecked husbands—even in the strictest privacy of life. I confess to an almost religious veneration for trailing drapery, and I pin my vestural faith with unflinching obstinacy to sweeping petticoats.

I knew a strong-minded bloomer at home, of some talent, and who was possessed, in a certain sense, of an excellent education. One day, after having flatteringly informed me that I really *had* a "soul above buttons" and the nursery, she gravely proposed that I should improve my *mind* by poring six hours a day over the metaphysical subtleties of Kant, Cousin, etc., and I remember that she called me a "piece of fashionable insipidity," and taunted me with not daring to go out of the beaten track, because I *truly* thought (for in those days I was an humble little thing enough, and sincerely desirous of walking in the right path as straitly as my feeble judgment would permit) that there were other authors more congenial to the flowerlike delicacy of the feminine intellect than her pet writers.

When will our sex appreciate the exquisite philosophy and truth of Lowell's remark upon the habits of Lady Redbreast and her esposo Robin, as illustrating the beautifully varied spheres of man and woman?—

He sings to the wide world, she to her nest;
In the nice ear of Nature, which song is the best?

Speaking of birds reminds me of a misfortune that I have lately experienced, which, in a life where there is so little to amuse and interest one, has been to me a subject of real grief. About three weeks ago, F. saw on the hill a California pheasant, which he chased into a coyote-hole and captured. Knowing how fond I am of pets, he brought it home and proposed that I should try to tame it. Now, from earliest childhood I have resolutely refused to keep *wild* birds, and when I have had them given to me (which has happened several times in this country,—young bluebirds, etc.), I have invariably set them free, and I proposed doing the same with the pretty pheasant, but as they are the most delicately exquisite in flavor of all game, F. said that if I did not wish to keep it he would wring its neck and have it served up for dinner. With the cruelty of kindness—often more diastrous than that of real malice—I shrank from having it killed, and consented to let it run about the cabin.

It was a beautiful bird, a little larger than the domestic hen. Its slender neck, which it curved with haughty elegance, was tinted with various shades of a shining steel color. The large, bright eye glanced with the prettiest shyness at its captors, and the cluster of feathers forming its tail drooped with the rare grace of an ostrich-plume. The colors of the body were of a subdued brilliancy, reminding one of a rich but somber mosaic.

As it seemed very quiet, I really believed that in time we should be able to tame it. Still, it *would* remain constantly under the sofa or bedstead. So F. concluded to place it in a cage for a few hours of each day, in order that it might become gradually accustomed to our presence. This was done, the bird appearing as well as ever, and after closing the door of its temporary prison one day I left it and returned to my seat by the fire. In less than two minutes afterwards, a slight struggle in the cage attracted my attention. I ran hastily back, and you may imagine my distress when I found the beautiful pheasant lying lifeless upon the ground. It never breathed or showed the faintest sign of life afterwards.

You may laugh at me if you please, but I firmly believe that it died of homesickness. What wonder that the free, beautiful, happy creature of God, torn from the sight of the broad blue sky, the smiling river, and the fresh, fragrant fir-trees of its mountain-home, and shut up in a dark, gloomy cabin, should have broken in twain its haughty little heart? Yes, you may laugh, call me sentimental, etc., but I shall never forgive myself for having killed, by inches, in my selfish and cruel kindness, that pretty creature.

Many people here call this bird a grouse, and those who have crossed the plains say that it is very much like the prairie-hen. The Spanish name is gallina del campo, literally, hen of the field. Since the death of my poor little victim, I have been told that it is utterly impossible to tame one of these birds, and it is said that if you put their eggs under a domestic fowl, the young, almost as soon as hatched, will instinctively run away to the beloved solitudes of their congenial homes, so passionately beats for liberty each pulse of their free and wild natures.

Among the noteworthy events which have occurred since my last, I don't know how I came to forget until the close of my letter two smart shocks of an earthquake to which we were treated a week ago. They were awe-inspiring, but, after all, were nothing in comparison to the timber-quake, an account of which I have given you above. But as F. is about to leave for the top of the Butte Mountains with a party of Rich Barians, and as I have much to do to prepare him for the journey, I must close.

Louise Amelia Knapp Smith Clapp (or, as she often spelled it, Clappe) was born in Elizabeth, New Jersey, in 1819 and was raised there and in Massachusetts. In 1848 or 1849 she married physician Dr. Fayette Clapp, and in 1849 the couple sailed to California. Dr. Clapp established a medical practice in Rich Bar, a mining camp on the Feather River. Here, under the pseudonym Dame Shirley, Clapp began writing accounts of gold-rush life for her sister, Molly; in 1854 and 1855 they were published as a series in The Pioneer, or California Monthly Magazine. *Clapp was a humorous and observant writer; her twenty-three letters provide vividly rendered portraits of gold-rush life. However, they were not collected into book form as* The Shirley Letters: From the California Mines, 1851–1852 *(Thomas C. Russell) until 1922. In 1853 Dr. Clapp left his wife and California; the couple divorced, and Louise Clapp, too, left Rich Bar and established herself as a public school teacher in San Francisco. In 1878 she returned to the East Coast; she died in New Jersey in 1906.*

⬬ *Joaquin Miller*

From *The Complete Poetical Works of Joaquin Miller*
THE GOLD THAT GREW BY SHASTA TOWN

    From Shasta town to Redding town
The ground is torn by miners dead;
The manzanita, rank and red,
Drops dusty berries up and down
Their grass-grown trails. Their silent
    mines
Are wrapped in chaparral and vines;
Yet one gray miner still sits down
'Twixt Redding and sweet Shasta town.

    The quail pipes pleasantly. The hare
Leaps careless o'er the golden oat
That grows below the water moat;
The lizard basks in sunlight there.
The brown hawk swims the perfumed air
Unfrightened through the livelong day;
And now and then a curious bear
Comes shuffling down the ditch by night,
And leaves some wide, long tracks in clay
So human-like, so stealthy light,
Where one lone cabin still stoops down
'Twixt Redding and sweet Shasta town.

    That great graveyard of hopes! of men
Who sought for hidden veins of gold;

Of young men suddenly grown old—
Of old men dead, despairing when
The gold was just within their hold!
That storied land, whereon the light
Of other days gleams faintly still;
Somelike the halo of a hill
That lifts above the falling night;
That warm, red, rich and human land,
That flesh-red soil, that warm red sand,
Where one gray miner still sits down!
'Twixt Redding and sweet Shasta town!

  "I know the vein is here!" he said;
For twenty years, for thirty years!
While far away fell tears on tears
From wife and babe who mourned him
    dead.
No gold! No gold! And he grew old
And crept to toil with bended head
Amid a graveyard of his dead,
Still seeking for that vein of gold.

  Then lo, came laughing down the years
A sweet grandchild! Between his tears
He laughed. He sat her by the door
The while he toiled; his day's toil o'er
He held her chubby cheeks between
His hard palms, laughed; and laughing
    cried.
You should have seen, have heard and
    seen
His boyish joy, his stout old pride,
When toil was done and he sat down
At night, below sweet Shasta town!

At last his strength was gone. "No
    more!"
I mine no more. I plant me now
A vine and fig-tree; worn and old,
I seek no more my vein of gold.
But, oh, I sigh to give it o'er;
These thirty years of toil! somehow
It seems so hard; but now, no more."

    And so the old man set him down
To plant, by pleasant Shasta town.
And it was pleasant; piped the quail
The full year through. The chipmunk
    stole,
His whiskered nose and tossy tail
Full buried in the sugar-bowl.

    And purple grapes and grapes of gold
Swung sweet as milk. While orange-trees
Grew brown with laden honey-bees.
Oh! it was pleasant up and down
That vine-set hill of Shasta town.

And then that cloud-burst came! Ah, me!
That torn ditch there! The mellow land
Rolled seaward like a rope of sand,
Nor left one leafy vine or tree
Of all that Eden nestling down
Below that moat by Shasta town!

The old man sat his cabin's sill,
His gray head bowed to hands and knee;
The child went forth, sang pleasantly,
Where burst the ditch the day before,
And picked some pebbles from the hill.
The old man moaned, moaned o'er and
    o'er:
"My babe is dowerless, and I
Must fold my helpless hands and die!
Ah, me! What curse comes ever down
On me and mine at Shasta town."

    "Good Grandpa, see!" the glad child
      said,
And so leaned softly to his side,—
Laid her gold head to his gray head,
And merry voiced and cheery cried,
"Good Grandpa, do not weep, but see!
I've found a peck of orange seeds!
I searched the hill for vine or tree;
No one!—not even oats or weeds;
But, oh! such heaps of orange seeds!

    "Come, good Grandpa! Now, once you
      said
That God is good. So this may teach
That we must plant each seed, and each
May grow to be an orange tree.
Now, good Grandpa, please raise your
      head,
And please come plant the seeds with me."
And prattling thus, or like to this,
The child thrust her full hands in his.

He sprang, sprang upright as of old.
"'Tis gold! 'tis gold! my hidden vein!
'Tis gold for you, sweet babe, 'tis gold!
Yea, God is good; we plant again!"
So one old miner still sits down
By pleasant, sunlit Shasta town.

Few authors have as clouded a biography as Joaquin Miller, whose own statements and writings about his life are so filled with exaggeration and fabrication that it's difficult to separate fact from fiction. Although he claimed to have been born in a covered wagon, he was most likely born Cincinnatus Hiner Miller in Liberty, Indiana, in 1837 and traveled west with his family to Oregon around 1850. His early careers included horse thief, miner, camp cook, lawyer, and failed candidate for the Oregon Supreme Court. In the late 1860s he left Oregon to travel throughout the eastern United States and England. Miller was living in London when he published two volumes of verse, Pacific Poems *(privately printed, 1871) and* Songs of the Sierras *(Roberts Brothers, 1871), which established him—in the eyes of the British, at least—as the bard of the American West. Other works include* Unwritten History: Life Amongst the Modocs *(American Publishing Company, 1873), a memoir based on the year he spent with the Northern California tribe;* The Complete Poetical Works of Joaquin Miller *(The Whitaker and Ray Company, 1902); and his best-known poem, "Columbus." In the 1880s Miller returned to California, building an eccentric estate in the hills above Oakland and reveling in his reputation as The Poet of the Sierras. He died in 1913.*

Clarence King

From *Mountaineering in the Sierra Nevada*
MOUNT WHITNEY 1871

T HERE LAY BETWEEN CARSON and Mount Whitney a ride of two hundred and eighty miles along the east base of the Sierra. Stage-driving, like other exact professions, gathers among its followers certain types of men and manners, either by some mode of natural selection, or else after a Darwinian way developing one set of traits to the exclusion of others. However interesting it might be to investigate the moulding power of whip and reins, or to discover what measure of coachman there is latent in every one of us, it cannot be questioned that the characters of drivers do resemble one another in surprising degree. That ostentatious silence and self-contained way of ignoring one's presence on the box for the first half hour, the tragi-comic, just-audible undertone in which they remonstrate with the swing team, and such single refrain of obsolete song as they drone and drone a hundred times, may be observed on every coach from San Diego to Montana.

So I found it natural enough that the driver, my sole companion from Carson to Aurora, should sit for the first hour in a silence etiquette forbade me to violate. His team, by strict attention to their duties, must have left his mind quite free, and I saw symptoms of suppressed sociability within forty minutes of our departure.

The nine-mile house, if my memory serves, was his landmark for taciturnity, for soon after passing it he began to skirmish along a sort of picket line of conversation. To the wheel mares he remarked, "Hot, gals; ain't it, tho'?" and to his off leader, who strained wild eyes in every direction for something to become excited about, "Look at him, Dixie; wouldn't you like a rabbit to shy at?"

With a true driver's pride in reading men, he scanned me from boots to barometer, and at last, to my immense delight, said, with the air of throwing his hat into a ring, "What mountain was you going down to measure?" Had he inquired after my grandfather by his first name, I could not have been more surprised. At once I told him the plain truth, and waited for further developments; but, like an indifferent shot who drives centre on a first trial, he proposed not to endanger his reputation for infallibility by other ventures, and withdrew again to that conspicuous stupidity which coachmen and Buddhists alike delight in.

Left to myself, I spent hours in looking out over the desert and up along that bold front of Sierra which rose on our right from the sage plains of Carson Valley up through ramparts of pine land to summits of rock and ravines with sunken snow-banks.

So far as Aurora, I remember little worth describing. Sierras, or outlying volcanic foot-hills, bound the west. About our road are desert plains and rolling sage-clad hills, fresh, light olive at this June season, and softly sloping in long *glacis* down to wide, impressive levels.

Green valleys and cultivated farms margin the Carson and Walker rivers. Sierras are not lofty enough to be grand, desert too gentle and overspread with sage to be terrible; yet the pale, high key of all its colors, and singular aërial brilliancy lend an otherwise dreary enough picture the charm,—as I once before said,—of water-color drawings. There is no perspective under this fierce white light; in midday intensely sharp reflections glare from hill and valley, except where the shadow of passing cloud spreads cool and blue over olive slopes.

Alas for Aurora, once so active and bustling with silver mines and its almost daily murder! Twenty-six whiskey hells and two Vigilance Committees graced those days of prosperity and mirthful gallows, of stock-board and the gay delirium of speculation. Now her sad streets are lined with closed doors; a painful silence broods over quartz mills, and through the whole deserted town one perceives that melancholy security of human life which is hereabouts one of the pathetic symptoms of bankruptcy. The "boys" have gone off to merrily shoot one another somewhere else, leaving poor Aurora in the hands of a sort of coroner's jury who gather nightly at the one saloon and hold dreary inquests over departed enterprise.

My landlord's tread echoed through a large, empty hotel, and when I responded to his call for lunch the silentest of girls became medium between me and a Chinaman, who gazed sad-eyed through his kitchen door as in pity for one who must choose between starving and his own cookery. But I have always felt it unpardonable egotism for a traveller to force the reader into sharing with him the inevitable miseries of roadside food. Whatever merit there may be in locking this prandial grief fast from public view, I feel myself entitled to in a high degree, for I hold it in my power to describe the most revolting cuisine on the planet, yet refrain.

From Aurora my road, still parallel with the mountains, though now hidden from them by banks of volcanic hills, climbed a long, wearisome slope from whose summit a glorious panorama of snowy Sierras lay before us. From our feet, steep declivities fell two thousand feet to the level of a wide desert basin, bounded upon the west by long ranks of high, white peaks, and otherwise walled in by chains of volcanic hills, smooth with dull sage flanks, and yet varied here and there by outcropping formations of eruptive rocks and dusky cedar forests.

Just at the Sierra foot, surrounded by bare, gray volcanoes and reaches of ashen plain, lies Mono lake, a broad oval darkened along its father shore by reflecting the shadowed mountains, and pale tranquil blue where among light desert levels it mirrors the silken softness of sky and cloud. Flocks of pelicans, high against the sky, floated in slow, wheeling flight, reflecting the sun from white wings, and, turning, were lost in the blue to gleam out again like flakes of snow.

The eye ranges over strange, forbidding hill-forms and leagues of desert, from which no familiarity can ever banish suggestions of death. Traced along boundary hills, straight terraces of an ancient beach indicate former water-levels, and afar in the Sierra, great, empty gorges, glacier-burnished and moraine-flanked, lead up to amphitheatres of rock once white with *névé*.

I recognized the old familiar summits: Mount Ritter, Lyell, Dana, and that firm peak with Titan strength and brow so square and solid it seems altogether natural we should have named it for California's statesman, John Conness.

We rumbled down hill and out upon the desert, plodding until evening through sand, and over rocky, cedar-wooded spurs, at last crossing adobe meadows, where were settlements and a herd of Spanish cattle which had escaped the drought of California, and now marched, northward bound, for Montana.

Frowning volcanic hills flanked our road as evening wore on, lifting dark forms against a sky singularly pale and luminous. Afar, we caught glimpses of the dark, swelling Sierra wave thrusting up "star-neighboring peaks," and then, descending into hollows among lava mounds, found ourselves shut completely in. A night at the Hot Springs of Partzwick was notably free from anything which may be recounted.

Morning found me waiting alone on the hotel veranda, and I suppose the luxuries of the establishment must have left a stamp of melancholy upon my face, for the little, solemn driver who drew up his vehicle at the door said in a tone of condolence, "The hearse is ready."

Stages, drivers and teams had been successively worse as I journeyed southward. This little old specimen, by whose side I sat from Partzwick to Independence, ought to be excepted, and I should neglect a duty were I not to portray one, at least, of his traits. He was a musical old fellow, and given to chanting in low tones songs, sometimes pathetic, often sentimental, but in every case preserved by him in most fragmentary recollection. Such singing suffered, too, from the necessary and frequent interruption of driving; the same breath quavering in cracked melody, and tossing some neatly rounded oath or horse-phrase at off or near wheeler, catching up an end of the refrain again in time to satisfy his musical requirements.

All the morning he had warned me most impressively to count myself favored if a certain bridge over Bishop's Creek should not sink under us and cast me upon wild waters. Rightly estimating my friend, I was not surprised when we reached the spot to find a good, solid structure bridging a narrow creek not more than four feet deep.

As we rolled on down Owen's Valley, he sang, chatted and drove in a manner which showed him capable of three distinct, yet simultaneous, mental processes. I follow his words as nearly as memory serves.

"That creek, sir, was six feet deep.
'Oh Lillie, sweet Lillie, dear Lillie Dale.'

What the devil are you shying at? You cursed mustang, come up out of that;

..... 'little green grave.'

Yes, seven feet, and if we'd have fell in, swimming wouldn't saved us.

"You, Balley, what are you a doin' on?

''Neath the hill in the flowing vale.'

And what's more, we couldn't have crawled up that bank, nohow.

'My own dear Lillie Dale.'

You'd like to kick over them traces, would you? Keep your doggoned neck up snug against that collar, and take that.

"We'd drowned, sir; drowned sure as thunder.

'In the place where the violets grow.'"

Desert hills, and low, mountain gateways, opening views of vast, sterile plains, no longer formed our eastern outlook. The White Mountains, a lofty, barren chain vying with the Sierras in altitude, rose in splendid rank and stretched southeast, parallel with the great range. Down the broad, intermediate trough flowed Owen's River, alternately through expanses of natural meadow and desolate reaches of sage.

The Sierra, as we travelled southward, became bolder and bolder, strong granite spurs plunging steeply down into the desert; above, the mountain sculpture grew grander and grander, until forms wild and rugged as the Alps stretched on in dense ranks as far as the eye could reach. More and more the granite came out in all its strength. Less and less soil covered the slopes: groves of pine became rarer, and sharp, rugged buttresses advanced boldly to the plain. Here and there a cañon-gate between rough granite pyramids, and flanked by huge moraines, opened its savage gallery back among peaks. Even around the summits there was but little snow, and the streams which at short intervals flowed from the mountain foot, traversing the plains, were sunken far below their ordinary volume.

The mountain forms and mode of sculpture of the opposite ranges are altogether different. The White and Inyo chains, formed chiefly of uplifted sedimentary beds, are largely covered with soil, and wherever the solid rock is exposed its easily traced strata plains and soft, wooded surface combined in producing a general aspect of breadth and smoothness; while the Sierra, here more than anywhere else, holds up a front of solid stone, carved into most intricate and highly ornamental forms: vast aiguilles, trimmed from summit to base with line of slender minarets; huge, broad domes, deeply fluted and surmounted with tall obelisks, and everywhere the greatest profusion of bristling points.

From the base of each range a long, sloping talus descends gently to the river, and here and there, bursting up through Sierra foot-hills, rise the red and black forms of recent volcanoes as regular and barren as if cooled but yesterday.

I had reason for not regretting my departure from the Inyo House at Independence next morning before sunrise; and when a young woman in an elaborate brown calico, copied evidently from some imperial evening toilet, pertly demanded my place by the driver, adding that she was not one of the "inside kind," I willingly yielded, and made myself contented on the back seat alone. Presently, however, a companion came to me in the person of a middle-aged Spanish doña, clad altogether in black, with a shawl worn over her head after the manner of a mantilla. When it began to rain violently and beat upon that brown calico, I made bold to offer the young woman my sheltered place, but she gayly declined, averring herself not made of sugar. So the doña and I shared my great coat across our laps and established relations of civility, though she spoke no English, and I only that little Spanish so much more embarrassing than none.

In her smile, in the large, soft eyes, and that tinge of Castilian blood which shone red-warm through olive cheek, I saw the signs of a race blessed with sturdier health than ours. With snowy hair growing low on a massive forehead, and just a glimpse now and then of large, gold beads, through a white handkerchief about her throat, she seemed to me a charming picture: though, perhaps, her fine looks gained something by contrasting with the sickly girl in front, whose pallor and cough could not have meant less than the pretubercular state.

Clouds covered the mountains on either hand, leaving me only ranches and people to observe. May I be forgiven if I am wrong in accounting for the late improvement of political tone in Tuolumne by the presence here of so large a share of her most degraded citizens; people whose faces and dress and life and manners are sadder than any possibilities held up to us by Darwin.

My long ride ended in a few hours at Lone Pine, where, from the hotel window, I watched a dark-blue mass of storm which covered and veiled the region where I knew my goal, the Whitney summit, must stand.

For two days storm-curtains hung low about the Sierra base, their vapor banks, dark with fringes of shower, at times drifting out over Lone Pine and quenching a thirsty earth. On the third afternoon blue sky shone through rifts overhead, and now and then a single peak, dashed with broken sunshine, rose for a moment over rolling clouds which swelled above it again like huge billows.

About an hour before sunset the storm began rapidly to sink into level fold, over which, in clear, yellow light, emerged "cloud-compelling" peaks. The liberated sun poured down shafts of light, piercing the mist which now in locks of gold and gray blew about the mountain heads in wonderful splendor.

How deep and solemn a blue filled the cañon depths! What passion of light glowed around the summits! With delight I watched them one after another fading till only the sharp, terrible crest of Whitney, still red with reflected light from the long-sunken sun, showed bright and glorious above the whole Sierra.

Upon observing the topography, I saw that one bold spur advanced from Mount Whitney to the plain; on either side of it profound cañons opened back to the summit. I remembered the impossibility of making a climb up those northern precipices, and at once chose the more southern gorge.

Next morning we set out on horseback for the mountain base, twelve miles across plains and through an outlying range of hills. My companion for the trip was Paul Pinson, as tough and plucky a mountaineer as France ever sent us, who consented readily to follow me. José, the mild-mannered and grinning Mexican boy who rode with us, was to remain in care of our animals at the foot-hills while we made the climb.

I left a Green barometer to be observed at Lone Pine, and carried my short high-mountain instrument, by the same excellent maker.

Gauzy mists again enveloped the Sierra, leaving us free minds to enjoy a ride, of which the very first mile supplied me food for days of thought.

The American residents of Lone Pine outskirts live in a homeless fashion; sullen, almost arrogant, neglect stares out from the open doors. There is no attempt at grace, no memory of comfort, no suggested hope for improvement.

Not so the Spanish homes, their low, adobe, wide-roofed cabins neatly enclosed with even, basket-work fence, and lining hedge of blooming hollyhock.

We stopped to bow good-morning to my friend and stage companion, the doña. She sat in the threshold of her open door, sewing; beyond her stretched a bare floor, clean and white: the few chairs, the table spread with snowy linen, everything, shone with an air of religious spotlessness. Symmetry reigned in the precise, well-kept garden, arranged in rows of pepper-plants and crisp heads of vernal lettuce.

I longed for a painter to catch her brilliant smile, and surround her on canvas as she was here, with order and dignity. The same plain, black dress clad her ample figure, and about the neck heavy, barbaric gold beads served again as collar.

Under low eaves above her, and quite around the house, hung, in triple row, festoons of flaming red peppers, in delicious contrast with the rich adobe gray.

It was a study of order and true womanly repose, fitted to cheer us, and a grouping of such splendid color as might tempt a painter to cross the world.

A little farther on we passed an Indian ranchero where several willow wickyups were built upon the bank of a cold brook. Half-naked children played about here and there; a few old squaws bustled at household work; but nearly all lay outstretched, dozing. A sort of tattered brilliancy characterized the place. Gay, high-colored squalor reigned. There seemed hardly more lack of thrift or sense of decorum than in the American ranches, yet somehow the latter send a stab of horror through one, while this quaint indolence and picturesque neglect seem aptly contrived to set off the Indian genius for loafing, and leave you with a sort of æsthetic satisfaction, rather than the sorrow their half development should properly evoke.

Leaving all this behind us, our road led westward across a long sage slope entering a narrow, tortuous pass through a low range of outlying granite hills. Strangely weathered forms towered on either side, their bare, brown surface contrasting pleasantly with the vivid ribbon of willows which wove a green and silver cover over swift water.

The granite was riven with innumerable cracks, showing here and there a strong tendency to concentric forms, and I judged the immense spheroidal bowlders which lay on all sides, piled one upon another, to be the kernels or nuclei of larger masses.

Quickly crossing this ridge, we came out upon the true Sierra foot-slope, a broad, inclined plain stretching north and south as far as we could see. Directly in front of us rose the rugged form of Mount Whitney spur, a single mass of granite, rough-hewn, and darkened with coniferous groves. The summits were lost in a cloud of almost indigo hue.

Putting our horses at a trot, we quickly ascended the *glacis,* and at the very foot of the rocks dismounted, and made up our packs. José, with the horses, left us and went back half a mile to a mountain ranch, where he was to await our return; and presently Pinson and I, with heavy burdens upon our backs, began slowly to work our way up the granite spur and toward the great cañon.

An hour's climb brought us around upon the south wall of our spur, and about a thousand feet above a stream which dashed and leaped along the cañon bottom, through wild ravines and over granite bluffs. Our slope was a rugged rock-face, giving foothold here and there to pine and juniper trees, but for the greater part bare and bold.

Far above, at an elevation of ten thousand feet, a dark grove of alpine pines gathered in the cañon bed. Thither we bent our steps, edging from cleft to cleft, making constant, though insignificant, progress. At length our wall became so wild and deeply cut with side cañons that we found it impossible to follow it longer, and descended carefully to the bottom.

Almost immediately, with heavy wind gusts and sound as of torrents, a storm broke upon us, darkening the air and drenching us to the skin. The three hours we toiled up over rocks, through dripping willow-brooks and among trains of *débris* were not noticeable for their cheerfulness.

The storm had ceased, but it was evening when, wet and exhausted, we at length reached the alpine grove, and threw ourselves down for rest under a huge, overhanging rock which offered its shelter for our bivouac.

Logs, soon brought in by Pinson, were kindled. The hot blaze seemed pleasant to us, though I cannot claim to have enjoyed those two hours spent in turning round and round before it while steaming and drying. But the broiled beef, the toast, and those generous cups of tea to which we devoted the hour between ten and eleven were quite satisfactory. So, too, was the pleasant chat till midnight warned us to roll up in overcoats and close our eyes to the fire, to the dark, sombre grove, and far stars crowding the now cloudless heavens.

The sun rose and shone on us while we breakfasted. Through all the visible sky not a cloud could be seen, and, thanks to yesterday's rain, the air was of crystal purity. Into it the granite summits above us projected forms of sunlit gray.

Up the glacier valley above camp we slowly tramped through a forest of noble Pinus Flexilis, the trunks of bright sienna contrasting richly with deep bronze foliage.

Minor flutings of a medial moraine offered gentle grade and agreeable footing for a mile and more, after which, by degrees, the woods gave way to a wide, open amphitheatre surrounded with cliffs.

I can never enter one of these great, hollow mountain chambers without a pause. There is a grandeur and spaciousness which expand and fit the mind for yet larger sensations when you shall stand on the height above.

Velvet of alpine sward edging an icy brooklet, by whose margin we sat down, reached to the right and left far enough to spread a narrow foreground, over which we saw a chain of peaks swelling from either side toward our amphitheatre's head, where, springing splendidly over them all, stood the sharp form of Whitney.

Precipices white with light and snow-fields of incandescent brilliance grouped themselves along walls and slopes. All around us, in wild, huge heaps, lay wrecks of glacier and avalanche.

We started again, passing the last tree, and began to climb painfully up loose *débris* and lodged blocks of the north wall. From here to the very foot of that granite pyramid which crowns the mountain, we found neither difficulty nor danger, only a long, tedious climb over footing which, from time to time, gave way provokingly.

By this time mist floated around the brow of Mount Whitney, forming a gray helmet, from which, now and then, the wind blew out long, waving plumes. After a brief rest we began to scale the southeast ridge, climbing from rock to rock, and making our way up steep fields of soft snow. Precipices, sharp and severe, fell away to east and west of us, but the rough pile above still afforded a way. We had to use extreme caution, for many blocks hung ready to fall at a touch, and the snow, where we were forced to work up it, often gave way, threatening to hurl us down into cavernous hollows.

When within a hundred feet of the top I suddenly fell through, but, supporting myself by my arms, looked down into a grotto of rock and ice, and out through a sort of window, over the western bluffs, and down thousands of feet to the far-away valley of the Kern.

I carefully and slowly worked my body out, and crept on hands and knees up over steep and treacherous ice-crests, where a slide would have swept me over a brink of the southern precipice.

We kept to the granite as much as possible, Pinson taking one train of blocks and I another. Above us but thirty feet rose a crest, beyond which we saw nothing. I dared not think it the summit till we stood there and Mount Whitney was under our feet.

Close beside us a small mound of rock was piled upon the peak, and solidly built into it an Indian arrow-shaft, pointing due west.

I climbed out to the southwest brink, and, looking down, could see that fatal precipice which had prevented me seven years before. I strained my eyes beyond, but already dense, impenetrable clouds had closed us in.

On the whole, this climb was far less dangerous than I had reason to hope. Only at the very crest, where ice and rock are thrown together insecurely, did we encounter any very trying work. The utter unreliableness of that honeycomb and cavernous cliff was rather uncomfortable, and might, at any moment, give the deathfall to one who had not coolness and muscular power at instant command.

I hung my barometer from the mound of our Indian predecessor, nor did I grudge his hunter pride the honor of first finding that one pathway to the summit of the United States, fifteen thousand feet above two oceans.

While we lunched I engraved Pinson's and my name upon a half dollar, and placed it in a hollow of the crest. Clouds still hung motionless over us, but in half an hour a west wind drew across, drifting the heavy vapors along with it. Light poured in, reddening the clouds, which soon rolled away, opening a grand view of the western Sierra ridge, and of the whole system of the Kern.

Only here and there could blue sky be seen, but, fortunately, the sun streamed through one of these windows in the storm, lighting up splendidly the snowy rank from Kaweah to Mount Brewer.

There they rose as of old, firm and solid; even the great snow-fields, though somewhat shrunken, lay as they had seven years before. I saw the peaks and passes and amphitheatres dear old Cotter and I had climbed: even that Mount Brewer pass where we looked back over the pathway of our dangers, and up with regretful hearts to the very rock on which I sat.

Deep below flowed the Kern, its hundred, snow-fed branches gleaming out amid rock and ice, or traced far away in the great glacier trough by dark lines of pine. There, only twelve miles northwest, stretched that ragged divide where Cotter and I came down the precipice with our rope. Beyond, into the vague blue of King's cañon, sloped the ice and rock of Mount Brewer wall.

Sombre storm-clouds and their even gloomier shadows darkened the northern sea of peaks. Only a few slant bars of sudden light flashed in upon purple granite and fields of ice. The rocky tower of Mount Tyndall, thrust up through rolling billows, caught for a moment the full light, and then sank into darkness and mist.

When all else was buried in cloud we watched the great west range. Weird and strange, it seemed shaded by some dark eclipse. Here and there through its gaps and passes serpent-like streams of mist floated in and crept slowly down the cañons of the hither slope, then all along the crest, torn and rushing spray of clouds whirled about the peaks, and in a moment a vast gray wave reared high, and broke, overwhelming all.

Just for a moment every trace of vapor cleared away from the east, unveiling for the first time spurs and gorges and plains. I crept to a brink and looked down into the Whitney Cañon, which was crowded with light. Great, scarred and ice-hewn precipices reached down four thousand feet, curving together like a ship, and holding in their granite bed a thread of brook, the small sapphire gems of alpine lake, bronze dots of pine, and here and there a fine enamelling of snow.

Beyond and below lay Owen's Valley, walled in by the barren Inyo chain, and afar, under a pale, sad sky, lengthened leagues and leagues of lifeless desert.

The storm had even swept across Kern Cañon, and dashed high against the peaks north and south of us. A few sharp needles and spikes struggled above it for a moment, but it rolled over them and rushed in torrents down the desert slope, burying everything in a dark, swift cloud.

We hastened to pack up our barometer and descend. A little way down the ice crust gave way under Pinson, but he saved himself, and we hurried on, reaching safely the cliff-base, leaving all dangerous ground above us.

So dense was the cloud we could not see a hundred feet, but tramped gayly down over rocks and sand, feeling quite assured of our direction, until suddenly we came upon the brink of a precipice and strained our eyes off into the mist. I threw a stone over and listened in vain for the sound of its fall. Pinson and I both thought we had deviated too far to the north, and were on the brink of Whitney Cañon, so we turned in the opposite direction, thinking to cross the ridge, entering our old amphitheatre, but in a few moments we again found ourselves upon the verge. This time a stone we threw over answered with a faint, dull crash from five hundred feet below. We were evidently upon a narrow blade. I remembered no such place, and sat down to recall carefully every detail of topography. At last I concluded that we had either strayed down upon the Kern side, or were on one of the cliffs overhanging the head of our true amphitheatre.

Feeling the necessity of keeping cool, I determined to ascend to the foot of the snow and search for our tracks. So we slowly climbed there again and took a new start.

By this time the wind howled fiercely, bearing a chill from snow-crystals and sleet. We hurried on before it, and, after one or two vain attempts, succeeded in finding our old trail down the amphitheatre slope, descending very rapidly to its floor.

From here, an exhausting tramp of five hours through the pine forest to our camp, and on down the rough, wearying slopes of the lower cañon, brought us to the plain where José and the horses awaited us.

From Lone Pine that evening, and from the open carriage in which I rode northward to Independence, I constantly looked back and up into the storm, hoping to catch one glimpse of Mount Whitney; but all the range lay submerged in dark, rolling cloud, from which now and then a sullen mutter of thunder reverberated.

For years our chief, Professor Whitney, has made brave campaigns into the unknown realm of Nature. Against low prejudice and dull indifference he has led the survey of California onward to success. There stand for him two monuments—one a great report made by his own hand; another, the loftiest peak in the Union, begun for him in the planet's youth and sculptured of enduring granite by the slow hand of Time.

Clarence King was born in Newport, Rhode Island, in 1842. After graduating from Yale University's Sheffield Scientific School in 1862, he traveled cross-country to the Comstock Lode in Nevada, then to California. There he met geologist and author William Brewer, who hired King to work on his California Geological Survey. For the next three years, King explored much of the state, and his travels inspired his 1872 memoir Mountaineering in the Sierra Nevada—*still one of the most vivid and entertaining accounts of exploration in the American West. After returning east in 1866, King convinced the U.S. Congress to fund a survey of the 40th parallel between eastern Colorado and California, and fieldwork for this survey brought him back west again over the next six years. In 1878 he was named first chief of the U.S. Geological Survey but resigned this post after three years to become a mining entrepreneur. Famed for his wit, intellect, and charm, King counted among his friends such luminaries as writer Henry Adams and diplomat John Hay. His last years were unhappy. In 1888 he secretly married an African-American woman, Ada Copeland, with whom he had four children; he let none of his distinguished friends know of this marriage, nor did he reveal his true name to Copeland until the end of his life. The stress of living a double life, coupled with financial struggles as a result of failed mining schemes, led King to be committed to a mental hospital in 1894. He died of tuberculosis in Phoenix, Arizona, in 1901.*

◉ John Muir

From *Our National Parks*
THE SEQUOIA AND
GENERAL GRANT NATIONAL PARKS

T HE BIG TREE *(SEQUOIA GIGANTEA)* is Nature's forest masterpiece, and, so far as I know, the greatest of living things. It belongs to an ancient stock, as its remains in old rocks show, and has a strange air of other days about it, a thoroughbred look inherited from the long ago—the auld lang syne of trees. Once the genus was common, and with many species flourished in the now desolate Arctic regions, in the interior of North America, and in Europe, but in long, eventful wanderings from climate to climate only two species have survived the hardships they had to encounter, the gigantea and sempervirens, the former now restricted to the western slopes of the Sierra, the other to the Coast Mountains, and both to California, excepting a few groves of Redwood which extend into Oregon. The Pacific Coast in general is the paradise of conifers. Here nearly all of them are giants, and display a beauty and magnificence unknown elsewhere. The climate is mild, the ground never freezes, and moisture and sunshine abound all the year. Nevertheless it is not easy to account for the colossal size of the Sequoias. The largest are about three hundred feet high and thirty feet in diameter. Who of all the dwellers of the plains and prairies and fertile home forests of round-headed oak and maple, hickory and elm, ever dreamed that earth could bear such growths,—trees that the familiar pines and firs seem to know nothing about, lonely, silent, serene, with a physiognomy almost godlike; and so old, thousands of them still living had already counted their years by tens of centuries when Columbus set sail from Spain and were in the vigor of youth or middle age when the star led the Chaldean sages to the infant Saviour's cradle! As far as man is concerned they are the same yesterday, to-day, and forever, emblems of permanence.

No description can give any adequate idea of their singular majesty, much less of their beauty. Excepting the sugar-pine, most of their neighbors with pointed tops seem to be forever shouting Excelsior, while the Big Tree, though soaring above them all, seems satisfied, its rounded head, poised lightly as a cloud, giving no impression of trying to go higher. Only in youth does it show like other conifers a heavenward yearning, keenly aspiring with a long quick-growing top. Indeed the whole tree for the first century or two, or until a hundred to a hundred and fifty feet high, is arrowhead in form, and, compared with the solemn rigidity of age, is as sensitive to the wind as a squirrel tail. The lower branches are gradually dropped as it grows older, and the upper ones thinned out until comparatively few are left. These, however, are developed to great size, divide again and again, and terminate in bossy rounded masses of leafy branchlets, while the head becomes dome-shaped. Then poised in fullness of strength and beauty, stern and solemn in mien, it glows with eager, enthusiastic life, quivering to the tip of every leaf and branch and far-reaching root, calm as a granite dome, the first to feel the touch of the rosy beams of the morning, the last to bid the sun good-night.

Perfect specimens, unhurt by running fires or lightning, are singularly regular and symmetrical in general form, though not at all conventional, showing infinite variety in sure unity and harmony of plan. The immensely strong, stately shafts, with rich purplish brown bark, are free of limbs for a hundred and fifty feet or so, though dense tufts of sprays occur here and there, producing an ornamental effect, while long parallel furrows give a fluted columnar appearance. It shoots forth its limbs with equal boldness in every direction, showing no weather side. On the old trees the main branches are crooked and rugged, and strike rigidly outward mostly at right angles from the trunk, but there is always a certain measured restraint in their reach which keeps them within bounds. No other Sierra tree has foliage so densely massed or outline so finely, firmly drawn and so obediently subordinate to an ideal type. A particularly knotty, angular, ungovernable-looking branch, five to eight feet in diameter and perhaps a thousand years old, may occasionally be seen pushing out from the trunk as if determined to break across the bounds of the regular curve, but like all the others, as soon as the general outline is approached the huge limb dissolves into massy bosses of branchlets and sprays, as if the tree were growing beneath an invisible bell glass against the sides of which the branches were moulded, while many small, varied departures from the ideal form give the impression of freedom to grow as they like.

Except in picturesque old age, after being struck by lightning and broken by a thousand snowstorms, this regularity of form is one of the Big Tree's most distinguishing characteristics. Another is the simple sculptural beauty of the trunk and its great thickness as compared with its height and the width of the branches, many of them being from eight to ten feet in diameter at a height of two hundred feet from the ground, and seeming more like finely modeled and sculptured architectural columns than the stems of trees, while the great strong limbs are like rafters supporting the magnificent dome head.

The root system corresponds in magnitude with the other dimensions of the tree, forming a flat far-reaching spongy network two hundred feet or more in width without any taproot, and the instep is so grand and fine, so suggestive of endless strength, it is long ere the eye is released to look above it. The natural swell of the roots, though at first sight excessive, gives rise to buttresses no greater than are required for beauty as well as strength, as at once appears when you stand back far enough to see the whole tree in its true proportions. The fineness of the taper of the trunk is shown by its thickness at great heights—a diameter of ten feet at a height of two hundred being, as we have seen, not uncommon. Indeed the boles of but few trees hold their thickness as well as Sequoia. Resolute, consummate, determined in form, always beheld with wondering admiration, the Big Tree always seems unfamiliar, standing alone, unrelated, with peculiar physiognomy, awfully solemn and earnest. Nevertheless, there is nothing alien in its looks. The Madrona, clad in thin, smooth, red and yellow bark and big glossy leaves, seems, in the dark coniferous forests of Washington and Vancouver Island, like some lost wanderer from the magnolia groves of the South, while the Sequoia, with all its strangeness, seems more at home than any of its neighbors, holding the best right to the ground as the oldest, strongest inhabitant. One soon becomes acquainted with new species of pine and fir and spruce as with friendly people, shaking their outstretched branches like shaking hands, and fondling their beautiful little ones; while the venerable aboriginal Sequoia, ancient of other days, keeps you at a distance, taking no notice of you, speaking only to the winds, thinking only of the sky, looking as strange in aspect and behavior among the neighboring trees as would the mastodon or hairy elephant among the homely bears and deer. Only the Sierra Juniper is at all like it, standing rigid and unconquerable on glacial pavements for thousands of years, grim, rusty, silent, uncommunicative, with an air of antiquity about as pronounced as that so characteristic of Sequoia.

The bark of full grown trees is from one to two feet thick, rich cinnamon brown, purplish on young trees and shady parts of the old, forming magnificent masses of color with the underbrush and beds of flowers. Toward the end of winter the trees themselves bloom while the snow is still eight or ten feet deep. The pistillate flowers are about three eighths of an inch long, pale green, and grow in countless thousands on the ends of the sprays. The staminate are still more abundant, pale yellow, a fourth of an inch long; and when the golden pollen is ripe they color the whole tree and dust the air and the ground far and near.

The cones are bright grass-green in color, about two and a half inches long, one and a half wide, and are made up of thirty or forty strong, closely packed, rhomboidal scales with four to eight seeds at the base of each. The seeds are extremely small and light, being only from an eighth to a fourth of an inch long and wide, including a filmy surrounding wing, which causes them to glint and waver in falling and enables the wind to carry them considerable distances from the tree.

The faint lisp of snowflakes as they alight is one of the smallest sounds mortal can hear. The sound of falling Sequoia seeds, even when they happen to strike on flat leaves or flakes of bark, is about as faint. Very different is the bumping and thudding of the falling cones. Most of them are cut off by the Douglas squirrel and stored for the sake of the seeds, small as they are. In the calm Indian summer these busy harvesters with ivory sickles go to work early in the morning, as soon as breakfast is over, and nearly all day the ripe cones fall in a steady pattering, bumping shower. Unless harvested in this way they discharge their seeds and remain on the trees for many years. In fruitful seasons the trees are fairly laden. On two small specimen branches one and a half and two inches in diameter I counted four hundred and eighty cones. No other California conifer produces nearly so many seeds, excepting perhaps its relative, the Redwood of the Coast Mountains. Millions are ripened annually by a single tree, and the product of one of the main groves in a fruitful year would suffice to plant all the mountain ranges of the world.

The dense tufted sprays make snug nesting places for birds, and in some of the loftiest, leafiest towers of verdure thousands of generations have been reared, the great solemn trees shedding off flocks of merry singers every year from nests, like the flocks of winged seeds from the cones.

The Big Tree keeps its youth far longer than any of its neighbors. Most silver firs are old in their second or third century, pines in their fourth or fifth, while the Big Tree growing beside them is still in the bloom of its youth, juvenile in every feature at the age of old pines, and cannot be said to attain anything like prime size and beauty before its fifteen hundredth year, or under favorable circumstances become old before its three thousandth. Many, no doubt, are much older than this. On one of the Kings River giants, thirty-five feet and eight inches in diameter exclusive of bark, I counted upwards of four thousand annual wood-rings, in which there was no trace of decay after all these centuries of mountain weather. There is no absolute limit to the existence of any tree. Their death is due to accidents, not, as of animals, to the wearing out of organs. Only the leaves die of old age, their fall is foretold in their structure; but the leaves are renewed every year and so also are the other essential organs—wood, roots, bark, buds. Most of the Sierra trees die of disease. Thus the magnificent silver firs are devoured by fungi, and comparatively few of them live to see their three hundredth birth year. But nothing hurts the Big Tree. I never saw one that was sick or showed the slightest sign of decay. It lives on through indefinite thousands of years until burned, blown down, undermined, or shattered by some tremendous lightning stroke. No ordinary bolt ever seriously hurts Sequoia. In all my walks I have seen only one that was thus killed outright. Lightning, though rare in the California lowlands, is common on the Sierra. Almost every day in June and July small thunderstorms refresh the main forest belt. Clouds like snowy mountains of marvelous beauty grow rapidly in the calm sky about midday and cast cooling shadows and showers that seldom last more than an hour. Nevertheless these brief, kind storms wound or kill a good many trees. I have seen silver firs two hundred feet high split into long peeled rails and slivers down to the roots, leaving not even a stump, the rails radiating like the spokes of a wheel from a hole in the ground where the tree stood. But the Sequoia, instead of being split and slivered, usually has forty or fifty feet of its brash knotty top smashed off in short chunks about the size of cord-wood, the beautiful rosy red ruins covering the ground in a circle a hundred feet wide or more. I never saw any that had been cut down to the ground or even to below the branches except one in the Stanislaus Grove, about twelve feet in diameter, the greater part of which was smashed to fragments, leaving only a leafless stump about seventy-five feet high. It is a curious fact that all the very old Sequoias have lost their heads by lightning. "All things come to him who waits." But of all living things Sequoia is perhaps the only one able to wait long enough to make sure of being struck by lightning. Thousands of years it stands ready and waiting, offering its head to every passing cloud as if inviting its fate, praying for heaven's fire as a blessing; and when at last the old head is off, another of the same shape immediately begins to grow on. Every bud and branch seems excited, like bees that have lost their queen, and tries hard to repair the damage. Branches that for many centuries have been growing out horizontally at once turn upward and all their branchlets arrange themselves with reference to a new top of the same peculiar curve as the old one. Even the small subordinate branches halfway down the trunk do their best to push up to the top and help in this curious head-making.

The great age of these noble trees is even more wonderful than their huge size, standing bravely up, millennium in, millennium out, to all that fortune may bring them, triumphant over tempest and fire and time, fruitful and beautiful, giving food and shelter to multitudes of small fleeting creatures dependent on their bounty. Other trees may claim to be about as large or as old: Australian Gums, Senegal Baobabs, Mexican Taxodiums, English Yews, and venerable Lebanon Cedars, trees of renown, some of which are from ten to thirty feet in diameter. We read of oaks that are supposed to have existed ever since the creation, but strange to say I can find no definite accounts of the age of any of these trees, but only estimates based on tradition and assumed average rates of growth. No other known tree approaches the Sequoia in grandeur, height and thickness being considered, and none as far as I know has looked down on so many centuries or opens such impressive and suggestive views into history. The majestic monument of the Kings River Forest is, as we have seen, fully four thousand years old, and measuring the rings of annual growth we find it was no less than twenty-seven feet in diameter at the beginning of the Christian era, while many observations lead me to expect the discovery of others ten or twenty centuries older. As to those of moderate age, there are thousands, mere youth as yet, that—

"Saw the light that shone
On Mahomet's uplifted crescent,
On many a royal gilded throne
And deed forgotten in the present,
… saw the age of sacred trees
And Druid groves and mystic larches,
And saw from forest domes like these
The builder bring his Gothic arches."

Great trees and groves used to be venerated as sacred monuments and halls of council and worship. But soon after the discovery of the Calaveras Grove one of the grandest trees was cut down for the sake of a stump! The laborious vandals had seen "the biggest tree in the world," then, forsooth, they must try to see the biggest stump and dance on it.

Generally considered the father of the American environmental movement, John Muir was born in Dunbar, Scotland, in 1838 and immigrated with his family to Wisconsin in 1849. He spent three years at the University of Wisconsin but left to travel—first walking the thousand miles from Indiana to the Gulf Coast, then crossing the Isthmus of Panama and sailing up the Pacific Coast to San Francisco, where he landed in 1868. That same year he traveled across the San Joaquin Valley to the Sierra Nevada, where he spent a summer herding sheep; he became interested in Sierra geology and was among the first to propose the then-controversial theory that the Yosemite Valley had been carved by Sierra glaciers. In 1874 he began publishing his natural history essays on the Sierra. For the rest of his life he divided his time between writing, working his family fruit ranch in Martinez, California, and passionately advocating the preservation of American wilderness. He led the campaign to have Yosemite set aside as a national park, which it was in 1890, and in 1892 he became one of the founders of the Sierra Club, of which he served as president until 1914. Muir's books include The Mountains of California *(Century, 1894),* Our National Parks *(Houghton Mifflin, 1901),* Stickeen *(Houghton Mifflin, 1909), and* My First Summer in the Sierra *(Houghton Mifflin, 1911). Muir was married to Louie Wanda Strentzel; they had two daughters. He died in 1914.*

Judy Van der Veer

Selection from *November Grass*

I N NOVEMBER THE GIRL BEGAN TAKING the cattle out to graze on roadside grass. All the dry grass was gone from the hill pasture and the last of the corn fodder was fed. Usually the corn fodder lasted until winter rains brought up new pasturage, but this summer the big field was turned for summer fallow; it was an old field and needed rest. The little field raised a good crop of corn but not enough to last until grass time. If the cattle got their fill of roadside forage they wouldn't need much hay, and saving hay was as good as saving money. By the roadside there were patches of Bermuda grass and plenty of tall brown grass; even the oldest cow could get enough to eat.

After the morning milking was done, the girl put a hackamore on Pete and rode him bareback, hazing the cows ahead of her. The old hound, Juno, walked at Pete's heels and Flaxie, the yearling filly, cavorted beside him. Sometimes the colt made sudden sallies, rushing up at the cows and making them trot until their empty udders swished back and forth. She was so beautiful and lively in the crisp morning that the girl took pleasure in watching her.

All the girl had to do was to stay near the cattle so they wouldn't wander too far or break into neighbors' fields. If any of them got in the road she shooed them out of the way when a car came along. But the road was so little traveled that the passing of a car became an event.

Some people thought herding cattle a monotonous job, but the girl enjoyed it. She liked the sound the browsing animals made, breaking off the sun-crisped grasses. It was satisfying to see the lean cows eat their fill.

Once the cattle settled down to grazing she turned Pete loose so he could eat, too. Flaxie the colt stopped her foolishness and grazed earnestly. The girl sat down and the hound went to sleep beside her. Sometimes the old dog dreamed. She whimpered and jerked her legs, thinking she was chasing rabbits over the hills.

The girl could drowse in the warm grass, or read a book if she brought one, or just sit and think. That was what made her occupation so pleasant. Apparently she was doing nothing but being lazy, yet she was tending to the very important job of feeding cattle.

This was the time of year for waiting. It was between the time of harvesting and the time of planting. The wild grass seeds were dormant in the hard earth. The farmers had to wait until rain came before they could plow and plant oats and barley. There was a hard dry crust over the fields where a few months ago corn had been tall and bright.

The corn had been so beautiful! The girl had helped with the irrigating and cultivating and because she worked with it so much it had grown, almost, to have a personality. She remembered how it had been when she went to walk up and down the rows one summer night. The corn was bright with light and deep with shadow, and breathless with growing under the August corn moon. And, soon after, all the stalks were cut and carried away. Now the field must wait a while, then it would receive oat seeds, and in the spring, oats would be cut and, after the cattle had gleaned the field, it would be plowed again and corn planted. Though the season now seemed slow of turning and nothing could be planted and nothing grew in the pastures, it was a good season. It was part of the cycle, though it seemed the stopping time.

The fields were waiting for their turn to be planted, first with grain, then with corn. The hills were waiting for the time of grass and wildflowers, for the time of young rabbits and coyote pups and fawns and grazing cattle again. Leaves dropped from sycamores, cottonwoods and willows, but the live oaks held their leaves, growing only a little more dusty looking as the days went on.

Though the land was very thirsty, so thirsty that even cactus looked as if it wanted rain, and dust was ankle deep in cattle trails, there was actually more surface water in places than in midsummer. Everywhere under the earth water was rising as if unbearably eager to meet water from the sky. You had only to dig a little hole in the sandy riverbed, and there was water.

Springs that had been nearly dry in August were reviving now, and where tules were yellowing in the swampy bits of riverbed, you saw that the water had risen. A remarkable thing to be happening after seven rainless months, but it happened every fall. Old folks said that it was because of colder nights, but the girl liked to think it was because water was anxious to be moving, now that it was time for rain. Once the rains really started there would be rushing torrents everywhere, everything would seem moving with excitement. It would be the time of year for hurry, tractors would drone until dark in the fields, horses and men would work themselves weary.

But now there was little work, and that, slow. Other men were doing what her father was doing, spreading manure on waiting fields, and between times hauling dead wood out of the river to burn when cold weather really came.

The only lively creatures this time of year were the turkeys. Their gobbling increased as the days went by. It was a sound you never heard in the spring; it belonged to fall as much as withered leaves and dry fields. It would seem to rise to a crescendo until Thanksgiving, then decrease until after Christmas, not to be heard until October again.

The cows were bred, except the heifer whose first calf stayed home in the corral. The cows and mares were quiet this time of year; in the spring they would rejoice in new calves and colts, then grow restless, longing to be bred again. But now it was their quiet time, and their hungry time, too. They probably had forgotten that grass is sometimes green.

The girl sat and looked around her at the waiting world. It was a yellow and brown world, with sparse touches of green. It was a world bordered by mountains. Their rocky sides turned red at sundown and gray blue at noon. It was all a little too bright, like a girl waiting eagerly for a lover coming. For though middays were hot and drowsy, there was a feeling of expectancy. There was a tenseness in the waiting; the world wasn't so relaxed as the dropping leaves might indicate.

But the girl felt relaxed. Summer had been a time of work, and a time of play, too. Summer had been a time of wonderment, and she must think about that later. Now this was different. This was a time to stop and look at the land before rain changed it. This was a time to look at herself before years changed her.

Judy Van der Veer was born in Oil City, Pennsylvania, in 1912. At age seven she moved with her family to a ranch near Ramona in San Diego County; ranch life and the San Diego County backcountry would become the subject and setting for all of her writing. Van der Veer published her first novel, The River Pasture *(Longmans, Green and Company), in 1936; it was followed by* Brown Hills *(Longmans, Green and Company, 1938) and* November Grass *(Longmans, Green and Company, 1940). She also wrote children's books, including* Wallace, the Wandering Pig *(Harcourt, Brace and World, 1967), and wrote frequently for the* Christian Science Monitor *and other newspapers. She died in 1982.*

✤ *Wallace Stegner*

Selection from *Angle of Repose*

S USAN WARD CAME WEST NOT TO JOIN a new society but to endure it, not to build anything but to enjoy a temporary experience and make it yield whatever instruction it contained. She anticipated her life in New Almaden as she had looked forward to the train journey across the continent—as a rather strenuous outdoor excursion. The day she spent resting with Oliver's sister Mary Prager in San Francisco she understood to be the last day of the East, not the first of the West. That sort of house, full of Oriental art, and that hidden garden with its pampas grass and palms and exotic flowers, were not for her, not yet. Mary Prager was such a beauty, and Conrad Prager so formidably elegant, that she wished she could introduce them to Augusta as proof of the acceptability of Oliver's connections. Because her trunks had not yet arrived, she had to wear Mary Prager's clothes, which made her feel, in the strange garden in the strange chilly air, like someone else—Mrs. Oliver Ward, perhaps, wife of the young mining engineer who as soon as he had established himself in his profession would he able to provide such a house and life as this, preferably near Guilford, Connecticut, or Milton, New York.

Nothing on the trip to New Almaden next day modified her understanding that her lot at first would be hardship. It was intensely hot, the valley roads seen through the train windows boiled with white dust, Lizzie's usually silent baby cried and would not be comforted. In San Jose a stage with black leather curtains waited; they were the only passengers. But her anticipation of a romantic Bret Harte stage ride lasted only minutes. Dust engulfed them. She had Oliver draw the curtains, but then the heat was so great that they suffered at a slow boil. After three minutes she had Oliver open the curtains again halfway. They were thus insured both heat and dust, and were almost entirely cut off from the view.

By that time Susan cared nothing about the view, she only wanted to get there. Whenever Oliver caught her eye she made a point of smiling bravely; when he said abusive things about the weather she looked at her perspiring hands, and made mute faces of comic endurance. Now and then, as the stage rocked and threw them around among their luggage, she looked up into Lizzie's stony face and envied her patience.

It seemed a fantastically long twelve miles. Whatever conversation they attempted faded. They sat on, suffering. Susan was aware of brutal sun outside, an intolerable glare above and through their dust. Then after a long time—two hours?—she happened to glance out through the half-open curtains and saw the white trunk and pointed leaves of a sycamore going by. Their wheels were rolling quietly in sand. She thought the air felt cooler. "Trees?" she said. "I thought it would be all barren."

Oliver, sitting with his hands braced on his knees, looked altogether too vigorous and untired. He had evidently been keeping silent for her sake, not because he himself felt this jolting, dust-choked, endless ride a hardship. "Are you disappointed?" he said.

"If there are trees maybe there's a stream. Is there?"

"Not up at our place."

"Where do we get our water?"

"Why, the housewife carries it from the spring," he said. "It's only a half mile up the hill. Things are not as uncivilized out here as you think."

Lizzie's face, bent over the finally sleeping baby, showed the faintest shadow of a smile. It was not well advised of Oliver to make jokes before her. She was a jewel, tidy, competent, and thoughtful, but she should not be spoiled with familiarity. Susan watched the trees pass, dusty but authentic.

The stage leveled off into what seemed a plain or valley. She leaned to see. Ahead of them, abrupt as the precipices up which little figures toil in Chinese paintings, she saw a wild wooded mountainside that crested at a long ridge spiky with conifers. She pulled the curtains wide. "But my goodness!" she cried. "You called them *hills!*"

He laughed at her, as pleased as if he had made them by hand. "You permiscus old consort," she said, "you deceived me. Don't tell me *anything*. I'm going to watch and draw my own conclusions."

The road became a street, and no dust rose around their wheels; she saw that it had been sprinkled. On one side of them was a stream nearly lost among trees and bushes, on the other a row of ugly identical cottages, each with a patch of lawn like a shirtfront and a row of red geraniums like a necktie. At the end of the street, below the wide veranda of a white house, a Mexican was watering flowers with a garden hose. She saw water gleam from the roadside ditch, smelled wet grass. The oaks had been pruned so that they went up high, like maples in a New England village. Their shade lay across road and lawn.

"This must be the Hacienda," she said.

"Draw your own conclusions."

"I conclude it is. It's nice."

"Would you rather we were going to live down here?"

She thought that cool grass the most delicious thing she had ever seen or smelled, but she appraised his tone and said cautiously, "I haven't seen our place yet."

"No. But this looks good to you, does it?"

She considered, or pretended to. "It's lovely and cool, but it looks as if it were trying to be something it isn't. It's a little too *proper* to be picturesque, isn't it?"

Oliver took her hand and shook it. "Good girl. And too close to too many people."

"Why? Aren't the manager and the others nice?"

"They're all right. I guess I prefer the Cousin Jacks and Mexicans up at the camps."

They were going right through the Hacienda at a trot. Some children scattered, turning to stare. A woman looked out a door. "Aren't we stopping here?" she asked.

"I slipped Eugene a little extra to deliver you right to your gate."

"Ah," she said, "that'll be nicer," and leaned to the window to see as the stage tilted through dry oaks along a trail dug out of the hillside. But her mind worried a question. He thought of making her arrival as pleasant as possible, and as easy for her, and he didn't hesitate to spend money to do it, but he hadn't thought to send her the fare to cross the continent—not only Lizzie's fare, which he might have forgotten, but her own, which he shouldn't have. Not the least unknown part of her unknown new life was the man beside her. From the time she had bought the tickets out of her savings she had not been entirely free of fear.

Grandmother, I feel like telling her, have a little confidence in the man you married. You're safer than you think.

The road climbed, kinked back on itself and started a sweeping curve around a nearly bare hill. Ahead she saw five parallel spurs of mountain, as alike as the ridges of a plowed field but huge and impetuous, plunging down into the canyon. The first was very dark, the next less dark, the third hazed, the fourth dim, the fifth almost gone. All day there had been no sky, but now she saw that there was one, a pale diluted blue.

At the turn a battered liveoak leaned on limbs that touched the ground on three sides. To its trunk were nailed many boxes, each with a name painted or chalked on it: Trengove, Fall, Tregoning, Tyrrell. Across a gulch on the left she saw roofs and heard the yelling of children.

"Cornish Camp?"

"Draw your own conclusions."

"What are the boxes? Is there a newspaper?"

"Oh Eastern effeteness," Oliver said. "Those are meat boxes. Every morning the meat wagon comes by and leaves Tregoning his leg of mutton and Trengove his soup bone and Mother Fall her pot roast. Tomorrow, if you want, I'll put up a box for Mother Ward."

"I don't think I should like everyone to know what I feed you," Susan said. "Doesn't anybody ever steal things?"

"Steals? This isn't the Hacienda."

"You don't *like* the Hacienda, do you?" she said. "Why not?"

He grunted.

"Well, I must say it's prettier than this."

"There I can't argue with you," he said. "It smells better, too."

The whole place had the air of having been dumped down the hillside—steep streets, houses at every angle white and incongruous and unpainted and shabby. Wash hung everywhere, the vacant lots were littered with cans and trash, dogs prowled and children screamed. At the water tank they slowed to pass through a reluctantly parting, densely staring tangle of men, boys, teamsters, cows, donkeys, mules. When Oliver leaned out and saluted some of them they waved, grinning, and stared with their hands forgotten in the air. Engineer and his new missus. She thought them coarse and cow-faced and strangely pale.

But they made sharp pictures, too: a boy hoisting a water yoke with a pail at each end, the pails sloshing silver over their rims; a teamster unyoking his mules; a donkey standing with his ears askew and his nose close to the ground, on his face a look of mournful patience that reminded her comically of Lizzie.

"Over there's Mother Fall's, where I lived," Oliver said, and pointed.

A white two-story house, square, blank, and ugly. Each window was a room, she supposed, one of them formerly his. The downstairs would smell of cabbage and grease. She could not even imagine living there. Her heart rose up and assured her that she would make him glad she had come.

"You said she was nice to you."

"Yes. A stout Cornish dame. She's been helping me get ready for you."

"I must call on her, I should think."

He looked at her a little queerly. "You sure must. If we don't have supper there tomorrow we'll never be forgiven."

Above and to the left, scattered down a long hogback ridge, the Mexican camp appeared. Its houses were propped with poles, timbers, ladders; its crooked balconies overflowed with flowers; in a doorway she saw a dark woman smoking a cigarette, on a porch a grandmother braided a child's hair. There were no white-painted cottages, but she thought this camp more attractive than the Cornish—it had a look of belonging, some gift of harmoniousness. The stage turned off to the right, below the camp, and left her craning, unsatisfied.

"Is there a Chinese Camp too?" she said.

"Around the hill and below us. We'll hear it a little, but we won't see it."

"Where's the mine?"

With his forefinger he jabbed straight down. "You don't see that either. Just a shaft house or a dump in a gulch here and there."

"You know what?" she said, holding the curtains back and watching ahead through the dusty little oaks, "I don't think you described this place very well."

"Draw your own conclusions," Oliver said. He offered a finger to

Lizzie's baby, just waking up and yawning and focusing his eyes. The stage stopped.

⟋⟍

THE COTTAGE SHE HAD IMAGINED exposed on a bare hill among ugly mine buildings was tucked back among liveoaks at the head of a draw. In her first quick devouring look she saw the verandas she had asked for and helped Oliver sketch, a rail fence swamped under geraniums. When she hopped out slapping dust from her clothes she saw that the yard showed the even tooth-marks of raking. He had prepared for her so carefully. Both mostly what she felt in the moment of arrival was space, extension, bigness. Behind the house the mountain went up steeply to the ridge, along which now lay, as soft as a sleeping cat, a roll of fog or cloud. Below the house it fell just as steeply down spurs and canyons to tumbled hills as bright as a lion's hide. Below those was the valley's dust, a level obscurity, and rising out of it, miles away, was another long mountain as high as their own. Turning back the way she had come in, she saw those five parallel spurs, bare gold on top, darkly wooded in the gulches, receding in layers of blue haze. I know that mountain, old Loma Prieta. In nearly a hundred years it has changed less than most of California. Once you get beyond the vineyards and subdivisions along its lower slopes there is nothing but a reservoir and an Air Force radar station.

"Well" Oliver said, "come on inside."

It was as she had visualized it from his sketches, but much more finished—a house, not a picturesque shack. It smelled cleanly of paint. Its floors and wainscot were dark redwood, its walls a soft gray. The light was dim and cool, as she thought the light in a house should be. A breeze went through the rooms, bringing inside the smell of aromatic sun-soaked plants. The Franklin stove was polished like a farmer's Sunday boots, water was piped into the sink, the kitchen cooler held sacks and cans and let out a rich smell of bacon. In the arch between dining room and living room Oliver had hung his spurs, bowie, and six-shooter. "The homey touch," he said. "And wait, there are some little housewarming presents."

From the piazza he brought one of the packages that had been part of their luggage down from San Francisco. She opened it and pulled out a grass fan. "Fiji," Oliver said. Next a large mat of the same grass, as finely woven as linen, and with a sweet hay smell. "More Fiji." Next a paper parasol that opened up to a view of Fujiyama. "Japan," Oliver said. "Don't open it inside—bad luck." At the bottom of the box was something heavy which, unwrapped, turned out to be a water jar with something in Spanish written across it. "Guadalajara," Oliver said. "Now you're supposed to feel that the place is yours. You know what that Spanish means? It says, 'Help thyself, little Tomasa.'"

There it sits, over on my window sill, ninety-odd years later, without even a nick out of it. The fan and the parasol went quickly, the mat lasted until Leadville and was mourned when it passed, the olla has come through three generations of us, as have the bowie, the spurs, and the six-shooter. It wasn't the worst set of omens that attended the beginning of my grandparents' housekeeping.

She was touched. Like the raked yard, the clean paint, his absurd masculine decorations in the archway, his gifts proved him what she had believed him to be. Yet the one small doubt stuck in her mind like a burr in tweed. In a small voice she said, "You'll spoil me."

"I hope so."

Lizzie came in with luggage in one hand and the baby in her other arm. "Right through the kitchen," Oliver said. "Your bed's made up. The best I could do for Georgie was a packing box with a pillow in it."

"That will be fine, thank you," Lizzie said, and went serenely on through.

Kind. He really was. And energetic. Within a minute he was making a fire so that Susan could have warm water to wash in. Then he said that he had a little errand at Mother Fall's, and before she could ask him what he was off the piazza and gone.

Susan took off her traveling dress and washed in the basin by the kitchen door. Below her were the tops of strange bushes, the steep mountainside tufted with sparse brown grass. Looking around the corner of Lizzie's room to the upward slopes, she saw exotic red-barked trees among the woods, and smelled the herb-cupboard smells of sage and bay. Another world. Thoughtfully she poured out the water and went inside, where Lizzie was slicing a round loaf she had found in the cooler. Even the bread here was strange.

"How does it seem, Lizzie? Is your room all right?"

"It's fine."

"Is it the way you imagined it?"

"I don't know that I imagined it much."

"Oh, I did," said Susan. "All wrong."

She looked at Lizzie's room, clean and bare; went out through the dining room where her gifts lay on the table and read the inscription on the olla: Help thyself, Tomasita. Out on the piazza she sat in the hammock and looked out over the green and gold mountain and thought *how strange, how strange.*

Rocks clattered in the trail, and Oliver came in sight with a great black dog padding beside him. He made it sit down in front of the hammock. "This is Stranger. We figure he's half Labrador and half St. Bernard. He thinks he's my dog, but he's mistaken. From now on he goes walking with nobody but you. Shake hands, Stranger."

With great dignity Stranger offered a paw like a firelog, first to Oliver, who pushed it aside, and then to Susan. He submitted to having his head stroked. "Stranger?" Susan said. "Is that your name, *Stranger?* That's wrong. You're the one who lives here. *I'm* the stranger."

Oliver went inside and came out with a piece of buttered bread. "Give him something. You're to feed him, always, so he'll get attached to you."

"But it's you he likes," Susan said. "Look at the way he watches every move you make."

"Just the same, he's going to learn to like *you.* "That's what we got him for, to look after you. If he doesn't, I'll make a rug of him. You hear that, you?"

The dog rolled his eyes and twisted his head back, keeping his bottom firmly on the boards. "Here, Stranger," Susan said, and broke off a piece of bread. The dog's eyes rolled down to fix on it. She tossed it, and he slupped it out of the air with a great sucking sound that made them both laugh. Over his broad black head Susan looked into Oliver's eyes. "You *will* spoil me."

"I hope so," he said for the second time.

Then she couldn't keep the question back any longer. "Oliver."

"Yes."

"Tell me something."

"Sure."

"I don't want you to be angry."

"Angry. At *you?*"

"It seems so petty. I shouldn't even mention it. I only want us to start without a single shadow between us."

"My God, what have I done?" Oliver said. Then a slow mulish look came into his face, a look like disgust or guilt or evasion. She stared at him in panic, remembering what his mother had said of him: that when he was put in the wrong he would never defend himself, he would only close up like a clam. She didn't want him to close up, she wanted to talk this out and be rid of it. Blue as blue stones in his sunburned face, his eyes touched hers and were withdrawn. Miserably she stood waiting. "I know what it is," he said. "You needn't tell me."

"You didn't just forget, then."

"No, I didn't forget,"

"But *why,* then?"

He looked over her head, he was interested in the valley. She could see shrugging impatience in his shoulders. "It isn't the money," she said. "I had the money, and there was nothing I would rather have spent it for than coming to you. But your letter never even mentioned it. I thought perhaps … I don't know. It shamed me before Father. I hated it that he had to send me off to someone he would think didn't know …"

"What my duty was?" Oliver said, almost sneering. "I knew."

"Then why?"

Impatiently he turned, he looked down at her directly. "Because I didn't have it."

"But you said you had something saved."

He swung an arm. "There it is."

"The house? I thought the mine agreed to pay for that."

"Kendall did. The manager. He changed his mind."

"But he *promised!*"

"Sure," Oliver said. "But then somebody overspent on one of the

Hacienda cottages and Kendall said no more renovations."

"But that's unfair!" she said. "You should have told Mr. Prager."

His laugh was incredulous. "Yes? Run crying to Conrad?"

"Well then you should just have stopped. We could have lived in it as it was."

"I could have," Oliver said. "You couldn't. I wouldn't have let you."

"Oh I'm sorry!" she said. "I didn't understand. I've been such an expense to you."

"It seems to me I've been an expense to you. How much did you spend for those tickets?"

"I won't tell you."

They stared at each other, near anger. She forgave him everything except that he hadn't explained. One word, and she would have been spared all her doubts about him. But she would certainly not let him pay her back. The hardship would not be all his. He was looking at her squarely, still mulish. She wanted to shake him. "You great … Why couldn't you have told me?"

She saw his eyebrows go up. His eyes, as they did when he smiled, closed into upside-down crescents. Young as he was, he had deep fans of wrinkles at the corners of his eyes that gave him a look of always being on the brink of smiling. And now he *was* smiling. He was not going to be sullen. They were past it.

"I was afraid you'd be sensible," he said. "I couldn't stand the thought of this place sitting here all ready for you and you not in it."

Although often considered less a California writer than a Western one, Wallace Stegner spent most of his career in California, and many of his books are set there. Stegner was born in Lake Mills, Iowa, in 1909. His family moved often, and Stegner spent portions of his childhood in Saskatchewan and Montana before settling in Salt Lake City, where he graduated from high school and, in 1930, from the University of Utah. He earned his M.A. and Ph.D. from the University of Iowa, then taught at the University of Wisconsin, Harvard, and Stanford, where he helped found the university's creative writing program and where he taught until 1971. Stegner's first novel, Remembering Laughter (Little, Brown and Company), was published in 1937; it was followed in 1943 by the semi-autobiographical The Big Rock Candy Mountain (Duell, Sloan and Pierce). Later works of fiction include The Women on the Wall (Houghton Mifflin Company, 1948), A Shooting Star (Viking Press, 1961), and Angle of Repose (Doubleday and Company, 1971). The last—which traces the life of cultured, eastern-born artist Susan Ward as she follows her mining engineer husband around the frontier West—earned Stegner the Pulitzer Prize in 1972. Stegner's nonfiction includes the biography of John Wesley Powell, Beyond the Hundredth Meridian (Houghton Mifflin, 1954); his memoir, Wolf Willow (The Viking Press, 1962); and his essay collection, The Sound of Mountain Water (Doubleday and Company, 1969). Stegner also became an ardent and eloquent advocate for the western environment. In 1934 Stegner married Mary Stuart Page; they had one son, writer Page Stegner. Wallace Stegner died in 1993.

Gary Snyder

From *The Gary Snyder Reader*

JOHN MUIR ON MT. RITTER

After scanning its face again and again,
I began to scale it, picking my holds
With intense caution. About half-way
To the top, I was suddenly brought to
A dead stop, with arms outspread
Clinging close to the face of the rock
Unable to move hand or foot
Either up or down. My doom
Appeared fixed. I MUST fall.
There would be a moment of
Bewilderment, and then,
A lifeless rumble down the cliff
To the glacier below.
My mind seemed to fill with a
Stifling smoke. This terrible eclipse
Lasted only a moment, when life blazed
Forth again with preternatural clearness.
I seemed suddenly to become possessed
Of a new sense. My trembling muscles
Became firm again, every rift and flaw in
The rock was seen as through a microscope,
My limbs moved with a positiveness and precision
With which I seemed to have
Nothing at all to do.

From *The Gary Snyder Reader*

HAY FOR THE HORSES

He had driven half the night
From far down San Joaquin
Through Mariposa, up the
Dangerous mountain roads,
And pulled in at eight a.m.
With his big truckload of hay
        behind the barn.
With winch and ropes and hooks
We stacked the bales up clean
To splintery redwood rafters
High in the dark, flecks of alfalfa
Whirling through shingle-cracks of light,
Itch of haydust in the
        sweaty shirt and shoes.
At lunchtime under Black oak
Out in the hot corral,
—The old mare nosing lunchpails,
Grasshoppers crackling in the weeds—
"I'm sixty eight," he said,
"I first bucked hay when I was seventeen.
I thought, that day I started,
I sure would hate to do this all my life.
And dammit, that's just what
I've gone and done."

From *The Gary Snyder Reader*

MID-AUGUST AT
SOURDOUGH MOUNTAIN LOOKOUT

Down valley a smoke haze
Three days heat, after five days rain
Pitch glows on the fir-cones
Across rocks and meadows
Swarms of new flies.

I cannot remember things I once read
A few friends, but they are in cities.
Drinking cold snow-water from a tin cup
Looking down for miles
Through high still air.

Poet and environmentalist Gary Snyder was born in San Francisco in 1930. His family moved to Washington state when he was two, and he grew up there and in Oregon. He attended Reed College in Portland, graduating in 1951; from 1953 to 1956 he studied Asian languages at the University of California, Berkeley. At the same time, Snyder was drawn to the western wilderness—he worked as a seasonal logger and fire lookout in the Sierra Nevada, experiences he drew upon in his first collection, Riprap *(Origin Press, 1959). In 1956 Snyder left San Francisco—where he was affiliated with Beat writers such as Jack Kerouac and Allen Ginsberg—to study Zen Buddhism in Japan. He remained abroad until the late 1960s, then returned to Northern California. In 1985 he became a professor of English at the University of California, Davis. His collections of poetry include* Myths and Texts *(Totem Press, 1960),* Turtle Island *(New Directions, 1974), and* The Gary Snyder Reader *(Counterpoint, 2000). Snyder has also been a strong voice for American environmentalism. His awards include the 1975 Pulitzer Prize (for* Turtle Island*) and the 1997 Bollingen Prize.*

THE VALLEYS

William Lewis Manly

Selection from *Death Valley in '49*

ONE THING WAS CERTAIN WE MUST MOVE somewhere at once. If we stay here we can live as long as the oxen do, and no longer, and if we go on it is uncertain where to go, to get a better place. We had guns and ammunition to be sure, but of late we had seen no living creature in this desert wild. Finally Mr. Bennett spoke and said:—

"Now I will make you a proposition. I propose that we select two of our youngest, strongest men and ask them to take some food and go ahead on foot to try to seek a settlement, and food, and we will go back to the good spring we have just left and wait for their return. It will surely not take them more than ten days for the trip, and when they get back we shall know all about the road and its character and how long it will take us to travel it. They can secure some other kind of food that will make us feel better, and when the oxen have rested a little at the spring we can get out with our wagons and animals and be safe. I think this is the best and safest way. Now what do you all say?"

After a little discussion all seemed to agree that this was the best, and now it remained to find the men to go. No one offered to accept the position of advance messengers. Finally Mr. Bennett said he knew one man well enough to know that he would come back if he lived, and he was sure he would push his way through. "I will take Lewis (myself) if he will consent to go." I consented, though I knew it was a hazardous journey, exposed to all sorts of things, Indians, climate and probable lack of water, but I thought I could do it and would not refuse. John Rogers a large strong Tennessee man was then chosen as the other one and he consented also.

Now preparations began, Mr. Arcane killed the ox which had so nearly failed, and all the men went to drying and preparing meat. Others made us some new mocassins out of rawhide, and the women made us each a knapsack.

Our meat was closely packed, and one can form an idea how poor our cattle were from the fact that John and I actually packed seven-eighths of all the flesh of an ox into our knapsacks and carried it away. They put in a couple of spoonfulls of rice and about as much tea. This seemed like robbery to the children, but the good women said that in case of sickness even that little bit might save our lives. I wore no coat or vest, but took half of a light blanket, while Rogers wore a thin summer coat and took no blanket. We each had a small tin cup and a small camp kettle holding a quart. Bennett had me take his seven-shooter rifle, and Rogers had a good double barreled shot gun. We each had a sheath knife, and our hats were small brimmed, drab affairs fitting close to the head and not very conspicuous to an enemy as we might rise up from behind a hill into possible views. We tried on our packs and fitted the straps a little so they would carry easy. They collected all the money there was in camp and gave it to us. Mr. Arcane had about $30 and others threw in small amounts from forty cents upward. We received all sorts of advice. Capt. Culverwell was an old sea faring man and was going to tell us how to find our way back, but Mr. Bennett told the captain that he had known Lewis as a hunter for many years, and that if he went over a place in the daytime he could find his way back at night every time. Others cautioned us about the Indians and told us how to manage. Others told us not to get caught in deep snow which we might find on the mountains.

This advice we received in all the kindness in which it was given, and then he bade them all good bye. Some turned away, too much affected to approach us, and others shook our hands with deep feeling, grasping them firmly and heartily hoping we would be successful and be able to pilot them out of this dreary place into a better land. Every one felt that a little food to make a change from the poor dried meat would be acceptable. Mr. and Mrs. Bennett and J. B. Arcane and wife were the last to remain when the others had turned away. They had most faith in the plan and felt deeply. Mrs. Bennett was the last, and she asked God to bless us and bring some food to her starving children.

We were so much affected that we could not speak and silently turned away and took our course again up the canyon we had descended the night before.

After a while we looked back and when they saw us turn around, all the hats and bonnets waved us a final parting.

Those left in the camp were Asabel, Bennett and Sarah his wife, with three children, George, Melissa, and Martha; J. B. Arcane and wife with son Charles. The youngest children were not more than two years old. There were also the two Earhart brothers, and a grown son, Capt. Culverwell, and some others I cannot recall; eleven grown people in all, besides a Mr. Wade, his wife and three children who did not mingle with our party, but usually camped a little distance off, followed our trail, but seemed to shun company. We soon passed round a bend of the cañon, and then walked on in silence.

We both of us meditated some over the homes of our fathers, but took new courage in view of the importance of our mission and passed on as fast as we could.

By night we were far up the mountain, near the perpendicular rough peak, and far above us on a slope we could see some bunches of grass and sage brush. We went to this and found some small water holes. No water ran from them they were so small. Here we staid all night. It did not seem very far to the snowy peak to the north of us. Just where we were seemed the lowest pass, for to the south were higher peaks and the rocks looked as if they were too steep to be got over.

Through this gap came a cold breeze, and we had to look round to get a sheltered place in which to sleep. We lay down close together, spoon fashion, and made the little blanket do as cover for the both of us. In the morning we filled our canteens, which we had made by binding two powder cans together with strips of cloth, and started for the summit near by. From this was the grandest sight we ever beheld. Looking east we could see the country we had been crawling over since November 4th. "Just look at the cursed country we have come over!" said Rogers as he pointed over it. To the north was the biggest mountain we ever saw, peaks on peaks and towering far above our heads, and covered with snow which was apparently everlasting.

This mountain seemed to have very few trees on it, and in extent, as it reached away to the north seemed interminable. South was a nearly level plain, and to the west I thought I could dimly see a range of mountains that held a little snow upon their summits, but on the main range to the south there was none. It seemed to me the dim snowy mountains must be as far as 200 miles away, but of course I could not judge accurately. After looking at this grand, but worthless landscape long enough to take in its principal features we asked each other what we supposed the people we left behind would think to see mountains so far ahead. We knew that they had an idea that the coast range was not very far ahead, but we saw at once to go over all these mountains and return within the limits of fifteen days which had been agreed upon between us, would probably be impossible, but we must try as best we could, so down the rocky steep we clambered and hurried on our way. In places the way was so steep that we had to help each other down, and the hard work made us perspire freely so that the water was a prime necessity. In one place near here, we found a little water and filled our canteens, besides drinking a good present supply. There were two low, black rocky ranges directly ahead of us which we must cross.

When part way down the mountain a valley or depression opened up in that direction up which it seemed as if we could look a hundred miles. Near by and a short distance north was a lake of water and when we reached the valley we crossed a clear stream of water flowing slowly toward the lake.

Being in need of water, we rushed eagerly to it and prepared to take a big drink, but the tempting fluid was as salt as brine and made our thirst all the more intolerable. Nothing grew on the bank of this stream and the bed was of hard clay, which glistened in the sun.

We now began the ascent of the next ridge, keeping a westernly course, and walked as fast as we could up the rough mountain side. We crossed the head of a cañon near the summit about dark, and here we found a trail, which from indications we knew to be that of the Jayhawkers, who had evidently been forced to the southward of the course they intended to take. They had camped here and had dug holes in the sand in search of water, but had found none.

We staid all night here and dug around in some other places in the bottom of the cañon, in the hope to have better luck than they did, but we got no water anywhere.

We seemed almost perishing for want of water, the hard exercise made us perspire so freely. In the morning we started on, and near the summit we came to the dead body of Mr. Fish, laying in the hot sun, as there was no material near here with which his friends could cover the remains. This Mr. Fish was the man who left camp some two weeks before in company with another and who carried the long whiplash wound about his body, in hope he could somewhere be able to trade it for bread. No doubt in this very place where he breathed his last, his bones still lie.

William Manly was born in Vermont in 1820 and moved with his family to Wisconsin, where he later worked as a lead miner. In July of 1849 he set out on the Oregon Trail for California, following it to Fort Bridger in Wyoming Territory. From there he floated down the Green and Colorado rivers to Arizona, then joined a pioneer party as it set out across the desert toward Southern California. The trip was an arduous one, with thirst and starvation threatening the lives of the men, women, and children as they wandered, lost, through the region now known as Death Valley. Manly and his friend John Rogers suffered additional hardships when they were sent ahead to seek help and return with supplies, which they were successful in doing. In 1894 Manly published an account of the journey titled Death Valley in '49 (Pacific Tree and Vine). *The book is likely at least partly ghost written; nevertheless, it remains one of the most gripping accounts of pioneer immigration to California—in the words of literary historian Lawrence Clark Powell, "a chronicle of death and disaster, survival and heroism, distinguished by narrative power, specific event, and precise observation." Manly died in 1903.*

Robert Louis Stevenson

From *The Silverado Squatters*
NAPA WINE

I WAS INTERESTED IN CALIFORNIAN WINE. Indeed, I am interested in all wines, and have been all my life, from the raisin wine that a schoolfellow kept secreted in his play-box up to my last discovery, those notable Valtellines, that once shone upon the board of Caesar.

Some of us, kind old Pagans, watch with dread the shadows falling on the age: how the unconquerable worm invades the sunny terraces of France, and Bordeaux is no more, and the Rhone a mere Arabia Petraea. Château Neuf is dead, and I have never tasted it; Hermitage—a hermitage indeed from all life's sorrows—lies expiring by the river. And in the place of these imperial elixirs, beautiful to every sense, gem-hued, flower-scented, dream-compellers:—behold upon the quays at Cette the chemicals arrayed; behold the analyst at Marseilles, raising hands in obsecration, attesting god Lyoeus, and the vats staved in, and the dishonest wines poured forth among the sea. It is not Pan only; Bacchus, too, is dead.

If wine is to withdraw its most poetic countenance, the sun of the white dinner-cloth, a deity to be invoked by two or three, all fervent, hushing their talk, degusting tenderly, and storing reminiscences—for a bottle of good wine, like a good act, shines ever in the retrospect—if wine is to desert us, go thy ways, old Jack! Now we begin to have compunctions, and look back at the brave bottles squandered upon dinner-parties, where the guests drank grossly, discussing politics the while, and even the schoolboy "took his whack," like liquorice water. And at the same time, we look timidly forward, with a spark of hope, to where the new lands, already weary of producing gold, begin to green with vineyards. A nice point in human history falls to be decided by Californian and Australian wines.

Wine in California is still in the experimental stage; and when you taste a vintage, grave economical questions are involved. The beginning of vine-planting is like the beginning of mining for the precious metals: the wine-grower also "prospects." One corner of land after another is tried with one kind of grape after another. This is a failure; that is better; a third best. So, bit by bit, they grope about for their Clos Vougeot and Lafite. Those lodes and pockets of earth, more precious than the precious ores, that yield inimitable fragrance and soft fire; those virtuous Bonanzas, where the soil has sublimated under sun and stars to something finer, and the wine is bottled poetry: these still lie undiscovered; chaparral conceals, thicket embowers them; the miner chips the rock and wanders farther, and the grizzly muses undisturbed. But there they bide their hour, awaiting their Columbus; and nature nurses and prepares them. The smack of Californian earth shall linger on the palate of your grandson.

Meanwhile the wine is merely a good wine; the best that I have tasted better than a Beaujolais, and not unlike. But the trade is poor; it lives from hand to mouth, putting its all into experiments, and forced to sell its vintages. To find one properly matured, and bearing its own name, is to be fortune's favourite.

Bearing its own name, I say, and dwell upon the innuendo.

"You want to know why California wine is not drunk in the States?" a San Francisco wine merchant said to me, after he had shown me through his premises. "Well, here's the reason."

And opening a large cupboard, fitted with many little drawers, he proceeded to shower me all over with a great variety of gorgeously tinted labels, blue, red, or yellow, stamped with crown or coronet, and hailing from such a profusion of *clos* and *châteaux,* that a single department could scarce have furnished forth the names. But it was strange that all looked unfamiliar.

"Chateau X—?" said I. "I never heard of that."

"I dare say not," said he. "I had been reading one of X—'s novels."

They were all castles in Spain! But that sure enough is the reason why California wine is not drunk in the States.

Napa valley has been long a seat of the wine-growing industry. It did not here begin, as it does too often, in the low valley lands along the river, but took at once to the rough foothills, where alone it can expect to prosper. A basking inclination, and stones, to be a reservoir of the day's heat, seem necessary to the soil for wine; the grossness of the earth must be evaporated, its marrow daily melted and refined for ages; until at length these clods that break below our footing, and to the eye appear but common earth, are truly and to the perceiving mind, a masterpiece of nature. The dust of Richebourg, which the wind carries away, what an apotheosis of the dust! Not man himself can seem a stranger child of that brown, friable powder, than the blood and sun in that old flask behind the faggots.

A Californian vineyard, one of man's outposts in the wilderness, has features of its own. There is nothing here to remind you of the Rhine or Rhone, of the low *côte d'or,* or the infamous and scabby deserts of Champagne; but all is green, solitary, covert. We visited two of them, Mr. Schram's and Mr. M'Eckron's, sharing the same glen.

Some way down the valley below Calistoga, we turned sharply to the south and plunged into the thick of the wood. A rude trail rapidly mounting; a little stream tinkling by on the one hand, big enough perhaps after the rains, but already yielding up its life; overhead and on all sides a bower of green and tangled thicket, still fragrant and still flower-bespangled by the early season, where thimble-berry played the part of our English hawthorn, and the buck-eyes were putting forth their twisted horns of blossom: through all this, we struggled toughly upwards, canted to and fro by the roughness of the trail, and continually switched across the face by sprays of leaf or blossom. The last is no great inconvenience at home; but here in California it is a matter of some moment. For in all woods and by every wayside there prospers an abominable shrub or weed, called poison-oak, whose very neighbourhood is venomous to some, and whose actual touch is avoided by the most impervious.

The two houses, with their vineyards, stood each in a green niche of its own in this steep and narrow forest dell. Though they were so near, there was already a good difference in level; and Mr. M'Eckron's head must be a long way under the feet of Mr. Schram. No more had been cleared than was necessary for cultivation; close around each oasis ran the tangled wood; the glen enfolds them; there they lie basking in sun and silence, concealed from all but the clouds and the mountain birds.

Mr. M'Eckron's is a bachelor establishment; a little bit of a wooden house, a small cellar hard by in the hillside, and a patch of vines planted and tended single-handed by himself. He had but recently begun; his vines were young, his business young also; but I thought he had the look of the man who succeeds. He hailed from Greenock: he remembered his father putting him inside Mons Meg, and that touched me home; and we exchanged a word or two of Scotch, which pleased me more than you would fancy.

Mr. Schram's, on the other hand, is the oldest vineyard in the valley, eighteen years old, I think; yet he began a penniless barber, and even after he had broken ground up here with his black malvoisies, continued for long to tramp the valley with his razor. Now, his place is the picture of prosperity: stuffed birds in the verandah, cellars far dug into the hillside, and resting on pillars like a bandit's cave:—all trimness, varnish, flowers, and sunshine, among the tangled wildwood. Stout, smiling Mrs. Schram, who has been to Europe and apparently all about the States for pleasure, entertained Fanny in the verandah, while I was tasting wines in the cellar. To Mr. Schram this was a solemn office; his serious gusto warmed my heart; prosperity had not yet wholly banished a certain neophite and girlish trepidation, and he followed every sip and read my face with proud anxiety. I tasted all. I tasted every variety and shade of Schramberger, red and white Schramberger, Burgundy Schramberger, Schramberger Hock, Schramberger Golden Chasselas, the latter with a notable bouquet, and I fear to think how many more. Much of it goes to London—most, I think; and Mr. Schram has a great notion of the English taste.

In this wild spot, I did not feel the sacredness of ancient cultivation. It was still raw, it was no Marathon, and no Johannisberg; yet the stirring sunlight, and the growing vines, and the vats and bottles in the cavern, made a pleasant music for the mind. Here, also, earth's cream was being skimmed and garnered; and the London customers can taste, such as it is, the tang of the earth in this green valley. So local, so quintessential is a wine, that it seems the very birds in the verandah might communicate a flavour, and that romantic cellar influence the bottle next to be uncorked in Pimlico, and the smile of jolly Mr. Schram might mantle in the glass.

But these are but experiments. All things in this new land are moving farther on: the wine-vats and the miner's blasting tools but picket for a night, like Bedouin pavillions; and to-morrow, to fresh woods! This stir of change and these perpetual echoes of the moving footfall, haunt the land. Men move eternally, still chasing Fortune; and, fortune found, still wander. As we drove back to Calistoga, the road lay empty of mere passengers, but its green side was dotted with the camps of travelling families: one cumbered with a great waggonful of household stuff, settlers going to occupy a ranche they had taken up in Mendocino, or perhaps Tehama County; another, a party in dust coats, men and women, whom we found camped in a grove on the roadside, all on pleasure bent, with a Chinaman to cook for them, and who waved their hands to us as we drove by.

Although born in Scotland and best known for his accounts of adventure on the high seas, Robert Louis Stevenson had a remarkable impact on California literature. Stevenson was born in Edinburgh in 1850. He earned a law degree but opted to make a life as a writer, publishing humorous essays in London periodicals. During a trip to France he met a married American woman named Fanny Osbourne, and the two fell in love; in 1879 he pursued her to Monterey, a trans-Atlantic, cross-country trip whose hardships brought the already frail Stevenson near death. Osbourne divorced her husband and married Stevenson in 1880. Virtually penniless, the couple honeymooned in a shack built on the side of Mount Saint Helena above the Napa Valley. The two months they spent there formed the basis for Stevenson's engaging portrait of the valley and its people, The Silverado Squatters *(Chatto and Windus, 1883). The pair returned to Scotland, where Stevenson's literary career blossomed; over the next few years he published his most famous works, including* Treasure Island *(Casell, 1883),* Kidnapped *(Casell, 1886), and* The Strange Case of Dr. Jekyll and Mr. Hyde *(Longmans, Green and Company, 1886). In 1888 the Stevensons returned to San Francisco, which became their launching point for an extended excursion to Hawaii, Tahiti, and Samoa. By this time Stevenson's health was failing, and he opted to remain in Samoa. He died there in 1894. Osbourne returned to California; she died in Santa Barbara in 1914.*

🍃 *Frank Norris*

Selection from *The Octopus*

THE PICNIC AND BARBECUE WERE TO BE HELD around the spring where Broderson Creek took its rise. Already two entire beeves were roasting there; teams were hitched, saddles removed, and men, women, and children, a great throng, spread out under the shade of the live-oaks. A vast confused clamour rose in the air, a babel of talk, a clatter of tin plates, of knives and forks. Bottles were uncorked, napkins and oilcloths spread over the ground. The men lit pipes and cigars, the women seized the occasion to nurse their babies.

Osterman, ubiquitous as ever, resplendent in his boots and English riding breeches, moved about between the groups, keeping up an endless flow of talk, cracking jokes, winking, nudging, gesturing, putting his tongue in his cheek, never at a loss for a reply, playing the goat.

"That josher, Osterman, always at his monkey-shines, but a good fellow for all that; brainy, too. Nothing stuck up about him either, like Magnus Derrick."

"Everything all right, Buck?" inquired Osterman, coming up to where Annixter, Hilma, and Mrs. Derrick were sitting down to their lunch.

"Yes, yes, everything right. But we've no corkscrew."

"No screwcork—no scare-crow? Here you are," and he drew from his pocket a silver-plated jack-knife with a corkscrew attachment.

Harran and Presley came up, bearing between them a great smoking, roasted portion of beef just off the fire. Hilma hastened to put forward a huge china platter.

Osterman had a joke to crack with the two boys, a joke that was rather broad, but as he turned about, the words almost on his lips, his glance fell upon Hilma herself, whom he had not seen for more than two months. She had handed Presley the platter, and was now sitting with her back against the tree, between two boles of the roots. The position was a little elevated and the supporting roots on either side of her were like the arms of a great chair—a chair of state. She sat thus, as on a throne, raised above the rest, the radiance of the unseen crown of motherhood glowing from her forehead, the beauty of the perfect woman surrounding her like a glory.

And the josh died away on Osterman's lips, and unconsciously and swiftly he bared his head. Something was passing there in the air about him that he did not understand, something, however, that imposed reverence and profound respect. For the first time in his life, embarrassment seized upon him, upon this joker, this wearer of clothes, this teller of funny stories, with his large red ears, bald head and comic actor's face. He stammered confusedly and took himself away, for the moment abstracted, serious, lost in thought.

By now everyone was eating. It was the feeding of the People, elemental, gross, a great appeasing of appetite, an enormous quenching of thirst. Quarters of beef, roasts, ribs, shoulders, haunches were consumed, loaves of bread by the thousands disappeared, whole barrels of wine went down the dry and dusty throats of the multitude. Conversation lagged while the People ate, while hunger was appeased. Everybody had his fill. One ate for the sake of eating, resolved that there should be nothing left, considering it a matter of pride to exhibit a clean plate.

After dinner, preparations were made for games. On a flat plateau at the top of one of the hills the contestants were to strive. There was to be a footrace of young girls under seventeen, a fat men's race, the younger fellows were to put the shot, to compete in the running broad jump, and the standing high jump, in the hop, skip, and step and in wrestling.

Presley was delighted with it all. It was Homeric, this feasting, this vast consuming of meat and bread and wine, followed now by games of strength. An epic simplicity and directness, an honest Anglo-Saxon mirth and innocence, commended it. Crude it was; coarse it was, but no taint of viciousness was here. These people were good people, kindly, benignant even, always readier to give than to receive, always more willing to help than to be helped. They were good stock. Of such was the backbone of the nation—sturdy Americans every one of them. Where else in the world round were such strong, honest men, such strong, beautiful women?

Annixter, Harran, and Presley climbed to the level plateau where the games were to be held, to lay out the courses, and mark the distances. It was the very place where once Presley had loved to lounge entire afternoons, reading his books of poems, smoking and dozing. From this high point one dominated the entire valley to the south and west. The view was superb. The three men paused for a moment on the crest of the hill to consider it.

Young Vacca came running and panting up the hill after them, calling for Annixter.

"Well, well, what is it?"

"Mr. Osterman's looking for you, sir, you and Mr. Harran. Vanamee, that cow-boy over at Derrick's, has just come from the Governor with a message. I guess it's important."

"Hello, what's up now?" muttered Annixter, as they turned back.

They found Osterman saddling his horse in furious haste. Near by him was Vanamee holding by the bridle an animal that was one lather of sweat. A few of the picnickers were turning their heads curiously in that direction. Evidently something of moment was in the wind.

"What's all up?" demanded Annixter, as he and Harran, followed by Presley, drew near.

"There's hell to pay," exclaimed Osterman under his breath. "Read that. Vanamee just brought it."

He handed Annixter a sheet of note paper, and turned again to the cinching of his saddle.

"We've got to be quick," he cried. "They've stolen a march on us."

Annixter read the note, Harran and Presley looking over his shoulder.

"Ah, it's them, is it," exclaimed Annixter.

Harran set his teeth. "Now for it," he exclaimed.

"They've been to your place already, Mr. Annixter," said Vanamee. "I passed by it on my way up. They have put Delaney in possession, and have set all your furniture out in the road."

Annixter turned about, his lips white. Already Presley and Harran had run to their horses.

"Vacca," cried Annixter, "where's Vacca? Put the saddle on the buckskin, *quick*. Osterman, get as many of the League as are here together at *this* spot, understand. I'll be back in a minute. I must tell Hilma this."

Hooven ran up as Annixter disappeared. His little eyes were blazing, he was dragging his horse with him.

"Say, dose fellers come, hey? Me, I'm alretty, see I hev der guhn."

"They've jumped the ranch, little girl," said Annixter, putting one arm around Hilma. "They're in our house now. I'm off. Go to Derrick's and wait for me there."

She put her arms around his neck.

"You're going?" she demanded.

"I must. Don't be frightened. It will be all right. Go to Derrick's and—good-bye."

She said never a word. She looked once long into his eyes, then kissed him on the mouth.

Meanwhile, the news had spread. The multitude rose to its feet. Women and men, with pale faces, looked at each other speechless, or broke forth into inarticulate exclamations. A strange, unfamiliar murmur took the place of the tumultuous gaiety of the previous moments. A sense of dread, of confusion, of impending terror weighed heavily in the air. What was now to happen?

When Annixter got back to Osterman, he found a number of the Leaguers already assembled. They were all mounted. Hooven was there and Harran, and besides these, Garnett of the Ruby ranch, and Gethings of the San Pablo, Phelps the foreman of Los Muertos, and, last of all, Dabney, silent as ever, speaking to no one. Presley came riding up.

"Best keep out of this, Pres," cried Annixter.

"Are we ready?" exclaimed Gethings.

"Ready, ready, we're all here."

"*All.* Is this all of us?" cried Annixter. "Where are the six hundred men who were going to rise when this happened?"

They had wavered, these other Leaguers. Now, when the actual crisis impended, they were smitten with confusion. Ah, no, they were not going to stand up and be shot at just to save Derrick's land. They were not armed. What did Annixter and Osterman take them for? No, sir; the Railroad had stolen a march on them. After all his big talk Derrick had allowed them to be taken by surprise. The only thing to do was to call a meeting of the

Executive Committee. That was the only thing. As for going down there with no weapons in their hands, *no,* sir. That was asking a little *too* much.

"Come on, then, boys," shouted Osterman, turning his back on the others. "The Governor says to meet him at Hooven's. We'll make for the Long Trestle and strike the trail to Hooven's there."

They set off. It was a terrible ride. Twice during the scrambling descent from the hills, Presley's pony fell beneath him. Annixter, on his buckskin, and Osterman, on his thoroughbred, good horsemen both, led the others, setting a terrific pace. The hills were left behind. Broderson Creek was crossed and on the levels of Quien Sabe, straight through the standing wheat, the nine horses, flogged and spurred, stretched out to their utmost. Their passage through the wheat sounded like the rip and tear of a gigantic web of cloth. The landscape on either hand resolved itself into a long blur. Tears came to the eyes, flying pebbles, clods of earth, grains of wheat flung up in the flight, stung the face like shot. Osterman's thoroughbred took the second crossing of Broderson's Creek in a single leap. Down under the Long Trestle tore the cavalcade in a shower of mud and gravel; up again on the farther bank, the horses blowing like steam engines; on into the trail to Hooven's, single file now, Presley's pony lagging, Hooven's horse bleeding at the eyes, the buckskin, game as a fighting cock, catching her second wind, far in the lead now, distancing even the English thoroughbred that Osterman rode.

At last Hooven's unpainted house, beneath the enormous live oak-tree, came in sight. Across the Lower Road, breaking through fences and into the yard around the house, thundered the Leaguers. Magnus was waiting for them.

The riders dismounted, hardly less exhausted than their horses.

"Why, where's all the men?" Annixter demanded of Magnus.

"Broderson is here and Cutter," replied the Governor, "no one else. I thought *you* would bring more men with you."

"There are only nine of us."

"And the six hundred Leaguers who were going to rise when this happened!" exclaimed Garnett bitterly.

"Rot the League," cried Annixter. "It's gone to pot—went to pieces at the first touch."

"We have been taken by surprise, gentlemen, after all," said Magnus. "Totally off our guard. But there are eleven of us. It is enough."

"Well, what's the game? Has the marshal come? How many men are with him?"

"The United States marshal from San Francisco," explained Magnus, "came down early this morning and stopped at Guadalajara. We learned it all through our friends in Bonneville about an hour ago. They telephoned me and Mr. Broderson. S. Behrman met him and provided about a dozen deputies. Delaney, Ruggles, and Christian joined them at Guadalajara. They left Guadalajara, going toward Mr. Annixter's ranch house on Quien Sabe. They are serving the writs in ejectment and putting the dummy buyers in possession. They are armed. S. Behrman is with them."

"Where are they now?"

"Cutter is watching them from the Long Trestle. They returned to Guadalajara. They are there now."

"Well," observed Gethings, "from Guadalajara they can only go to two places. Either they will take the Upper Road and go on to Osterman's next, or they will take the Lower Road to Mr. Derrick's."

"That is as I supposed," said Magnus. "That is why I wanted you to come here. From Hooven's, here, we can watch both roads simultaneously."

"Is anybody on the lookout on the Upper Road?"

"Cutter. He is on the Long Trestle."

"Say," observed Hooven, the instincts of the old-time soldier stirring him, "say, dose feller pretty demn schmart, I tink. We got to put some picket way oudt bei der Lower Roadt alzoh, und he tek dose glassus Mist'r Ennixt'r got bei um. Say, look at dose irregation ditsch. Dot ditsch he run righd across *both* dose road, hey? Dat's some fine entrenchment, you bedt. We fighd um from dose ditsch."

In fact, the dry irrigating ditch was a natural trench, admirably suited to the purpose, crossing both roads as Hooven pointed out and barring approach from Guadalajara to all the ranches save Annixter's—which had already been seized.

Gethings departed to join Cutter on the Long Trestle, while Phelps and Harran, taking Annixter's field glasses with them, and mounting their horses, went out toward Guadalajara on the Lower Road to watch for the marshal's approach from that direction.

After the outposts had left them, the party in Hooven's cottage looked to their weapons. Long since, every member of the League had been in the habit of carrying his revolver with him. They were all armed and, in addition, Hooven had his rifle. Presley alone carried no weapon.

The main room of Hooven's house, in which the Leaguers were now assembled, was barren, poverty-stricken, but tolerably clean. An old clock ticked vociferously on a shelf. In one corner was a bed, with a patched, faded quilt. In the centre of the room, straddling over the bare floor, stood a pine table. Around this the men gathered, two or three occupying chairs, Annixter sitting sideways on the table, the rest standing.

"I believe, gentlemen," said Magnus, "that we can go through this day without bloodshed. I believe not one shot need be fired. The Railroad will not force the issue, will not bring about actual fighting. When the marshal realizes that we are thoroughly in earnest, thoroughly determined, I am convinced that he will withdraw."

There were murmurs of assent.

"Look here," said Annixter, "if this thing can by any means be settled peaceably, I say let's do it, so long as we don't give in."

The others stared. Was this Annixter who spoke—the Hotspur of the League, the quarrelsome, irascible fellow who loved and sought a quarrel? Was it Annixter, who now had been the first and only one of them all to suffer, whose ranch had been seized, whose household possessions had been flung out into the road?

"When you come right down to it," he continued, "killing a man, no matter what he's done to you, is a serious business. I propose we make one more attempt to stave this thing off. Let's see if we can't get to talk with the marshal himself; at any rate, warn him of the danger of going any further. Boys, let's not fire the first shot. What do you say?"

The others agreed unanimously and promptly; and old Broderson, tugging uneasily at his long beard, added:

"No—no—no violence, no *unnecessary* violence, that is. I should hate to have innocent blood on my hands—that is, if it *is* innocent. I don't know, that S. Behrman—ah, he is a—a—surely he had innocent blood on *his* head. That Dyke affair, terrible, terrible; but then Dyke *was* in the wrong—driven to it, though; the Railroad did drive him to it. I want to be fair and just to everybody—"

"There's a team coming up the road from Los Muertos," announced Presley from the door.

"Fair and just to everybody," murmured old Broderson, wagging his head, frowning perplexedly. "I don't want to—to—to harm anybody unless they harm me."

"Is the team going toward Guadalajara?" enquired Garnett, getting up and coming to the door.

"Yes, it's a Portuguese, one of the garden truck men."

"We must turn him back," declared Osterman. "He can't go through here. We don't want him to take any news on to the marshal and S. Behrman."

"I'll turn him back," said Presley.

He rode out toward the market cart, and the others, watching from the road in front of Hooven's, saw him halt it. An excited interview followed. They could hear the Portuguese expostulating volubly, but in the end he turned back.

"Martial law on Los Muertos, isn't it?" observed Osterman. "Steady all," he exclaimed as he turned about, "here comes Harran."

Harran rode up at a gallop. The others surrounded him.

"I saw them," he cried. "They are coming this way. S. Behrman and Ruggles are in a two-horse buggy. All the others are on horseback. There are eleven of them. Christian and Delaney are with them. Those two have rifles. I left Hooven watching them."

"Better call in Gethings and Cutter right away," said Annixter. "We'll need all our men."

"I'll call them in," Presley volunteered at once. "Can I have the buckskin? My pony is about done up."

He departed at a brisk gallop, but on the way met Gethings and Cutter returning. They, too, from their elevated position, had observed the marshal's party leaving Guadalajara by the Lower Road. Presley told them of the decision of the Leaguers not to fire until fired upon.

"All right," said Gethings. "But if it comes to a gun-fight, that means it's all up with at least one of us. Delaney never misses his man."

When they reached Hooven's again, they found that the Leaguers had already taken their position in the ditch. The plank bridge across it had been torn up. Magnus, two long revolvers lying on the embankment in front of him, was in the middle, Harran at his side. On either side, some five feet intervening between them, stood the other Leaguers, their revolvers ready. Dabney, the silent old man, had taken off his coat.

"Take your places between Mr. Osterman and Mr. Broderson," said Magnus, as the three men rode up. "Presley," he added, "I forbid you to take any part in this affair."

"Yes, keep him out of it," cried Annixter from his position at the extreme end of the line. "Go back to Hooven's house, Pres, and look after the horses," he added. "This is no business of yours. And keep the road behind us clear. Don't let *anyone* come near, not *anyone,* understand?"

Presley withdrew, leading the buckskin and the horses that Gethings and Cutter had ridden. He fastened them under the great live-oak and then came out and stood in the road in front of the house to watch what was going on.

In the ditch, shoulder deep, the Leaguers, ready, watchful, waited in silence, their eyes fixed on the white shimmer of the road leading to Guadalajara.

"Where's Hooven?" enquired Cutter.

"I don't know," Osterman replied. "He was out watching the Lower Road with Harran Derrick. Oh, Harran," he called, "isn't Hooven coming in?"

"I don't know what he is waiting for," answered Harran. "He was to have come in just after me. He thought maybe the marshal's party might make a feint in this direction, then go around by the Upper Road, after all. He wanted to watch them a little longer. But he ought to be here now."

"Think he'll take a shot at them on his own account?"

"Oh, no, he wouldn't do that."

"Maybe they took him prisoner."

"Well, that's to be thought of, too."

Suddenly there was a cry. Around the bend of the road in front of them came a cloud of dust. From it emerged a horse's head.

"Hello, hello, there's something."

"Remember, we are not to fire first."

"Perhaps that's Hooven; I can't see. Is it? There only seems to be one horse."

"Too much dust for one horse."

Annixter, who had taken his field glasses from Harran, adjusted them to his eyes.

"That's not them," he announced presently, "nor Hooven, either. That's a cart." Then, after another moment, he added, "The butcher's cart from Guadalajara."

The tension was relaxed. The men drew long breaths, settling back in their places.

"Do we let him go on, Governor?"

"The bridge is down. He can't go by and we must not let him go back. We shall have to detain him and question him. I wonder the marshal let him pass."

The cart approached at a lively trot.

"Anybody else in that cart, Mr. Annixter?" asked Magnus. "Look carefully. It may be a ruse. It is strange the marshal should have let him pass."

The Leaguers roused themselves again. Osterman laid his hand on his revolver.

"No," called Annixter, in another instant, "no, there's only one man in it."

The cart came up, and Cutter and Phelps, clambering from the ditch, stopped it as it arrived in front of the party.

"Hey—what—what?" exclaimed the young butcher, pulling up. "Is that bridge broke?"

But at the idea of being held, the boy protested at top voice, badly frightened, bewildered, not knowing what was to happen next.

"No, no, I got my meat to deliver. Say, you let me go. Say, I ain't got nothing to do with you."

He tugged at the reins, trying to turn the cart about. Cutter, with his jack-knife, parted the reins just back of the bit.

"You'll stay where you are, m'son, for a while. We're not going to hurt you. But you are not going back to town till we say so. Did you pass anybody on the road out of town?"

In reply to the Leaguers' questions, the young butcher at last told them he had passed a two-horse buggy and a lot of men on horseback just beyond the railroad tracks. They were headed for Los Muertos.

"That's them, all right," muttered Annixter. "They're coming by this road, sure."

The butcher's horse and cart were led to one side of the road, and the horse tied to the fence with one of the severed lines. The butcher, himself, was passed over to Presley, who locked him in Hooven's barn.

"Well, what the devil," demanded Osterman, "has become of Bismarck?"

In fact, the butcher had seen nothing of Hooven. The minutes were passing, and still he failed to appear.

"What's he up to, anyways?"

"Bet you what you like, they caught him. Just like that crazy Dutchman to get excited and go too near. You can always depend on Hooven to lose his head."

Five minutes passed, then ten. The road toward Guadalajara lay empty, baking and white under the sun.

"Well, the marshal and S. Behrman don't seem to be in any hurry, either."

"Shall I go forward and reconnoitre, Governor?" asked Harran.

But Dabney, who stood next to Annixter, touched him on the shoulder and, without speaking, pointed down the road. Annixter looked, then suddenly cried out:

"Here comes Hooven."

The German galloped into sight, around the turn of the road, his rifle laid across his saddle. He came on rapidly, pulled up, and dismounted at the ditch.

"Dey're commen," he cried, trembling with excitement. "I watch um long dime bei der side oaf der roadt in der busches. Dey shtop bei der gate oder side der relroadt trecks and talk long dime mit one n'udder. Den dey gome on. Dey're gowun sure do zum monkey-doodle pizeness. Me, I see Gritschun put der kertridges in his guhn. I tink dey gowun to gome *my* blace first. Dey gowun to try to put me off, tek my home, bei Gott."

"All right, get down in here and keep quiet, Hooven. Don't fire unless—"

"Here they are."

A half-dozen voices uttered the cry at once.

There could be no mistake this time. A buggy, drawn by two horses, came into view around the curve of the road. Three riders accompanied it, and behind these, seen at intervals in a cloud of dust, were two—three—five—six others.

This, then, was S. Behrman with the United States marshal and his posse. The event that had been so long in preparation, the event which it had been said would never come to pass, the last trial of strength, the last fight between the Trust and the People, the direct, brutal grapple of armed men, the law defied, the Government ignored, behold, here it was close at hand.

Osterman cocked his revolver, and in the profound silence that had fallen upon the scene the click was plainly audible from end to end of the line.

"Remember our agreement, gentlemen," cried Magnus, in a warning voice. "Mr. Osterman, I must ask you to let down the hammer of your weapon."

No one answered. In absolute quiet, standing motionless in their places, the Leaguers watched the approach of the marshal.

Five minutes passed. The riders came on steadily. They drew nearer. The grind of the buggy wheels in the grit and dust of the road, and the prolonged clatter of the horses' feet began to make itself heard. The Leaguers could distinguish the faces of their enemies.

In the buggy were S. Behrman and Cyrus Ruggles, the latter driving. A tall man in a frock coat and slouched hat—the marshal, beyond question—rode at the left of the buggy; Delaney, carrying a Winchester, at the right. Christian, the real-estate broker, S. Behrman's cousin, also with a rifle, could be made out just behind the marshal. Back of these, riding well up, was a group of horsemen, indistinguishable in the dust raised by the buggy's wheels.

Steadily the distance between the Leaguers and the posse diminished.

"Don't let them get too close, Governor," whispered Harran.

When S. Behrman's buggy was about one hundred yards distant from the irrigating ditch, Magnus sprang out upon the road, leaving his revolvers behind him. He beckoned Garnett and Gethings to follow, and the three ranchers, who, with the exception of Broderson, were the oldest men present, advanced, without arms, to meet the marshal.

Magnus cried aloud:

"Halt where you are."

From their places in the ditch, Annixter, Osterman, Dabney, Harran, Hooven, Broderson, Cutter, and Phelps, their hands laid upon their revolvers, watched silently, alert, keen, ready for anything.

At the Governor's words, they saw Ruggles pull sharply on the reins. The buggy came to a standstill, the riders doing likewise. Magnus approached the marshal, still followed by Garnett and Gethings, and began to speak. His voice was audible to the men in the ditch, but his words could not be made out. They heard the marshal reply quietly enough and the two shook hands. Delaney came around from the side of the buggy, his horse standing before the team across the road. He leaned from the saddle, listening to what was being said, but made no remark. From time to time, S. Behrman and Ruggles, from their seats in the buggy, interposed a sentence or two into the conversation, but at first, so far as the Leaguers could discern, neither Magnus nor the marshal paid them any attention. They saw, however, that the latter repeatedly shook his head and once they heard him exclaim in a loud voice:

"I only know my duty, Mr. Derrick."

Then Gethings turned about, and seeing Delaney close at hand, addressed an unheard remark to him. The cowpuncher replied curtly and the words seemed to anger Gethings. He made a gesture, pointing back to the ditch, showing the intrenched Leaguers to the posse. Delaney appeared to communicate the news that the Leaguers were on hand and prepared to resist, to the other members of the party. They all looked toward the ditch and plainly saw the ranchers there, standing to their arms.

But meanwhile Ruggles had addressed himself more directly to Magnus, and between the two an angry discussion was going forward. Once even Harran heard his father exclaim:

"The statement is a lie and no one knows it better than yourself."

"Here," growled Annixter to Dabney, who stood next him in the ditch, "those fellows are getting too close. Look at them edging up. Don't Magnus see that?"

The other members of the marshal's force had come forward from their places behind the buggy and were spread out across the road. Some of them were gathered about Magnus, Garnett, and Gethings; and some were talking together, looking and pointing toward the ditch. Whether acting upon signal or not the Leaguers in the ditch could not tell, but it was certain that one or two of the posse had moved considerably forward. Besides this, Delaney had now placed his horse between Magnus and the ditch, and two others riding up from the rear had followed his example. The posse surrounded the three ranchers, and by now, everybody was talking at once.

"Look here," Harran called to Annixter, "this won't do. I don't like the looks of this thing. They all seem to be edging up, and before we know it they may take the Governor and the other men prisoners."

"They ought to come back," declared Annixter.

"Somebody ought to tell them that those fellows are creeping up."

By now, the angry argument between the Governor and Ruggles had become more heated than ever. Their voices were raised; now and then they made furious gestures.

"They ought to come back," cried Osterman. "We couldn't shoot now if anything should happen, for fear of hitting them."

"Well, it sounds as though something were going to happen pretty soon."

They could hear Gethings and Delaney wrangling furiously; another deputy joined in.

"I'm going to call the Governor back," exclaimed Annixter, suddenly clambering out of the ditch.

"No, no," cried Osterman, "keep in the ditch. They can't drive us out if we keep here."

Hooven and Harran, who had instinctively followed Annixter, hesitated at Osterman's words and the three halted irresolutely on the road before the ditch, their weapons in their hands.

"Governor," shouted Harran, "come on back. You can't do anything."

Still the wrangle continued, and one of the deputies, advancing a little from out the group, cried out:

"Keep back there! Keep back there, you!"

"Go to hell, will you?" shouted Harran on the instant. "You're on my land."

"Oh, come back here, Harran," called Osterman. "That ain't going to do any good."

"There—listen," suddenly exclaimed Harran. "The Governor is calling us. Come on; I'm going."

Osterman got out of the ditch and came forward, catching Harran by the arm and pulling him back.

"He didn't call. Don't get excited. You'll ruin everything. Get back into the ditch again."

But Cutter, Phelps, and the old man Dabney, misunderstanding what was happening, and seeing Osterman leave the ditch, had followed his example. All the Leaguers were now out of the ditch, and a little way down the road, Hooven, Osterman, Annixter, and Harran in front, Dabney, Phelps, and Cutter coming up from behind.

"Keep back, you," cried the deputy again.

In the group around S. Behrman's buggy, Gethings and Delaney were yet quarrelling, and the angry debate between Magnus, Garnett, and the marshal still continued.

Till this moment, the real-estate broker, Christian, had taken no part in the argument, but had kept himself in the rear of the buggy. Now, however, he pushed forward. There was but little room for him to pass, and, as he rode by the buggy, his horse scraped his flank against the hub of the wheel. The animal recoiled sharply, and, striking against Garnett, threw him to the ground. Delaney's horse stood between the buggy and the Leaguers gathered on the road in front of the ditch; the incident, indistinctly seen by them, was misinterpreted.

Garnett had not yet risen when Hooven raised a great shout:

"Hoch, der Kaiser! Hoch, der Vaterland!"

With the words, he dropped to one knee, and sighting his rifle carefully, fired into the group of men around the buggy.

Instantly the revolvers and rifles seemed to go off of themselves. Both sides, deputies and Leaguers, opened fire simultaneously. At first, it was nothing but a confused roar of explosions; then the roar lapsed to an irregular, quick succession of reports, shot leaping after shot; then a moment's silence, and, last of all, regular as clock-ticks, three shots at exact intervals. Then stillness.

Delaney, shot through the stomach, slid down from his horse, and, on his hands and knees, crawled from the road into the standing wheat. Christian fell backward from the saddle toward the buggy, and hung suspended in that position, his head and shoulders on the wheel, one stiff leg still across his saddle. Hooven, in attempting to rise from his kneeling position, received a rifle ball squarely in the throat, and rolled forward upon his face. Old Broderson, crying out, "Oh, they've shot me, boys," staggered sideways, his head bent, his hands rigid at his sides, and fell into the ditch. Osterman, blood running from his mouth and nose, turned about and walked back. Presley helped him across the irrigating ditch and Osterman laid himself down, his head on his folded arms. Harran Derrick dropped where he stood, turning over on his face, and lay motionless, groaning terribly, a pool of blood forming under his stomach. The old man Dabney, silent as ever, received his death, speechless. He fell to his knees, got up again, fell once more, and died without a word. Annixter, instantly killed, fell his length to the ground, and lay without movement, just as he had fallen, one arm across his face.

Frank Norris was born in Chicago in 1870 and at age fourteen moved with his family to San Francisco. He began writing fiction while a student at the University of California, Berkeley, and at Harvard. Norris then worked as a reporter in South Africa, later returning to San Francisco to work as an editor at The Wave *magazine. In 1899 he published* McTeague *(Doubleday and McClure), which follows the doomed paths of a San Francisco dentist, his wife, and his best friend; in 1924 director Erich von Stroheim made it into a notable silent film,* Greed. *Norris moved to New York and began work on a trilogy he called "The Epic of the Wheat." Its first volume,* The Octopus *(Doubleday, Page and Company, 1901), focused on the battles between San Joaquin Valley wheat farmers and the Southern Pacific Railroad; it was inspired by the real-life battle of Mussel Slough in Tulare County in 1880. Norris's second volume,* The Pit *(Doubleday, Page and Company, 1903), is set in the Chicago wheat exchange. Norris did not live to write the third and final volume; he died following an appendectomy in 1902.*

❦ Mary Austin

Selection from *The Land of Little Rain*

EAST AWAY FROM THE SIERRAS, south from Panamint and Amargosa, east and south many an uncounted mile, is the Country of Lost Borders.

Ute, Paiute, Mojave, and Shoshone inhabit its frontiers, and as far into the heart of it as a man dare go. Not the law, but the land sets the limit. Desert is the name it wears upon the maps, but the Indian's is the better word. Desert is a loose term to indicate land that supports no man; whether the land can be bitted and broken to that purpose is not proven. Void of life it never is, however dry the air and villainous the soil.

This is the nature of that country. There are hills, rounded, blunt, burned, squeezed up out of chaos, chrome and vermilion painted, aspiring to the snow-line. Between the hills lie high level-looking plains full of intolerable sun glare, or narrow valleys drowned in a blue haze. The hill surface is streaked with ash drift and black, unweathered lava flows. After rains water accumulates in the hollows of small closed valleys, and, evaporating, leaves hard dry levels of pure desertness that get the local name of dry lakes. Where the mountains are steep and the rains heavy, the pool is never quite dry, but dark and bitter, rimmed about with the efflorescence of alkaline deposits. A thin crust of it lies along the marsh over the vegetating area, which has neither beauty nor freshness. In the broad wastes open to the wind the sand drifts in hummocks about the stubby shrubs, and between them the soil shows saline traces. The sculpture of the hills here is more wind than water work, though the quick storms do sometimes scar them past many a year's redeeming. In all the Western desert edges there are essays in miniature at the famed, terrible Grand Cañon, to which, if you keep on long enough in this country, you will come at last.

Since this is a hill country one expects to find springs, but not to depend upon them; for when found they are often brackish and unwholesome, or maddening, slow dribbles in a thirsty soil. Here you find the hot sink of Death Valley, or high rolling districts where the air has always a tang of frost. Here are the long heavy winds and breathless calms on the tilted mesas where dust devils dance, whirling up into a wide, pale sky. Here you have no rain when all the earth cries for it, or quick downpours called cloud-bursts for violence. A land of lost rivers, with little in it to love; yet a land that once visited must be come back to inevitably. If it were not so there would be little told of it.

This is the country of three seasons. From June on to November it lies hot, still, and unbearable, sick with violent unrelieving storms; then on until April, chill, quiescent, drinking its scant rain and scanter snows; from April to the hot season again, blossoming, radiant, and seductive. These months are only approximate; later or earlier the rain-laden wind may drift up the water gate of the Colorado from the Gulf, and the land sets its seasons by the rain.

The desert floras shame us with their cheerful adaptations to the seasonal limitations. Their whole duty is to flower and fruit, and they do it hardly, or with tropical luxuriance, as the rain admits. It is recorded in the report of the Death Valley expedition that after a year of abundant rains, on the Colorado desert was found a specimen of Amaranthus ten feet high. A year later the same species in the same place matured in the drought at four inches. One hopes the land may breed like qualities in her human offspring, not tritely to "try," but to do. Seldom does the desert herb attain the full stature of the type. Extreme aridity and extreme altitude have the same dwarfing effect, so that we find in the high Sierras and in Death Valley related species in miniature that reach a comely growth in mean temperatures. Very fertile are the desert plants in expedients to prevent evaporation, turning their foliage edgewise toward the sun, growing silky hairs, exuding viscid gum. The wind, which has a long sweep, harries and helps them. It rolls up dunes about the stocky stems, encompassing and protective, and above the dunes, which may be, as with the mesquite, three times as high as a man, the blossoming twigs flourish and bear fruit.

There are many areas in the desert where drinkable water lies within a few feet of the surface, indicated by the mesquite and the bunch grass *(Sporobolus airoides)*. It is this nearness of unimagined help that makes the tragedy of desert deaths. It is related that the final breakdown of that hapless party that gave Death Valley its forbidding name occurred in a locality where shallow wells would have saved them. But how were they to know that? Properly equipped it is possible to go safely across that ghastly sink, yet every year it takes its toll of death, and yet men find there sun-dried mummies, of whom no trace or recollection is preserved. To underestimate one's thirst, to pass a given landmark to the right or left, to find a dry spring where one looked for running water—there is no help for any of these things.

Along springs and sunken watercourses one is surprised to find such water-loving plants as grow widely in moist ground, but the true desert breeds its own kind, each in its particular habitat. The angle of the slope, the frontage of a hill, the structure of the soil determines the plant. South-looking hills are nearly bare, and the lower tree-line higher here by a thousand feet. Cañons running east and west will have one wall naked and one clothed. Around dry lakes and marshes the herbage preserves a set and orderly arrangement. Most species have well-defined areas of growth, the best index the voiceless land can give the traveler of his whereabouts.

If you have any doubt about it, know that the desert begins with the creosote. This immortal shrub spreads down into Death Valley and up to the lower timber-line, odorous and medicinal as you might guess from the name, wandlike, with shining fretted foliage. Its vivid green is grateful to the eye in a wilderness of gray and greenish white shrubs. In the spring it exudes a resinous gum which the Indians of those parts know how to use with pulverized rock for cementing arrow points to shafts. Trust Indians not to miss any virtues of the plant world!

Nothing the desert produces expresses it better than the unhappy growth of the tree yuccas. Tormented, thin forests of it stalk drearily in the high mesas, particularly in that triangular slip that fans out eastward from the meeting of the Sierras and coastwise hills where the first swings across the southern end of the San Joaquin Valley. The yucca bristles with bayonet-pointed leaves, dull green, growing shaggy with age, tipped with panicles of fetid, greenish bloom. After death, which is slow, the ghostly hollow network of its woody skeleton, with hardly power to rot, makes the moonlight fearful. Before the yucca has come to flower, while yet its bloom is a creamy cone-shaped bud of the size of a small cabbage, full of sugary sap, the Indians twist it deftly out of its fence of daggers and roast it for their own delectation. So it is that in those parts where man inhabits one sees young plants of *Yucca arborensis* infrequently. Other yuccas, cacti, low herbs, a thousand sorts, one finds journeying east from the coastwise hills. There is neither poverty of soil nor species to account for the sparseness of desert growth, but simply that each plant requires more room. So much earth must be preëmpted to extract so much moisture. The real struggle for existence, the real brain of the plant, is underground; above there is room for a rounded perfect growth. In Death Valley, reputed the very core of desolation, are nearly two hundred identified species.

Above the lower tree-line, which is also the snow-line, mapped out abruptly by the sun, one finds spreading growth of piñon, juniper, branched nearly to the ground, lilac and sage, and scattering white pines.

There is no special preponderance of self-fertilized or wind-fertilized plants, but everywhere the demand for and evidence of insect life. Now where there are seeds and insects there will be birds and small mammals, and where these are, will come the slinking, sharp-toothed kind that prey on them. Go as far as you dare in the heart of a lonely land, you cannot go so far that life and death are not before you. Painted lizards slip in and out of rock crevices, and pant on the white hot sands. Birds, hummingbirds even, nest in the cactus scrub; woodpeckers befriend the demoniac yuccas; out of the stark, treeless waste rings the music of the night-singing mockingbird. If it be summer and the sun well down, there will be a burrowing owl to call. Strange, furry, tricksy things dart across the open places, or sit motionless in the conning towers of the creosote. The poet may have "named all the birds without a gun," but not the fairy-footed, ground-inhabiting, furtive, small folk of the rainless regions. They are too many and too swift; how many you would not believe without seeing the footprint tracings in the sand. They are nearly all night workers, finding the days too hot and white. In mid-desert where there are no cattle, there are no birds of carrion, but if you go far in that direction the chances are that you will find yourself shadowed by their tilted wings. Nothing so large as a man can move unspied upon in that country, and they know well how the land deals with strangers. There are hints to be had here of the way in which a land forces new habits on its dwellers. The quick increase of suns at the end of spring sometimes overtakes birds in their nesting and effects a reversal of the ordinary manner of incubation. It becomes necessary to keep eggs cool rather than warm. One hot, stifling spring in the Little Antelope I had occasion to pass and repass frequently the nest of a pair of meadowlarks, located unhappily in the shelter of a very slender weed. I never caught them sitting except near night, but at midday they stood, or drooped above it, half fainting with pitifully parted bills, between their treasure and the sun. Sometimes both of them together with wings spread and half lifted continued a spot of shade in a temperature that constrained me at last in a fellow feeling to spare them a bit of canvas for permanent shelter. There was a fence in that country shutting in a cattle range, and along its fifteen miles of posts one could be sure of finding a bird or two in every strip of shadow; sometimes the sparrow and the hawk, with wings trailed and beaks parted, drooping in the white truce of noon.

If one is inclined to wonder at first how so many dwellers came to be in the loneliest land that ever came out of God's hands, what they do there and why stay, one does not wonder so much after having lived there. None other than this long brown land lays such a hold on the affections. The rainbow hills, the tender bluish mists, the luminous radiance of the spring, have the lotus charm. They trick the sense of time, so that once inhabiting there you always mean to go away without quite realizing that you have not done it. Men who have lived there, miners and cattle-men, will tell you this, not so fluently, but emphatically, cursing the land and going back to it. For one thing there is the divinest, cleanest air to be breathed anywhere in God's world. Some day the world will understand that, and the little oases on the windy tops of hills will harbor for healing its ailing, house-weary broods. There is promise there of great wealth in ores and earths, which is no wealth by reason of being so far removed from water and workable conditions, but men are bewitched by it and tempted to try the impossible.

You should hear Salty Williams tell how he used to drive eighteen and twenty-mule teams from the borax marsh to Mojave, ninety miles, with the trail wagon full of water barrels. Hot days the mules would go so mad for drink that the clank of the water bucket set them into an uproar of hideous, maimed noises, and a tangle of harness chains, while Salty would sit on the high seat with the sun glare heavy in his eyes, dealing out curses of pacification in a level, uninterested voice until the clamor fell off from sheer exhaustion. There was a line of shallow graves along that road; they used to count on dropping a man or two of every new gang of coolies brought out in the hot season. But when he lost his swamper, smitten without warning at the noon halt, Salty quit his job; he said it was "too durn hot." The swamper he buried by the way with stones upon him to keep the coyotes from digging him up, and seven years later I read the penciled lines on the pine head-board, still bright and unweathered.

But before that, driving up on the Mojave stage, I met Salty again crossing Indian Wells, his face from the high seat, tanned and ruddy as a harvest moon, looming through the golden dust above his eighteen mules. The land had called him.

The palpable sense of mystery in the desert air breeds fables, chiefly of lost treasure. Somewhere within its stark borders, if one believes report, is a hill strewn with nuggets; one seamed with virgin silver; an old clayey water-bed where Indians scooped up earth to make cooking pots and shaped them reeking with grains of pure gold. Old miners drifting about the desert edges, weathered into the semblance of the tawny hills, will tell you tales like these convincingly. After a little sojourn in that land you will believe them on their own account. It is a question whether it is not better to be bitten by the little horned snake of the desert that goes sidewise and strikes without coiling, than by the tradition of a lost mine.

And yet—and yet—is it not perhaps to satisfy expectation that one falls into the tragic key in writing of desertness? The more you wish of it the more you get, and in the mean time lose much of pleasantness. In that country which begins at the foot of the east slope of the Sierras and spreads out by less and less lofty hill ranges toward the Great Basin, it is possible to live with great zest, to have red blood and delicate joys, to pass and repass about one's daily performance an area that would make an Atlantic seaboard State, and that with no peril, and, according to our way of thought, no particular difficulty. At any rate, it was not people who went into the desert merely to write it up who invented the fabled Hassaympa, of whose waters, if any drink, they can no more see fact as naked fact, but all radiant with the color of romance. I, who must have drunk of it in my twice seven years' wanderings, am assured that it is worth while.

For all the toil the desert takes of a man it gives compensations, deep breaths, deep sleep, and the communion of the stars. It comes upon one with new force in the pauses of the night that the Chaldeans were a desert-bred people. It is hard to escape the sense of mastery as the stars move in the wide clear heavens to risings and settings unobscured. They look large and near and palpitant; as if they moved on some stately service not needful to declare. Wheeling to their stations in the sky, they make the poor world-fret of no account. Of no account you who lie out there watching, nor the lean coyote that stands off in the scrub from you and howls and howls.

Mary Austin was born in Carlinville, Illinois, in 1868 and graduated from Blackburn College in 1888. She then moved with her mother and brother to California, where they attempted to homestead in the San Joaquin Valley. In 1891 she married teacher and farmer Stafford Wallace Austin. The couple moved to the Owens Valley, where Stafford taught in Bishop and Lone Pine, before relocating to Los Angeles; they later divorced. In the 1890s Austin began selling literary sketches of the region to The Overland Monthly; *in 1903 these were published as* The Land of Little Rain *(Houghton Mifflin, 1903). Her next three books were set in the Southern California desert:* The Basket Woman *(Houghton Mifflin, 1904), which discussed the lives of the Paiute Indians;* Isidro *(Houghton Mifflin, 1905), a novel focusing on Mexican California; and* The Flock *(Houghton Mifflin, 1906), about sheepherding. Later works include* California, the Land of the Sun *(Macmillan, 1914) and* Earth Horizon: Autobiography *(Houghton Mifflin, 1932). Soon after the publication of* The Land of Little Rain, *Austin moved to the writers and artists colony of Carmel, on Monterey Bay; later she lived in New York and in Santa Fe, where she died in 1934.*

John Steinbeck

Selection from *The Grapes of Wrath*

T HE TRUCK TOOK THE ROAD and moved up the long hill, through the broken, rotten rock. The engine boiled very soon and Tom slowed down and took it easy. Up the long slope, winding and twisting through dead country, burned white and gray, and no hint of life in it. Once Tom stopped for a few moments to let the engine cool, and then he traveled on. They topped the pass while the sun was still up, and looked down on the desert—black cinder mountains in the distance, and the yellow sun reflected on the gray desert. The little starved bushes, sage and greasewood, threw bold shadows on the sand and bits of rock. The glaring sun was straight ahead. Tom held his hand before his eyes to see at all. They passed the crest and coasted down to cool the engine. They coasted down the long sweep to the floor of the desert, and the fan turned over to cool the water in the radiator. In the driver's seat, Tom and Al and Pa, and Winfield on Pa's knee, looked into the bright descending sun, and their eyes were stony, and their brown faces were damp with perspiration. The burnt land and the black, cindery hills broke the even distance and made it terrible in the reddening light of the setting sun.

Al said, "Jesus, what a place. How'd you like to walk acrost her?"

"People done it," said Tom. "Lots a people done it; an' if they could, we could."

"Lots must a died," said Al.

"Well, we ain't come out exac'ly clean."

Al was silent for a while, and the reddening desert swept past. "Think we'll ever see them Wilsons again?" Al asked.

Tom flicked his eyes down to the oil gauge. "I got a hunch nobody ain't gonna see Mis' Wilson for long. Jus' a hunch I got."

Winfield said, "Pa, I wanta get out."

Tom looked over at him. "Might's well let ever'body out 'fore we settle down to drivin' tonight." He slowed the car and brought it to a stop. Winfield scrambled out and urinated at the side of the road. Tom leaned out. "Anybody else?"

"We're holdin' our water up here," Uncle John called.

Pa said, "Winfiel', you crawl up on top. You put my legs to sleep a-settin' on 'em." The little boy buttoned his overalls and obediently crawled up the back board and on his hands and knees crawled over Granma's mattress and forward to Ruthie.

The truck moved on into the evening, and the edge of the sun struck the rough horizon and turned the desert red.

Ruthie said, "Wouldn' leave you set up there, huh?"

"I didn' want to. It wasn't so nice as here. Couldn' lie down."

"Well, don' you bother me, a-squawkin' an' a-talkin'," Ruthie said, "'cause I'm goin' to sleep, an' when I wake up, we gonna be there! 'Cause Tom said so! Gonna seem funny to see pretty country."

The sun went down and left a great halo in the sky. And it grew very dark under the tarpaulin, a long cave with light at each end—a flat triangle of light.

Connie and Rose of Sharon leaned back against the cab, and the hot wind tumbling through the tent struck the backs of their heads, and the tarpaulin whipped and drummed above them. They spoke together in low tones, pitched to the drumming canvas, so that no one could hear them. When Connie spoke he turned his head and spoke into her ear, and she did the same to him. She said, "Seems like we wasn't never gonna do nothin' but move. I'm so tar'd."

He turned his head to her ear. "Maybe in the mornin'. How'd you like to be alone now?" In the dusk his hand moved out and stroked her hip.

She said, "Don't. You'll make me crazy as a loon. Don't do that." And she turned her head to hear his response.

"Maybe—when ever'body's asleep."

"Maybe," she said. "But wait till they get to sleep. You'll make me crazy, an' maybe they won't get to sleep."

"I can't hardly stop," he said.

"I know. Me neither. Le's talk about when we get there; an' you move away 'fore I get crazy."

He shifted away a little. "Well, I'll get to studyin' nights right off," he said. She sighed deeply. "Gonna get one a them books that tells about it an' cut the coupon, right off."

"How long, you think?" she asked.

"How long what?"

"How long 'fore you'll be makin' big money an' we got ice?"

"Can't tell," he said importantly. "Can't really rightly tell. Fella oughta be studied up pretty good 'fore Christmus."

"Soon's you get studied up we could get ice an' stuff, I guess."

He chuckled. "It's this here heat," he said. "What you gonna need ice roun' Christmus for?"

She giggled. "Tha's right. But I'd like ice any time. Now don't. You'll get me crazy!"

The dusk passed into dark and the desert stars came out in the soft sky, stars stabbing and sharp, with few points and rays to them, and the sky was velvet. And the heat changed. While the sun was up, it was a beating, flailing heat, but now the heat came from below, from the earth itself, and the heat was thick and muffling. The lights of the truck came on, and they illuminated a little blur of highway ahead, and a strip of desert on either side of the road. And sometimes eyes gleamed in the lights far ahead, but no animal showed in the lights. It was pitch dark under the canvas now. Uncle John and the preacher were curled in the middle of the truck, resting on their elbows, and staring out the back triangle. They could see the two bumps that were Ma and Granma against the outside. They could see Ma move occasionally, and her dark arm moving against the outside.

Uncle John talked to the preacher. "Casy," he said, "you're a fella oughta know what to do."

"What to do about what?"

"I dunno," said Uncle John.

Casy said, "Well, that's gonna make it easy for me!"

"Well, you been a preacher."

"Look, John, ever'body takes a crack at me 'cause I been a preacher. A preacher ain't nothin' but a man."

"Yeah, but—he's—a *kind* of a man, else he wouldn' be a preacher. I wanna ast you—well, you think a fella could bring bad luck to folks?"

"I dunno," said Casy. "I dunno."

"Well—see—I was married—fine, good girl. An' one night she got a pain in her stomach. An' she says, 'You better get a doctor.' An' I says, 'Hell, you jus' et too much.'" Uncle John put his hand on Casy's knee and he peered through the darkness at him. "She give me a *look*. An' she groaned all night, an' she died the next afternoon." The preacher mumbled something. "You see," John went on, "I kil't her. An' sence then I tried to make it up—mos'ly to kids. An' I tried to be good, an' I can't. I get drunk, an' I go wild."

"Ever'body goes wild," said Casy. "I do too."

"Yeah, but you ain't got a sin on your soul like me."

Casy said gently, "Sure I got sins. Ever'body got sins. A sin is somepin you ain't sure about. Them people that's sure about ever'thing an' ain't got no sin—well, with that kind a son-of-a-bitch, if I was God I'd kick their ass right outa heaven! I couldn' stand 'em!"

Uncle John said, "I got a feelin' I'm bringin' bad luck to my own folks. I got a feelin' I oughta go away an' let 'em be. I ain't comf'table bein' like this."

Casy said quickly, "I know this—a man got to do what he got to do. I can't tell you. I don't think they's luck or bad luck. On'y one thing in this worl' I'm sure of, an' that's I'm sure nobody got a right to mess with a fella's life. He got to do it all hisself. Help him, maybe, but not tell him what to do."

Uncle John said disappointedly, "Then you don' know?"

"I don' know."

"You think it was a sin to let my wife die like that?"

"Well," said Casy, "for anybody else it was a mistake, but if you think it was a sin—then it's a sin. A fella builds his own sins right up from the groun'."

"I got to give that a goin'-over," said Uncle John, and he rolled on his back and lay with his knees pulled up.

The truck moved on over the hot earth, and the hours passed. Ruthie and Winfield went to sleep. Connie loosened a blanket from the load and covered himself and Rose of Sharon with it, and in the heat they struggled together, and held their breaths. And after a time Connie threw off the blanket and the hot tunneling wind felt cool on their wet bodies.

On the back of the truck Ma lay on the mattress beside Granma, and she could not see with her eyes, but she could feel the struggling body and the struggling heart; and the sobbing breath was in her ear. And Ma said over and over, "All right. It's gonna be all right." And she said hoarsely, "You know the family got to get acrost. You know that."

Uncle John called, "You all right?"

It was a moment before she answered. "All right. Guess I dropped off to sleep." And after a time Granma was still, and Ma lay rigid beside her.

The night hours passed, and the dark was in against the truck. Sometimes cars passed them, going west and away; and sometimes great trucks came up out of the west and rumbled eastward. And the stars flowed down in a slow cascade over the western horizon. It was near midnight when they neared Daggett, where the inspection station is. The road was floodlighted there, and a sign illuminated, "KEEP RIGHT AND STOP." The officers loafed in the office, but they came out and stood under the long covered shed when Tom pulled in. One officer put down the license number and raised the hood.

Tom asked, "What's this here?"

"Agricultural inspection. We got to look over your stuff. Got any vegetables or seeds?"

"No," said Tom.

"Well, we got to look over your stuff. You got to unload."

Now Ma climbed heavily down from the truck. Her face was swollen and her eyes were hard. "Look, mister. We got a sick ol' lady. We got to get her to a doctor. We can't wait." She seemed to fight with hysteria. "You can't make us wait."

"Yeah? Well, we got to look you over."

"I swear we ain't got any thing!" Ma cried. "I swear it. An' Granma's awful sick."

"You don't look so good yourself," the officer said.

Ma pulled herself up the back of the truck, hoisted herself with huge strength. "Look," she said.

The officer shot a flashlight beam up on the old shrunken face. "By God, she is," he said. "You swear you got no seeds or fruits or vegetables, no corn, no oranges?"

"No, no. I swear it!"

"Then go ahead. You can get a doctor in Barstow. That's only eight miles. Go on ahead."

Tom climbed in and drove on.

The officer turned to his companion. "I couldn' hold 'em."

"Maybe it was a bluff," said the other.

"Oh, Jesus, no! You should of seen that ol' woman's face. That wasn't no bluff."

Tom increased his speed to Barstow, and in the little town he stopped, got out, and walked around the truck. Ma leaned out. "It's awright," she said. "I didn' wanta stop there, fear we wouldn' get acrost."

"Yeah! But how's Granma?"

"She's awright—awright. Drive on. We got to get acrost." Tom shook his head and walked back.

"Al," he said, "I'm gonna fill her up, an' then you drive some." He pulled to an all-night gas station and filled the tank and the radiator, and filled the crank case. Then Al slipped under the wheel and Tom took the outside, with Pa in the middle. They drove away into the darkness and the little hills near Barstow were behind them.

Tom said, "I don' know what's got into Ma. She's flighty as a dog with a flea up his ass. Wouldn' a took long to look over the stuff. An' she says Granma's sick; an' now she says Granma's awright. I can't figger her out. She ain't right. S'pose she wore her brains out on the trip."

Pa said, "Ma's almost like she was when she was a girl. She was a wild one then. She wasn' scairt of nothin'. I thought havin' all the kids an' workin' took it out a her, but I guess it ain't. Christ! When she got that jack handle back there, I tell you I wouldn' wanna be the fella took it away from her."

"I dunno what's got into her," Tom said. "Maybe she's jus' tar'd out."

Al said, "I won't be doin' no weepin' an' a-moanin' to get through. I got this goddamn car on my soul."

Tom said, "Well, you done a damn good job a pickin'. We ain't had hardly no trouble with her at all."

All night they bored through the hot darkness, and jackrabbits scuttled into the lights and dashed away in long jolting leaps. And the dawn came up behind them when the lights of Mojave were ahead. And the dawn showed high mountains to the west. They filled the water and oil at Mojave and crawled into the mountains, and the dawn was about them.

Tom said, "Jesus, the desert's past! Pa, Al, for Christ sakes! The desert's past!"

"I'm too goddamn tired to care," said Al.

"Want me to drive?"

"No, wait awhile."

They drove through Tehachapi in the morning glow, and the sun came up behind them, and then—suddenly they saw the great valley below them. Al jammed on the brake and stopped in the middle of the road, and, "Jesus Christ! Look!" he said. The vineyards, the orchards, the great flat valley, green and beautiful, the trees set in rows, and the farm houses.

And Pa said, "God Almighty!" The distant cities, the little towns in the orchard land, and the morning sun, golden on the valley. A car honked behind them. Al pulled to the side of the road and parked.

"I want ta look at her." The grain fields golden in the morning, and the willow lines, the eucalyptus trees in rows.

Pa sighed, "I never knowed they was anything like her." The peach trees and the walnut groves, and the dark green patches of oranges. And red roofs among the trees, and barns—rich barns. Al got out and stretched his legs.

He called, "Ma—come look. We're there!"

Ruthie and Winfield scrambled down from the car, and then they stood, silent and awestruck, embarrassed before the great valley. The distance was thinned with haze, and the land grew softer and softer in the distance. A windmill flashed in the sun, and its turning blades were like a little heliograph, far away. Ruthie and Winfield looked at it, and Ruthie whispered, "It's California."

Winfield moved his lips silently over the syllables. "There's fruit," he said aloud.

Casy and Uncle John, Connie and Rose of Sharon climbed down. And they stood silently. Rose of Sharon had started to brush her hair back, when she caught sight of the valley and her hand dropped slowly to her side.

Tom said, "Where's Ma? I want Ma to see it. Look, Ma! Come here, Ma." Ma was climbing slowly, stiffly, down the back board. Tom looked at her. "My God, Ma, you sick?" Her face was stiff and putty-like, and her eyes seemed to have sunk deep into her head, and the rims were red with weariness. Her feet touched the ground and she braced herself by holding the truck-side.

Her voice was a croak. "Ya say we're acrost?"

Tom pointed to the great valley. "Look!"

She turned her head, and her mouth opened a little. Her fingers went to her throat and gathered a little pinch of skin and twisted gently. "Thank God!" she said. "The fambly's here." Her knees buckled and she sat down on the running board.

"You sick, Ma?"

"No, jus' tar'd."

"Didn' you get no sleep?"

"No."

"Was Granma bad?"

Ma looked down at her hands, lying together like tired lovers in her lap. "I wisht I could wait an' not tell you. I wisht it could be all—nice."

Pa said, "Then Granma's bad."

Ma raised her eyes and looked over the valley. "Granma's dead."

They looked at her, all of them, and Pa asked, "When?"

"Before they stopped us las' night."

"So that's why you didn' want 'em to look."

"I was afraid we wouldn' get acrost," she said. "I tol' Granma we couldn' he'p her. The fambly had ta get acrost. I tol' her, tol' her when she was a-dyin'. We couldn' stop in the desert. There was the young ones—an' Rosasharn's baby. I tol' her." She put up her hands and covered her face for a moment. "She can get buried in a nice green place," Ma said softly. "Trees aroun' an' a nice place. She got to lay her head down in California."

The family looked at Ma with a little terror at her strength.

Tom said, "Jesus Christ! You layin' there with her all night long!"

"The fambly hadda get acrost," Ma said miserably.

Tom moved close to put his hand on her shoulder.

"Don' touch me," she said. "I'll hol' up if you don' touch me. That'd get me."

Pa said, "We got to go on now. We got to go on down."

Ma looked up at him. "Can—can I set up front? I don' wanna go back there there no more—I'm tar'd. I'm awful tar'd."

They climbed back on the load, and they avoided the long stiff figure covered and tucked in a comforter, even the head covered and tucked. They moved to their places and tried to keep their eyes from it—from the hump on the comfort that would be the nose, and the steep cliff that would be the jut of the chin. They tried to keep their eyes away, and they could not. Ruthie and Winfield, crowded in a forward corner as far away from the body as they could get, stared at the tucked figure.

And Ruthie whispered, "Tha's Granma, an' she's dead."

Winfield nodded solemnly. "She ain't breathin' at all. She's awful dead."

And Rose of Sharon said softly to Connie, "She was a-dyin' right when we—"

"How'd we know?" he reassured her.

Al climbed on the load to make room for Ma in the seat. And Al swaggered a little because he was sorry. He plumped down beside Casy and Uncle John. "Well, she was ol'. Guess her time was up," Al said. "Ever'body got to die." Casy and Uncle John turned eyes expressionlessly on him and looked at him as though he were a curious talking bush. "Well, ain't they?" he demanded. And the eyes looked away, leaving Al sullen and shaken.

Casy said in wonder, "All night long, an' she was alone." And he said, "John, there's a woman so great with love—she scares me. Makes me afraid an' mean."

John asked, "Was it a sin? Is they any part of it you might call a sin?"

Casy turned on him in astonishment, "A sin? No, there ain't no part of it that's a sin."

"I ain't never done nothin' that wasn't part sin," said John, and he looked at the long wrapped body.

Tom and Ma and Pa got into the front seat. Tom let the truck roll and started on compression. And the heavy truck moved, snorting and jerking and popping down the hill. The sun was behind them, and the valley golden and green before them. Ma shook her head slowly from side to side. "It's purty," she said. "I wisht they could of saw it."

"I wisht so too," said Pa.

Tom patted the steering wheel under his hand. "They was too old," he said. "They wouldn't of saw nothin' that's here. Grampa would a been a-seein' the Injuns an' the prairie country when he was a young fella. An' Granma would a remembered an' seen the first home she lived in. They was too ol'. Who's really seein' it is Ruthie an' Winfiel'."

Pa said, "Here's Tommy talkin' like a growed-up man, talkin' like a preacher almos'."

And Ma smiled sadly. "He is. Tommy's growed way up—way up so I can't get aholt of 'im sometimes."

They popped down the mountain, twisting and looping, losing the valley sometimes, and then finding it again. And the hot breath of the valley came up to them, with hot green smells on it, and with resinous sage and tarweed smells. The crickets crackled along the road. A rattlesnake crawled across the road and Tom hit it and broke it and left it squirming.

Tom said, "I guess we got to go to the coroner, wherever he is. We got to get her buried decent. How much money might be lef', Pa?"

"'Bout forty dollars," said Pa.

Tom laughed. "Jesus, are we gonna start clean! We sure ain't bringin' nothin' with us." He chuckled a moment, and then his face straightened quickly. He pulled the visor of his cap down low over his eyes. And the truck rolled down the mountain into the great valley.

‿⌐

Arguably the most famous writer California has produced, John Steinbeck was born in Salinas, California, in 1902, the son of a Monterey County treasurer and a former schoolteacher. He attended Stanford University but left before graduating. He published his first novel in 1929: Cup of Gold *(McBride), based on the exploits of pirate Sir Henry Morgan. Steinbeck's later and more successful works focused on rural California life and were often set in his native Salinas Valley or along the coast in nearby Monterey. These include* Pastures of Heaven *(Brewer, Warren and Putnam, 1932),* To a God Unknown *(Ballou, 1933), and* Tortilla Flat *(Covici-Friede, 1935), followed by* In Dubious Battle *(Covici-Friede, 1936),* Of Mice and Men *(Covici-Friede, 1937), and the short-story collection* The Long Valley *(Viking Press, 1938). That same year, Steinbeck began research for his most famous work, visiting migrant labor camps in the San Joaquin Valley to collect the stories and impressions that would inspire* The Grapes of Wrath *(Viking Press, 1939). The epic novel tells the story of the Joad family's Depression-era migration from Dust Bowl Oklahoma to California. Its eloquent but unsparing depictions of the prejudices the new arrivals faced made* The Grapes of Wrath *both successful and controversial; awarded the Pulitzer Prize, it was also banned from some California libraries and, in at least one instance, burned. In 1940 it was made into a notable film. Steinbeck's later books included the nonfiction* Sea of Cortez *(Viking Press, 1941), written with his friend marine biologist Ed Ricketts;* Cannery Row *(Viking Press, 1945);* The Pearl *(Viking Press, 1948); and* East of Eden *(Viking Press, 1952), a recounting of the Biblical Cain and Abel story transplanted to the Salinas Valley. In 1962 Steinbeck was awarded the Nobel Prize in Literature. He died in New York in 1968.*

Wilma McDaniel

From *The Last Dust Storm*
1939 IN CALIFORNIA

It was a year of farewells
and great movies

Goodbye Mister Chips
Robert Donat did well
by you
in that role

Goodbye nineteen
you did as well for me
as nineteen could do

when cousins
went off to Berkeley
leaving me
to mourn my ignorance

Hello heaven
one of mine went there
so suddenly
I couldn't say good-bye

He was Gone With the Wind
it seemed to me
at my age of ten plus nine

But
the wind is never gone
for good
it will blow that year
back again
bringing everything I lost

From *Sister Vayda's Song*
VALLEY FOG

She arrived
fashionably late this year
cloaked in classic trailing gray
dripping with diamonds
so many
when she even moved a finger
they fell by millions
teardrop perfect on houses
lawns
railroad tracks
wasted their beauty on growling
trucks
and gave the water tower
a noble tiara

From *A Primer for Buford*
THE LONG WAIT

Entering town
from either direction, a billboard announces
Tulare, The City With A Smile
I cannot agree and do not smile

This town is grim
flat
pure sand
and ugly in color when you take a hard
look at it

Searching for one good feature in summer
you have to wait half a lifetime
until 110 degree heat has melted asphalt
burned out swamp coolers
ruined marriages that were
the least bit shaky
then cooled into Tule fog
until next April Fools' Day

From *A Primer for Buford*
WATCHING TRUCK DRIVERS
AT PANCAKE HOUSE

Boys
I always order pancakes
he told his buddies
slathered butter on them
poured syrup
like thick maple rain
Nothing much a cook
can do to ruin a pancake
if the stove don't blow up

Wilma McDaniel was born in Stroud, Oklahoma, in 1918. When she was eighteen, she and her family made the journey John Steinbeck writes about in The Grapes of Wrath—traveling from Dust Bowl Oklahoma to California, settling first in Livingston, in Merced County. She worked as a maid and on San Joaquin Valley farms; not until she was in her fifties did she begin to earn recognition as a poet, after bringing a shoebox filled with her work into the office of the Tulare Advance-Register. McDaniel would go on to publish twenty-five volumes of poetry, including Sister Vayda's Song *(Hanging Loose Press, 1982)*, A Primer for Buford *(Hanging Loose Press, 1990), and* The Last Dust Storm *(Hanging Loose Press, 1995)*. McDaniel died in Tulare in 2007.

Joan Didion

From *Slouching Toward Bethlehem*
NOTES FROM A NATIVE DAUGHTER

I T IS VERY EASY TO SIT AT THE BAR IN, say, La Scala in Beverly Hills, or Ernie's in San Francisco, and to share in the pervasive delusion that California is only five hours from New York by air. The truth is that La Scala and Ernie's are only five hours from New York by air. California is somewhere else.

Many people in the East (or "back East," as they say in California, although not in La Scala or Ernie's) do not believe this. They have been to Los Angeles or to San Francisco, have driven through a giant redwood and have seen the Pacific glazed by the afternoon sun off Big Sur, and they naturally tend to believe that they have in fact been to California. They have not been, and they probably never will be, for it is a longer and in many ways a more difficult trip than they might want to undertake, one of those trips on which the destination flickers chimerically on the horizon, ever receding, ever diminishing. I happen to know about that trip because I come from California, come from a family, or a congeries of families, that has always been in the Sacramento Valley.

You might protest that no family has been in the Sacramento Valley for anything approaching "always." But it is characteristic of Californians to speak grandly of the past as if it had simultaneously begun, *tabula rasa,* and reached a happy ending on the day the wagons started west. *Eureka*—"I Have Found It"—as the state motto has it. Such a view of history casts a certain melancholia over those who participate in it; my own childhood was suffused with the conviction that we had long outlived our finest hour. In fact that is what I want to tell you about: what it is like to come from a place like Sacramento. If I could make you understand that, I could make you understand California and perhaps something else besides, for Sacramento *is* California, and California is a place in which a boom mentality and a sense of Chekhovian loss meet in uneasy suspension; in which the mind is troubled by some buried but ineradicable suspicion that things had better work here, because here, beneath that immense bleached sky, is where we run out of continent.

In 1847 Sacramento was no more than an adobe enclosure, Sutter's Fort, standing alone on the prairie; cut off from San Francisco and the sea by the Coast Range and from the rest of the continent by the Sierra Nevada, the Sacramento Valley was then a true sea of grass, grass so high a man riding into it could tie it across his saddle. A year later gold was discovered in the Sierra foothills, and abruptly Sacramento was a town, a town any moviegoer could map tonight in his dreams—a dusty collage of assay offices and wagonmakers and saloons. Call that Phase Two. Then the settlers came—the farmers, the people who for two hundred years had been moving west on the frontier, the peculiar flawed strain who had cleared Virginia, Kentucky, Missouri; they made Sacramento a farm town. Because the land was rich, Sacramento became eventually a rich farm town, which meant houses in town, Cadillac dealers, a country club. In that gentle sleep Sacramento dreamed until perhaps 1950, when something happened. What happened was that Sacramento woke to the fact that the outside world was moving in, fast and hard. At the moment of its waking Sacramento lost, for better or for worse, its character, and that is part of what I want to tell you about.

⌐

BUT THE CHANGE IS NOT what I remember first. First I remember running a boxer dog of my brother's over the same flat fields that our great-great-grandfather had found virgin and had planted; I remember swimming (albeit nervously, for I was a nervous child, afraid of sinkholes and afraid of snakes, and perhaps that was the beginning of my error) the same rivers we had swum for a century: the Sacramento, so rich with silt that we could barely see our hands a few inches beneath the surface; the American, running clean and fast with melted Sierra snow until July, when it would slow down, and rattlesnakes would sun themselves on its newly exposed rocks. The Sacramento, the American, sometimes the Cosumnes, occasionally the Feather. Incautious children died every day in those rivers; we read about it in the paper, how they had miscalculated a current or stepped into a hole down where the American runs into the Sacramento, how the Berry Brothers had been called in from Yolo County to drag the river but how the bodies remained unrecovered. "They were from away," my grandmother would extrapolate from the newspaper stories. "Their parents had no *business* letting them in the river. They were visitors from Omaha." It was not a bad lesson, although a less than reliable one; children we knew died in the rivers too.

When summer ended—when the State Fair closed and the heat broke, when the last green hop vines had been torn down along the H Street road and the tule fog began rising off the low ground at night—we would go back to memorizing the Products of Our Latin American Neighbors and to visiting the great-aunts on Sunday, dozens of great-aunts, year after year of Sundays. When I think now of those winters I think of yellow elm leaves wadded in the gutters outside the Trinity Episcopal Pro-Cathedral on M Street. There are actually people in Sacramento now who call M Street Capitol Avenue, and Trinity has one of those featureless new buildings, but perhaps children still learn the same things there on Sunday mornings:

Q. In what way does the Holy Land resemble the Sacramento Valley?
A. In the type and diversity of its agricultural products.

And I think of the rivers rising, of listening to the radio to hear at what height they would crest and wondering if and when and where the levees would go. We did not have as many dams in those years. The bypasses would be full, and men would sandbag all night. Sometimes a levee would go in the night, somewhere upriver; in the morning the rumor would spread that the Army Engineers had dynamited it to relieve the pressure on the city.

After the rains came spring, for ten days or so; the drenched fields would dissolve into a brilliant ephemeral green (it would be yellow and dry as fire in two or three weeks) and the real-estate business would pick up. It was the time of year when people's grandmothers went to Carmel; it was the time of year when girls who could not even get into Stephens or Arizona or Oregon, let alone Stanford or Berkeley, would be sent to Honolulu, on the *Lurline*. I have no recollection of anyone going to New York, with the exception of a cousin who visited there (I cannot imagine why) and reported that the shoe salesmen at Lord & Taylor were "intolerably rude." What happened in New York and Washington and abroad seemed to impinge not at all upon the Sacramento mind. I remember being taken to call upon a very old woman, a rancher's widow, who was reminiscing (the favored conversational mode in Sacramento) about the son of some contemporaries of hers. "That Johnston boy never did amount to much," she said. Desultorily, my mother protested: Alva Johnston, she said, had won the Pulitzer Prize, when he was working for *The New York Times*. Our hostess looked at us impassively. "He never amounted to anything in Sacramento," she said.

Hers was the true Sacramento voice, and, although I did not realize it then, one not long to be heard, for the war was over and the boom was on and the voice of the aerospace engineer would be heard in the land. VETS NO DOWN! EXECUTIVE LIVING ON LOW FHA!

LATER, WHEN I WAS LIVING IN NEW YORK, I would make the trip back to Sacramento four and five times a year (the more comfortable the flight, the more obscurely miserable I would be, for it weighs heavily upon my kind that we could perhaps not make it by wagon), trying to prove that I had not meant to leave at all, because in at least one respect California— the California we are talking about—resembles Eden: it is assumed that those who absent themselves from its blessings have been banished, exiled by some perversity of heart. Did not the Donner-Reed Party, after all, eat its own dead to reach Sacramento?

I have said that the trip back is difficult, and it is—difficult in a way that magnifies the ordinary ambiguities of sentimental journeys. Going back to California is not like going back to Vermont, or Chicago; Vermont and Chicago are relative constants, against which one measures one's own change. All that is constant about the California of my childhood is the rate at which it disappears. An instance: on Saint Patrick's Day of

1948 I was taken to see the legislature "in action," a dismal experience; a handful of florid assemblymen, wearing green hats, were reading Pat-and-Mike jokes into the record. I still think of the legislators that way—wearing green hats, or sitting around on the veranda of the Senator Hotel fanning themselves and being entertained by Artie Samish's emissaries. (Samish was the lobbyist who said, "Earl Warren may be the governor of the state, but I'm the governor of the legislature.") In fact there is no longer a veranda at the Senator Hotel—it was turned into an airline ticket office, if you want to embroider the point—and in any case the legislature has largely deserted the Senator for the flashy motels north of town, where the tiki torches flame and the steam rises off the heated swimming pools in the cold Valley night.

It is hard to *find* California now, unsettling to wonder how much of it was merely imagined or improvised; melancholy to realize how much of anyone's memory is no true memory at all but only the traces of someone else's memory, stories handed down on the family network. I have an indelibly vivid "memory," for example, of how Prohibition affected the hop growers around Sacramento: the sister of a grower my family knew brought home a mink coat from San Francisco, and was told to take it back, and sat on the floor of the parlor cradling that coat and crying. Although I was not born until a year after Repeal, that scene is more "real" to me than many I have played myself.

I remember one trip home, when I sat alone on a night jet from New York and read over and over some lines from a W. S. Merwin poem I had come across in a magazine, a poem about a man who had been a long time in another country and knew that he must go home:

… But it should be
Soon. Already I defend hotly
Certain of our indefensible faults,
Resent being reminded; already in my mind
Our language becomes freighted with a richness
No common tongue could offer, while the mountains
Are like nowhere on earth, and the wide rivers.

You see the point. I want to tell you the truth, and already I have told you about the wide rivers.

IT SHOULD BE CLEAR BY NOW that the truth about the place is elusive, and must be tracked with caution. You might go to Sacramento tomorrow and someone (although no one I know) might take you out to Aerojet-General, which has, in the Sacramento phrase, "something to do with rockets." Fifteen thousand people work for Aerojet, almost all of them imported; a Sacramento lawyer's wife told me, as evidence of how Sacramento was opening up, that she believed she had met one of them, at an open house two Decembers ago. ("Couldn't have been nicer, actually," she added enthusiastically. "I think he and his wife bought the house next *door* to Mary and Al, something like that, which of course was how *the* met him.") So you might go to Aerojet and stand in the big vendors' lobby where a couple of thousand components salesmen try every week to sell their wares and you might look up at the electrical wallboard that lists Aerojet personnel, their projects and their location at any given time, and you might wonder if I have been in Sacramento lately. MINUTEMAN, POLARIS, TITAN, the lights flash, and all the coffee tables are littered with airline schedules, very now, very much in touch.

But I could take you a few miles from there into towns where the banks still bear names like The Bank of Alex Brown, into towns where the one hotel still has an octagonal-tile floor in the dining room and dusty potted palms and big ceiling fans; into towns where everything—the seed business, the Harvester franchise, the hotel, the department store and the main street—carries a single name, the name of the man who built the town. A few Sundays ago I was in a town like that, a town smaller than that, really, no hotel, no Harvester franchise, the bank burned out, a river town. It was the golden anniversary of some of my relatives and it was 110° and the guests of honor sat on straight-backed chairs in front of a sheaf of gladioluses in the Rebekah Hall. I mentioned visiting Aerojet-General to a cousin I saw there, who listened to me with interested disbelief. Which is the true California? That is what we all wonder.

LET US TRY OUT A FEW irrefutable statements, on subjects not open to interpretation. Although Sacramento is in many ways the least typical of the Valley towns, it *is* a Valley town, and must be viewed in that context. When you say "the Valley" in Los Angeles, most people assume that you mean the San Fernando Valley (some people in fact assume that you mean Warner Brothers), but make no mistake: we are talking not about the valley of the sound stages and the ranchettes but about the real Valley, the Central Valley, the fifty thousand square miles drained by the Sacramento and the San Joaquin Rivers and further irrigated by a complex network of sloughs, cutoffs, ditches, and the Delta-Mendota and Friant-Kern Canals.

A hundred miles north of Los Angeles, at the moment when you drop from the Tehachapi Mountains into the outskirts of Bakersfield, you leave Southern California and enter the Valley. "You look up the highway and it is straight for miles, coming at you, with the black line down the center coming at you and at you ... and the heat dazzles up from the white slab so that only the black line is clear, coming at you with the whine of the tires, and if you don't quit staring at that line and don't take a few deep breaths and slap yourself hard on the back of the neck you'll hypnotize yourself."

Robert Penn Warren wrote that about another road, but he might have been writing about the Valley road, U.S. 99, three hundred miles from Bakersfield to Sacramento, a highway so straight that when one flies on the most direct pattern from Los Angeles to Sacramento one never loses sight of U.S. 99. The landscape it runs through never, to the untrained eye, varies. The Valley eye can discern the point where miles of cotton seedlings fade into miles of tomato seedlings, or where the great corporation ranches—Kern County Land, what is left of DiGiorgio—give way to private operations (somewhere on the horizon, if the place is private, one sees a house and a stand of scrub oaks), but such distinctions are in the long view irrelevant. All day long, all that moves is the sun, and the big Rainbird sprinklers.

Every so often along 99 between Bakersfield and Sacramento there is a town: Delano, Tulare, Fresno, Madera, Merced, Modesto, Stockton. Some of these towns are pretty big now, but they are all the same at heart, one- and two- and three-story buildings artlessly arranged, so that what appears to be the good dress shop stands beside a W. T. Grant store, so that the big Bank of America faces a Mexican movie house. *Dos Peliculas, Bingo Bingo Bingo.* Beyond the downtown (pronounced *down*town, with the Okie accent that now pervades Valley speech patterns) lie blocks of old frame houses—paint peeling, sidewalks cracking, their occasional leaded amber windows overlooking a Foster's Freeze or a five-minute car wash or a State Farm Insurance office; beyond those spread the shopping centers and the miles of tract houses, pastel with redwood siding, the unmistakable signs of cheap building already blossoming on those houses which have survived the first rain. To a stranger driving 99 in an air-conditioned car (he would be on business, I suppose, any stranger driving 99, for 99 would never get a tourist to Big Sur or San Simeon, never get him to the California he came to see), these towns must seem so flat, so impoverished, as to drain the imagination. They hint at evenings spent hanging around gas stations, and suicide pacts sealed in drive-ins.

But remember:

Q. In what way does the Holy Land resemble the Sacramento Valley?
A. In the type and diversity of its agricultural products.

U.S. 99 in fact passes through the richest and most intensely cultivated agricultural region in the world, a giant outdoor hothouse with a billion-dollar crop. It is when you remember the Valley's wealth that the monochromatic flatness of its towns takes on a curious meaning, suggests a habit of mind some would consider perverse. There is something in the Valley mind that reflects a real indifference to the stranger in his air-conditioned car, a failure to perceive even his presence, let alone his thoughts or wants. An implacable insularity is the seal of these towns. I once met a woman in Dallas, a most charming and attractive woman accustomed to the hospitality and social hypersensitivity of Texas, who told me that during the four war years her husband had been stationed in Modesto, she had never once been invited inside anyone's house. No one in Sacramento would find this story remarkable ("She probably had no *re*latives there," said someone to whom I told it), for the Valley towns understand one another, share a peculiar spirit. They think alike and they look alike. *I* can tell Modesto from Merced, but I have visited there, gone to dances there; besides, there is over the main street of Modesto an arched sign which reads:

WATER—WEALTH
CONTENTMENT—HEALTH

There is no such sign in Merced.

⌒

I SAID THAT SACRAMENTO WAS the least typical of the Valley towns, and it is—but only because it is bigger and more diverse, only because it has had the rivers and the legislature; its true character remains the Valley character, its virtues the Valley virtues, its sadness the Valley sadness. It is just as hot in the summertime, so hot that the air shimmers and the grass bleaches white and the blinds stay drawn all day, so hot that August comes on not like a month but like an affliction; it is just as flat, so flat that a ranch of my family's with a slight rise on it, perhaps a foot, was known for the hundred-some years which preceded this year as "the hill ranch." (It is known this year as a subdivision in the making, but that is another part of the story.) Above all, in spite of its infusions from outside, Sacramento retains the Valley insularity.

To sense that insularity a visitor need do no more than pick up a copy of either of the two newspapers, the morning *Union* or the afternoon *Bee.* The *Union* happens to be Republican and impoverished and the *Bee* Democratic and powerful ("THE VALLEY OF THE BEES!" as the McClatchys, who own the Fresno, Modesto, and Sacramento *Bees,* used to headline their advertisements in the trade press. "ISOLATED FROM ALL OTHER MEDIA INFLUENCE!"), but they read a good deal alike, and the tone of their chief editorial concerns is strange and wonderful and instructive. The *Union,* in a county heavily and reliably Democratic, frets mainly about the possibility of a local takeover by the John Birch Society; the *Bee,* faithful to the letter of its founder's will, carries on overwrought crusades against phantoms it still calls "the power trusts." Shades of Hiram Johnson, whom the *Bee* helped elect governor in 1910. Shades of Robert La Follette, to whom the *Bee* delivered the Valley in 1924. There is something about the Sacramento papers that does not quite connect with the way Sacramento lives now, something pronouncedly beside the point. The aerospace engineers, one learns, read the San Francisco *Chronicle.*

The Sacramento papers, however, simply mirror the Sacramento peculiarity, the Valley fate, which is to be paralyzed by a past no longer relevant. Sacramento is a town which grew up on farming and discovered to its shock that land has more profitable uses. (The chamber of commerce will give you crop figures, but pay them no mind—what matters is the feeling, the knowledge that where the green hops once grew is now Larchmont Riviera, that what used to be the Whitney ranch is now Sunset City, thirty-three thousand houses and a country-club complex.) It is a town in which defense industry and its absentee owners are suddenly the most important facts; a town which has never had more people or more money, but has lost its *raison d'être.* It is a town many of whose most solid citizens sense about themselves a kind of functional obsolescence. The old families still see only one another, but they do not see even one another as much as they once did; they are closing ranks, preparing for the long night, selling their rights-of-way and living on the proceeds. Their children still marry one another, still play bridge and go into the real-estate business together. (There is no other business in Sacramento, no reality other than land—even I, when I was living and working in New York, felt impelled to take a University of California correspondence course in Urban Land Economics.) But late at night when the ice has melted there is always somebody now, some Julian English, whose heart is not quite in it. For out there on the outskirts of town are marshaled the legions of aerospace engineers, who talk their peculiar condescending language and tend their dichondra and plan to stay in the promised land; who are raising a new generation of native Sacramentans and who do not care, really do not care, that they are not asked to join the Sutter Club. It makes one wonder, late at night when the ice is gone; introduces some air into the womb, suggests that the Sutter Club is perhaps not, after all, the Pacific Union or the Bohemian; that Sacramento is not *the city.* In just such self-doubts do small towns lose their character.

I WANT TO TELL YOU A SACRAMENTO STORY. A few miles out of town is a place, six or seven thousand acres, which belonged in the beginning to a rancher with one daughter. That daughter went abroad and married a title, and when she brought the title home to live on the ranch, her father built them a vast house—music rooms, conservatories, a ballroom. They needed a ballroom because they entertained: people from abroad, people from San Francisco, house parties that lasted weeks and involved special trains. They are long dead, of course, but their only son, aging and unmarried, still lives on the place. He does not live in the house, for the house is no longer there. Over the years it burned, room by room, wing by wing. Only the chimneys of the great house are still standing, and its heir lives in their shadow, lives by himself on the charred site, in a house trailer.

That is a story my generation knows; I doubt that the next will know it, the children of the aerospace engineers. Who would tell it to them? Their grandmothers live in Scarsdale, and they have never met a great-aunt. "Old" Sacramento to them will be something colorful, something they read about in *Sunset*. They will probably think that the Redevelopment has always been there, that the Embarcadero, down along the river, with its amusing places to shop and its picturesque fire houses turned into bars, has about it the true flavor of the way it was. There will be no reason for them to know that in homelier days it was called Front Street (the town was not, after all, settled by the Spanish) and was a place of derelicts and missions and itinerant pickers in town for a Saturday-night drunk: VICTORIOUS LIFE MISSION, JESUS SAVES, BEDS 25¢ A NIGHT, CROP INFORMATION HERE. They will have lost the real past and gained a manufactured one, and there will be no way for them to know, no way at all, why a house trailer should stand alone on seven thousand acres outside town.

But perhaps it is presumptuous of me to assume that they will be missing something. Perhaps in retrospect this has been a story not about Sacramento at all, but about the things we lose and the promises we break as we grow older; perhaps I have been playing out unawares the Margaret in the poem:

Margaret, are you grieving
Over Goldengrove unleaving?...
It is the blight man was born for,
It is Margaret you mourn for.

1965

Joan Didion was born in Sacramento in 1934. Her family has deep ties to the Sacramento Valley, and the area plays a prominent role in both her fiction and nonfiction. Didion attended the University of California, Berkeley, graduating in 1956. She then moved to New York to work for Vogue magazine; her nonfiction also appeared in The National Review and Life, among other publications. In 1963 she published her first novel, Run River (Ivan Obolensky). Her 1968 collection of essays and journalism titled Slouching Toward Bethlehem (Farrar, Straus and Giroux) placed her at the forefront of 1960s "New Journalists." Later nonfiction works include The White Album (Simon and Schuster, 1979), Salvador (Simon and Schuster, 1983), Miami (Simon and Schuster, 1987), Where I Was From (Alfred A. Knopf, 2003), and The Year of Magical Thinking (Alfred A. Knopf, 2005); the last earned the National Book Award. Didion's novels include Play It As It Lays (Farrar, Straus and Giroux, 1970), Democracy (1984), and The Last Thing He Wanted (Alfred A. Knopf, 1996). With her husband, writer John Gregory Dunne, Didion also wrote screenplays for films, including Play It As It Lays, True Confessions, and Up Close and Personal.

❦ *Gary Soto*

From *Gary Soto: New and Selected Poems*
THE ELEMENTS OF SAN JOAQUIN
For César Chávez

Field

The wind sprays pale dirt into my mouth
The small, almost invisible scars
On my hands.

The pores in my throat and elbows
Have taken in a seed of dirt of their own.

After a day in the grape fields near Rolinda
A fine silt, washed by sweat,
Has settled into the lines
On my wrists and palms.

Already I am becoming the valley,
A soil that sprouts nothing.
For any of us.

Wind

A dry wind over the valley
Peeled mountains, grain by grain,
To small slopes, loose dirt
Where red ants tunnel.

The wind strokes
The skulls and spines of cattle
To white dust, to nothing,

Covers the spiked tracks of beetles,
Of tumbleweed, of sparrows
That pecked the ground for insects.

Evenings, when I am in the yard weeding,
The wind picks up the breath of my armpits
Like dust, swirls it
Miles away

And drops it
On the ear of a rabid dog,
And I take on another life.

Wind

When you got up this morning the sun
Blazed an hour in the sky,

A lizard hid
Under the curled leaves of manzanita
And winked its dark lids.

Later, the sky grayed,
And the cold wind you breathed
Was moving under your skin and already far
From the small hives of your lungs.

Stars

At dusk the first stars appear.
Not one eager finger points toward them.

A little later the stars spread with the night
And an orange moon rises
To lead them, like a shepherd, toward dawn.

Sun

In June the sun is a bonnet of light
Coming up,
Little by little,
From behind a skyline of pine.

The pastures sway with fiddle-neck,
Tassels of foxtail.
At Piedra
A couple fish on the river's edge,
Their shadows deep against the water.
Above, in the stubbled slopes,
Cows climb down
As the heat rises
In a mist of blond locusts,
Returning to the valley.

Rain

When autumn rains flatten sycamore leaves,
The tiny volcanos of dirt
Ants raised around their holes,
I should be out of work.

My silverwear and stack of plates will go unused
Like the old, my two good slacks
Will smother under a growth of lint
And smell of the old dust
That rises
When the closet door opens or closes.

The skin of my belly will tighten like a belt
And there will be no reason for pockets.

Harvest

East of the sun's slant, in the vineyard that never failed,
A wind crossed my face, moving the dust
And a portion of my voice a step closer to a new year.

The sky went black in the ninth hour of rolling trays,
And in the distance ropes of rain dropped to pull me
From the thick harvest that was not mine.

Fog

If you go to your window
You will notice a fog drifting in.

The sun is no stronger than a flashlight.
Not all the sweaters
Hung in closets all summer

Could soak up this mist. The fog:
A mouth nibbling everything to its origin,
Pomegranate trees, stolen bicycles,

The string of lights at a used-car lot,
A Pontiac with scorched valves.

In Fresno the fog is passing
The young thief prying a window screen,
Graying my hair that falls
And goes unfound, my fingerprints
Slowly growing a fur of dust—
One hundred years from now

There should be no reason to believe
I lived.

Daybreak

In this moment when the light starts up
In the east and rubs
The horizon until it catches fire,

We enter the fields to hoe,
Row after row, among the small flags of onion,
Waving off the dragonflies
That ladder the air.

And tears the onions raise
Do not begin in your eyes but in ours,
In the salt blown
From one blister into another;

They begin in knowing
You will never waken to bear
The hour timed to a heart beat,
The wind pressing us closer to the ground.

When the season ends,
And the onions are unplugged from their sleep,
We won't forget what you failed to see,
And nothing will heal
Under the rain's broken fingers.

Gary Soto was born in Fresno, California, in 1952, the grandchild of Mexican immigrants. He discovered poetry while attending Fresno City College, and he later studied with Philip Levine at Fresno State University. Soto earned an M.F.A. in creative writing from the University of California, Irvine. He published his first book of poetry, The Elements of San Joaquin, *(University of Pittsburgh Press) in 1977; it was followed by* The Tale of Sunlight *(University of Pittsburgh Press) in 1978 and* Gary Soto: New and Selected Poems *(Chronicle Books) in 1995. Soto is also a prolific author of children's books; among these are works of poetry, including* A Fire in My Hands *(Harcourt, 1991) and* Canto Familiar *(Harcourt, 1995), and young adult novels, including* Jesse *(Harcourt, 1994).*

SAN FRANCISCO BAY

✳ *Mark Twain*

EARLY RISING, AS REGARDS EXCURSIONS TO THE CLIFF HOUSE

Early to bed, and early to rise,
Makes a man healthy, wealthy and wise
—Benjamin Franklin

I don't see it.
—George Washington

NOW BOTH OF THESE ARE HIGH AUTHORITIES—very high and respectable authorities—but I am with General Washington first, last, and all the time on this proposition.

Because I don't see it, either.

I have tried getting up early, and I have tried getting up late—and the latter agrees with me best. As for a man's growing any wiser, or any richer, or any healthier, by getting up early, I know it is not so; because I have got up early in the station-house many and many a time, and got poorer and poorer for the next half a day, in consequence, instead of richer and richer. And sometimes, on the same terms, I have seen the sun rise four times a week up there at Virginia, and so far from my growing healthier on account of it, I got to looking blue, and pulpy, and swelled, like a drowned man, and my relations grew alarmed and thought they were going to lose me. They entirely despaired of my recovery, at one time, and began to grieve for me as one whose days were numbered—whose fate was sealed—who was soon to pass away from them forever, and from the glad sunshine, and the birds, and the odorous flowers, and murmuring brooks, and whispering winds, and all the cheerful scenes of life, and go down into the dark and silent tomb—and they went forth sorrowing, and jumped a lot in the graveyard, and made up their minds to grin and bear it with that fortitude which is the true Christian's brightest ornament.

You observe that I have put a stronger test on the matter than even Benjamin Franklin contemplated, and yet it would not work. Therefore, how is a man to grow healthier, and wealthier, and wiser by going to bed early and getting up early, when he fails to accomplish these things even when he does not go to bed at all? And as far as becoming wiser is concerned, you might put all the wisdom I acquired in these experiments in your eye, without obstructing your vision any to speak of.

As I said before, my voice is with George Washington's on this question.

Another philosopher encourages the world to get up at sunrise because "it is the early bird that catches the worm."

It is a seductive proposition, and well calculated to trap the unsuspecting. But its attractions are all wasted on me, because I have no use for the worm. If I had, I would adopt the Unreliable's plan. He was much interested in this quaint proverb, and directed the powers of his great mind to its consideration for three or four consecutive hours. He was supposing a case. He was supposing, for instance, that he really wanted the worm—that the possession of the worm was actually necessary to his happiness—that he yearned for it and hankered after it, therefore, as much as a man *could* yearn for and hanker after a worm under such circumstances—and he was supposing, further, that he was opposed to getting up early in order to catch it (which was much the more plausible of the two suppositions). Well, at the end of three or four hours' profound meditation upon the subject, the Unreliable rose up and said: "If he were so anxious about the worm, and he couldn't get along without him, and he didn't want to get up early in the morning to catch him—why then, by George, he would just lay for him the night before!" I never would have thought of that. I looked at the youth, and said to myself, he is malicious, and dishonest, and unhandsome, and does not smell good—yet how quickly do these trivial demerits disappear in the shadow when the glare from his great intellect shines out above them!

I have always heard that the only time in the day that a trip to the Cliff House could be thoroughly enjoyed, was early in the morning; (and I suppose it might be as well to withhold an adverse impression while the flow-tide of public opinion continues to set in that direction.)

I tried it the other morning with Harry, the stock-broker, rising at 4 A. M., to delight in the following described things, to wit:

A road unencumbered by carriages, and free from wind and dust; a bracing atmosphere; the gorgeous spectacle of the sun in the dawn of his glory; the fresh perfume of flowers still damp with dew; a solitary drive on the beach while its smoothness was yet unmarred by wheel or hoof, and a vision of white sails glinting in the morning light far out at sea.

These were the considerations, and they seemed worthy a sacrifice of seven or eight hours' sleep.

We sat in the stable, and yawned, and gaped, and stretched, until the horse was hitched up, and then drove out into the bracing atmosphere. (When another early voyage is proposed to me, I want it understood that there is to be no bracing atmosphere in the programme. I can worry along without it.) In half an hour we were so thoroughly braced up with it that it was just a scratch that we were not frozen to death. Then the harness came unshipped, or got broken, or something, and I waxed colder and drowsier while Harry fixed it. I am not fastidious about clothes, but I am not used to wearing fragrant, sweaty horse-blankets, and not partial to them, either; I am not proud, though, when I am freezing, and I added the horse-blanket to my overcoats, and tried to wake up and feel warm and cheerful. It was useless, however—all my senses slumbered, and continued to slumber, save the sense of smell.

When my friend drove past suburban gardens and said the flowers never exhaled so sweet an odor before, in his experience, I dreamily but honestly endeavored to think so too, but in my secret soul I was conscious that they only smelled like horse-blankets. (When another early voyage is proposed to me, I want it understood that there is to be no "fresh perfume of flowers" in the programme, either. I do not enjoy it. My senses are not attuned to the flavor—there is too much horse about it and not enough eau de cologne.)

The wind was cold and benumbing, and blew with such force that we could hardly make headway against it. It came straight from the ocean, and I think there are ice-bergs out there somewhere. True, there was not much dust, because the gale blew it all to Oregon in two minutes; and by good fortune, it blew no gravel-stones, to speak of—only one, of any consequence, I believe—a three-cornered one—it struck me in the eye. I have it there yet. However, it does not matter—for the future I suppose I can manage to see tolerably well out of the other. (Still, when another early voyage is proposed to me, I want it understood that the dust is to be put in, and the gravel left out of the programme. I might want my other eye if I continue to hang on until my time comes; and besides, I shall not mind the dust much hereafter, because I have only got to shut one eye, now, when it is around.)

No, the road was not encumbered by carriages—we had it all to ourselves. I suppose the reason was, that most people do not like to enjoy themselves too much, and therefore they do not go out to the Cliff House in the cold and the fog, and the dread silence and solitude of four o'clock in the morning. They are right. The impressive solemnity of such a pleasure trip is only equalled by an excursion to Lone Mountain in a hearse. Whatever of advantage there may be in having that Cliff House road all to yourself, we had—but to my mind a greater advantage would lie in dividing it up in small sections among the entire community; because, in consequence of the repairs in progress on it just now, it is as rough as a corduroy bridge—(in a good many places,) and consequently the less you have of it, the happier you are likely to be, and the less shaken up and disarranged on the inside. (Wherefore, when another early voyage is proposed to me, I want it understood that the road is not to be unencumbered with carriages, but just the reverse—so that the balance of the people shall be made to stand their share of the jolting and the desperate lonesomeness of the thing.)

From the moment we left the stable, almost, the fog was so thick that we could scarcely see fifty yards behind or before, or overhead; and for a while, as we approached the Cliff House, we could not see the horse at all, and were obliged to steer by his ears, which stood up dimly out of the dense white mist that enveloped him. But for those friendly beacons, we must have been cast away and lost.

I have no opinion of a six-mile ride in the clouds; but if I ever have to take another, I want to leave the horse in the stable and go in a balloon. I shall prefer to go in the afternoon, also, when it is warm, so that I may gape, and yawn, and stretch, if I am drowsy, without disarranging my horse-blanket and letting in a blast of cold wind.

We could scarcely see the sportive seals out on the rocks, writhing and squirming like exaggerated maggots, and there was nothing soothing in their discordant barking, to a spirit so depressed as mine was.

Harry took a cocktail at the Cliff House, but I scorned such ineffectual stimulus; I yearned for fire, and there was none there; they were about to make one, but the bar-keeper looked altogether too cheerful for me—I could not bear his unnatural happiness in the midst of such a ghastly picture of fog, and damp, and frosty surf, and dreary solitude. I could not bear the sacrilegious presence of a pleasant face at such a time; it was too much like sprightliness at a funeral, and we fled from it down the smooth and vacant beach.

We had that all to ourselves, too, like the road—and I want it divided up, also, hereafter. We could not drive in the roaring surf and seem to float abroad on the foamy sea, as one is wont to do in the sunny afternoon, because the very thought of any of that icy-looking water splashing on you was enough to congeal your blood, almost. We saw no white-winged ships sailing away on the billowy ocean, with the pearly light of morning descending upon them like a benediction—"because the fog had the bulge on the pearly light," as the Unreliable observed when I mentioned it to him afterwards; and we saw not the sun in the dawn of his glory, for the same reason. Hill and beach, and sea and sun were all wrapped in a ghostly mantle of mist, and hidden from our mortal vision. (When another early voyage is proposed to me, I want it understood that the sun in his glory, and the morning light, and the ships at sea, and all that sort of thing are to be left out of the programme, so that when we fail to see them, we shall not be so infernally disappointed.)

We were human icicles when we got to the Ocean House, and there was no fire there, either. I banished all hope, then, and succumbed to despair; I went back on my religion, and sought surcease of sorrow in soothing blasphemy. I am sorry I did it, now, but it was a great comfort to me, then. We could have had breakfast at the Ocean House, but we did not want it; can statues of ice feel hunger? But we adjourned to a private room and ordered red-hot coffee, and it was a sort of balm to my troubled mind to observe that the man who brought it was as cold, and as silent, and as solemn as the grave itself. His gravity was so impressive, and so appropriate and becoming to the melancholy surroundings, that it won upon me and thawed out some of the better instincts of my nature, and I told him he might ask a blessing if he thought it would lighten him up any—because he looked as if he wanted to, very bad—but he only shook his head resignedly and sighed.

That coffee did the business for us. It was made by a master artist, and it had not a fault; and the cream that came with it was so rich and thick that you could hardly have strained it through a wire fence. As the generous beverage flowed down our frigid throats, our blood grew warm again, our muscles relaxed, our torpid bodies awoke to life and feeling, anger and uncharitableness departed from us and we were cheerful once more. We got good cigars, also, at the Ocean House, and drove into town over a smooth road lighted by the sun and unclouded by fog.

Near the Jewish cemeteries we turned a corner too suddenly, and got upset, but sustained no damage, although the horse did what he honestly could to kick the buggy out of the State while we were grovelling in the sand. We went on down to the steamer, and while we were on board, the buggy was upset again by some outlaw, and an axle broken.

However, these little accidents, and all the deviltry and misfortune that preceded them, were only just and natural consequences of the absurd experiment of getting up at an hour in the morning when all God-fearing Christians ought to be in bed. I consider that the man who leaves his pillow, deliberately, at sun-rise, is taking his life in his own hands, and he ought to feel proud if he don't have to put it down again at the coroner's office before dark.

Now, for that early trip, I am not any healthier or any wealthier than I was before, and only wiser in that I know a good deal better than to go and do it again. And as for all those notable advantages, such as the sun in the dawn of his glory, and the ships, and the perfume of the flowers, etc., etc., etc., I don't see them, any more than myself and Washington see the soundness of Benjamin Franklin's attractive little poem.

If you go to the Cliff House at any time after seven in the morning, you cannot fail to enjoy it—but never start out there before daylight, under the impression that you are going to have a pleasant time and come back insufferably healthier and wealthier and wiser than your betters on account of it. Because if you do you will miss your calculation, and it will keep you swearing about it right straight along for a week to get even again.

Put no trust in the benefits to accrue from early rising, as set forth by the infatuated Franklin—but stake the last cent of your substance on the judgment of old George Washington, the Father of his Country, who said "he couldn't see it."

And you hear me endorsing that sentiment.

California played an important part in the career of Mark Twain. Born Samuel Clemens in Florida, Missouri, in 1835, he grew up in nearby Hannibal. At age twenty-two, Clemens taught himself to pilot riverboats on the Mississippi River; his pen name, Mark Twain, derives from a river pilot's shout indicating water of two fathoms or deeper. In 1861 Twain began working as a reporter; the following year he traveled west with his brother Orion, who had been appointed secretary to the territorial governor of Nevada. They rode a stagecoach across the Great Plains and the Rocky Mountains to Virginia City, Nevada; from there Twain continued on to San Francisco and the California Gold Country. His travels through Gold Country provided material for Twain's first major work, "The Celebrated Jumping Frog of Calaveras County," published in The New York Saturday Press *in 1865. The entire trip inspired his book* Roughing It *(American Publishing Company), which was published in 1872. By that time Twain had married and moved to the East Coast; there he wrote his best-known books,* Tom Sawyer *(American Publishing Company, 1876) and* Huckleberry Finn *(Charles L. Webster and Company, 1885). He died in 1910.*

✿ *Bret Harte*

From *The Poetical Works of Bret Harte*
SAN FRANCISCO
(FROM THE SEA)

Serene, indifferent of Fate,
Thou sittest at the Western Gate;

Upon thy heights so lately won
Still slant the banners of the sun;

Thou seest the white seas strike their tents,
O Warder of two Continents!

And, scornful of the peace that flies
Thy angry winds and sullen skies,

Thou drawest all things, small or great,
To thee, beside the Western Gate.

O lion's whelp, that hidest fast
In jungle growth of spire and mast,

I know thy cunning and thy greed,
Thy hard high lust and wilful deed,

And all thy glory loves to tell
Of specious gifts material.

Drop down, O fleecy Fog, and hide
Her skeptic sneer, and all her pride!

Wrap her, O Fog, in gown and hood
Of her Franciscan Brotherhood.

Hide me her faults, her sin and blame;
With thy gray mantle cloak her shame!

So shall she, cowled, sit and pray
Till morning bears her sins away.

Then rise, O fleecy Fog, and raise
The glory of her coming days;

Be as the cloud that flecks the seas
Above her smoky argosies,

When forms familiar shall give place
To stranger speech and newer face;

When all her throes and anxious fears
Lie hushed in the repose of years;

When Art shall raise and Culture lift
The sensual joys and meaner thrift,

And all fulfilled the vision, we
Who watch and wait shall never see,—

Who, in the morning of her race,
Toiled fair or meanly in our place,—

But, yielding to the common lot,
Lie unrecorded and forgot.

Among the writers who fixed gold rush–era California most firmly in the American public's imagination is Bret Harte. Born Francis Brett Harte in Albany, New York, in 1836, he followed his mother to Oakland in 1854. In 1860 he began working as a typesetter for the newspaper the Golden Era; he soon began contributing his writing to the paper and to other publications, including the Atlantic Monthly. In 1868 he became editor of The Overland Monthly, where he began publishing the gold-rush tales that would make him famous—among them, The Luck of Roaring Camp (1868) and The Outcasts of Poker Flat (1869). He also published volumes of essays and poetry, among them The Poetical Works of Bret Harte (Houghton Mifflin, 1870). Harte left California for Boston in the early 1870s and later lived in Germany, Scotland, and London, where he died in 1902.

Ina Coolbrith

From *Songs from the Golden Gate*
COPA DE ORO
(CALIFORNIA POPPY)

THY satin vesture richer is than looms
  Of Orient weave for raiment of her kings!
  Not dyes of olden Tyre, not precious things
Regathered from the long-forgotten tombs
Of buried empires, not the iris plumes
  That wave upon the tropics' myriad wings,
  Not all proud Sheba's queenly offerings,
Could match the golden marvel of thy blooms.
For thou art nurtured from the treasure-veins
  Of this fair land: thy golden rootlets sup
    Her sands of gold—of gold thy petals spun.
Her golden glory, thou! on hills and plains,
  Lifting, exultant, every kingly cup
    Brimmed with the golden vintage of the sun.

FROM RUSSIAN HILL

July 1915
Night and the hill to me!
  Silence no sound that jars;
Above, of stars a sea;
  Below, a sea of stars!

Trancèd in slumber's sway,
  The city at its feet.
A tang of salty spray
  Blends with the odors sweet

From garden-close and wall,
  Where the madroño stood,
And tangled chaparral,
  In the old solitude.

Here, from the Long Ago,
  Rezánov's sailors sleep;
There the Presidio;
  Beyond the plumèd steep;

The waters, mile on mile,
  Foam-fringed with feathery white;
The beaconed fortress isle,
  And Yerba Buena's light.

O hill of memories!
  Thy scroll so closely writ
With song, that bough and breeze
  And bird should utter it:

Hill of desire and dream,
  Youth's visions manifold,
That still in beauty gleam
  From the sweet days of old!

Ring out thy solemn tone,
  O far off Mission bell!
I keep the tryst, alone
  With one who loved me well.

A voice I may not hear!
  Face that I may not see,
Yet know a Presence near
  To watch the hour with me . . .

How stately and serene
  The moon moves up the sky;
How silverly between
  The shores her footprints lie!

Peace that no shadow mars!
  Night and the hill to me!
Below, a sea of stars!
  Above, of stars a sea!

Ina Coolbrith was born in the Mormon settlement of Nauvoo, Illinois, in 1841, the niece of Joseph Smith, Mormon prophet and founder of the Church of Jesus Christ of Latter-day Saints. In 1851 she traveled to California with her mother—by her account, escorted over the Sierra Nevada by African-American explorer James P. Beckwourth. She lived in Los Angeles for a time, then moved to the San Francisco Bay area. She established herself as a poet, contributing to magazines such as The Overland Monthly *while working as a librarian at the Oakland Free Library. There she became a mentor to a young aspiring writer named Jack London. Coolbrith's many other literary friends included Mark Twain and Joaquin Miller. Her collections of poems include* A Perfect Day *(J. H. Carmany and Company, 1881) and* Songs of the Golden Gate *(Houghton Mifflin, 1895). She died in 1928.*

✿ *Mary Edith Griswold*

THREE DAYS ADRIFT

PRIL 18—EVENING. In sand lot near foot of Van Ness avenue. I'm writing by the light of the burning city. The fire is still twenty blocks from my house, but we came out here to spend the night because we have been afraid since the first earthquake shock. Then, the house swayed and creaked and trembled; rose and fell like a ship in a tempest. I couldn't walk on the floor at all—had to crawl to the door on my hands and knees. Just as I opened the door my big plaster cast of "The Winged Victory" fell from her pedestal and smashed on the floor. She made a big heap of rubbish. I was too terrified to think. I tried to call to the Dixons, but couldn't articulate. They didn't hear a sound from me throughout those terrible forty seconds. I thought it was the end—but neither the beautiful dreams nor the horrors that are supposed to panorama instant death came to me. My heart beat double quick somewhere up in my throat. I felt nauseated. But I managed to save my toppling mirror; saved it while all other breakable objects in my room went smash. I held on to it with one hand and braced myself against the door frame with the other and watched the crystal scent bottles slide off and spill their precious fragrance on the drunken floor; my statuette of Psyche fell from her shelf and broke her head off. But my little Aztec idol Huitzpochitle took his tumble like a valiant god-of-war without a scratch. He rolled about on the floor in an undignified way but he never changed expression. The final jerk almost upset the bureau on top of me, but after that my house rocked regularly for awhile like a swing when you "let the old cat die." I felt the ease which followed the cessation of great pain. When I felt quite sure that the floor was firm under my feet again I went out on the balcony. A cloud of dust rose from the city as though a race of giants were shaking their great carpet.

Almost all the chimneys were down. Almost instantly columns of smoke began to rise from the other side of town.

We dressed. When we wanted to wash we found there was no water. Next, we hurried down town to see if Maynard Dixon's studio was all right. On Union street the cable slot looked as if it had been run through a Chinese wash house fluting machine.

We had to walk, there being no cars.

In the Latin Quarter the streets were full of terrified people all crowding to keep in the middle of the street. It was the quietest crowd I was ever in. Scarcely any one spoke. The children didn't cry. The fear of God was upon us all. Everyone was afraid of another shock.

Maynard's studio was in chaos. The canvases were uninjured but his Navajo pottery was sadly smashed and mingled on the floor with the rest of his studio litter. A box of matches had been ignited by the shock and extinguished again by a vase of water spilling over it.

From the studio we went down Montgomery street to the Palace hotel. It was uninjured. Things inside seemed quiet and in order. There was no broken glass, no plaster—everything was quiet and in place. A Chinese servant in a white linen blouse was calmly dusting the furniture in the Palm Garden. Men were passing to and fro in the corridor, others were reading the newspapers in the office; the clerks were at the desk. The proud boast that the Palace was earthquake proof had been vindicated.

From there we went along Market street to Lotta's fountain. The old buildings east of Sansome street were blazing. We saw the cupola on the roof of the "Fly in the Pudding" restaurant turn into a beautiful "set piece" and other old wood buildings of early days catch fire. People in the street were kept busy dodging the speeding automobiles. Suddenly there was another earthquake shock. The crowds scurried panic stricken to the middle of the street. There they waited breathless for another disaster. But it never came.

By nine the fire had come up to the Grand Opera House. Third street was a mass of people from south of Market street trying to escape with their household goods. There were women pushing sewing machines in front of them, children carrying phonographs, men dragging trunks. The screeching sound of the trunks dragging on the cable slots went to my marrow. At the corner a fireman stood beside a hydrant from which trailed a string of empty hose. A woman darted out of the crowd and ran up to him.

"What's the matter, Tom?"

"There's no water."

Up to now we had only felt fear, now we knew fear. No water, and fires on every side! The fireman kissed the woman and told her to go back to the folks, assuring her that he was all right. The woman did not cry but her lips trembled. She realized better than we could the terrible import of these words.

We then started for the editorial rooms of Sunset Magazine in the Sunset Press building at the other end of Market street. At every cross street streams of people from south of Market came, staggering under the weight of the burden of their loads. "San Francisco will burn," said somebody. Dixon thought he ought to try and save something from his studio—he and his wife turned back—I obstinately insisted upon going to Sunset offices—insisted that I wasn't afraid to proceed alone. So soon as they left me I was sorry and tried to catch them, but they were lost in the confusion. There was much to see. Earthquakes uncover strange secrets. The ruins of our monster seven million dollar City Hall cried to heaven the shame of the men who built it. At Sunset Press the printers were gathered in the street. The front wall of the top story had fallen, revealing the machinery of the engraving plant.

While I waited there feeling like a shipwrecked sailor on a drifting sea one of my fellow editors, Allan Dunn, hove in sight. I hailed him. He threw me a line, as it were, and towed me up to his house on the top of Hyde street hill. Mrs. Dunn was walking up and down in front of the house clad in her best tailor suit, her pretty new opera cloak on her arm. We went inside and burned up all the gas left in the pipes making coffee.

A slight temblor sent us helter-skelter into the street where the crowd going toward the fire caught us up and whirled us along to the top of the hill on Sacramento street. The fire was roaring over an immense territory. We wanted to get into the thick of things and went on down to Union Square. It was full of refugees sitting on their household goods. There were gathered Chinamen, Italians, "muckers" from south of Market street, Grand Opera singers; painted women who blinked as though they had not seen daylight for months; and fashionable people in evening dress donned hurriedly when they were awakened by the earthquake—a succotash of civilization—I didn't see any policemen. There was no need of any—the crowd was perfectly quiet—it was this unearthly, unnatural calm which made me afraid to speak. I saw only one talkative person. She was a beautiful creature of stunning style who walked between two men, her hands in her muff. I believe she was the only woman in all San Francisco that day who acted unconcerned. As the trio sailed past me I heard her say "O, we'll have a good time as long as our money lasts."

As we stopped on Stockton street to watch a toppling wall I found myself next to an old colored man. As he spoke I recognized in him the negro exhorter. I had sometimes listened when he was holding forth from his open-air platforms. Now he was exclaiming:

"Haven't I prophesied all this? Haven't I told you this wicked town would be consumed with fire and brimstone? But now I'm sorry I spoke."

At the Sequoia Club we rescued Mrs. Solly Walter. Later she and I detached ourselves from the Dunns and walked back to my house. The residence streets looked like circus day in a country village. The women were all sitting on chairs in their front yards, secure in the feeling that Van Ness avenue was too wide for fire to cross it. By noon today both sides of the wide boulevard were lined with people and furniture. Sometimes a woman would have saved only one easy chair and was comfortably rocking in it. Again it was a bedroom set that had been snatched from the burning—but always there were phonographs and parrots and dogs and canary birds. Here, as everywhere, the crowd showed no emotion, except when the earth trembled, as it did now and then, slightly. Then everyone would rush for the middle of the street.

This afternoon my old friend Mr. Whitney called for me with a buggy. We made a complete circuit of the fire zone. The people seem to feel that a power too stupendous to combat had taken charge of their destiny, and that the fury of the forces of nature cannot be met by the puny hands of man. We are all learning the lesson of the inevitable.

The open lot near my house is full of people and new comers are constantly arriving. The pillar of fire mounts higher and higher. The heavens south are burning red, while north over Fort Mason smoke hangs low. It frightens me, the smoke, even more than the fire. It is an unreasonable fear I know, and I'm ashamed to tell anyone of it—the fear that the heavens will fall—the sky looks so near. What if we should get caught up in a maelstrom of smoke and only four blocks of unstable earth between us and the bay!

Thursday, April 19. At Fort Mason. Yesterday's sights and sounds and experiences are forgotten in today's. We rose when the sun looked up over Union street hill—red as wine through the smoke—and dragged our mattresses back to my house with the fire still many blocks away. While we were eating cold food on the balcony, Xavier Martinez, the artist, came up with some friends to see if there was a way of making coffee. There was not, but I offered an acceptable substitute and threw in the house. They accepted. This was certainly lucky because Maynard and Lillian wanted to go home to Sausalito. They urged me to come along, but I refused. I know now why the people who live at the foot of Vesuvius all stay till it is too late to escape the lava.

The Dixons departed taking with them a few cherished things on a two-wheeled push-cart.

Vail Bakewell, the lawyer, came over from Oakland on a tug to rescue us and take us over to his home in Oakland. We all refused to go. I, for one, must see the closing act of this monster tragedy, a whole city for a stage, 500,000 actors and everyone playing his part. We were joined by Porter Garnett, the critic, but soon he left us to save his mother from danger.

At four this afternoon a big cloud of smoke came over us—cinders as big as dollars began to fall and a shower of plaster dust. This frightened us. I packed three trunks and the boys carried them into the neighbor's garden. I wrapped a wet blanket around the band-box containing my new spring hat and hid it in a rose bush. We bought a four-wheeled cart from a small boy, made two two-wheeled carts out of it by using the pantry shelves for the body, loaded up one with food and the other with clothes and started out for my friends', the Towarts, sand lots on the other side of the Presidio. Van Ness avenue was full of people and movings—so full it spilled out into every vacant lot and side street. Going was difficult. Our cart broke down. I experienced the most terrible and senseless fear that this great mass of people, animals and things would stampede. After a council we decided to stop here in Fort Mason for the night.

We are in the middle of an immense field—there must be thousands camping here—people of all nations thrown together higglety-pigglety. Our nearest neighbor is an Italian vegetable peddler and he has brought his entire family and household effects. When they went for the second load they left the baby here wailing an obligato to the accompaniment of a German fellow with a fiddle. Behind us sit a newly wed couple beside their trunk. The little bride is quietly weeping while her inexperienced spouse shows plainly that this is too much for one day. In the camps of the Latin races the men are doing all the talking, while among us English speaking people only the women can be heard. On the top of the hill stood a bearded Italian waving a large chromo of St. Francis at the ever approaching fire, while he called upon the patron saint to save his city.

11 P.M. Vail Bakewell and Rob Towart have just returned from an adventure. They went over to see if the Towarts' house had burned. It is still standing but it is only a question of a few hours. Fire is coming up all sides of Russian Hill. I started out with Vail on an exploring expedition. The first startling sight was a rose garden, with hundreds of huge roses glowing red in the light of the flames. We had the luck to get inside the fire lines. It was a thrilling experience while it lasted, until we were peremptorily ordered out by the Colonel in command of the troops. We went so close to the fire that I felt my hair curl. We saw some people loot a grocery and bar—the proprietor inviting everyone to help themselves. We went inside. There were no lights, only that ghastly light coming in the windows of the fire across the street. It made me sick.

Outside a puppy sat whining. I took it up in my arms and it was trembling. There were many dogs and cats that had been forgotten or abandoned by their masters. Some we saw ran away from us, back into the burning houses. A cry was raised that we were surrounded by fire, but there was an avenue of escape down the north side where the hill makes a sheer drop of 50 feet. My nerves still tingle with the excitement of this. Everything has been on such a big scale today! Has Fate thus set a measure which will make all other experiences which are to come to me seem puny?

Still later a span of horses broke their tethering straps and came charging into our camp. We scared them away with umbrellas, which we are using for tents. This so upset the tranquility of our crowd that Vail and I volunteered to go back to my house to fetch some restoratives. We went by way of Van Ness avenue. Everything has burned from there to the ferry up to Vallejo street. It was the most wonderful sight! Many miles—a limitless space of blue flames with the last red glow of big timbers between—of dancing, palpitating, living light.

The great dwelling houses on the west side of Van Ness avenue were ablaze. Soldiers were dynamiting them. It was like the booming of artillery fire.

On our way back we saw two men sitting on the front steps of a big house. They asked us in to see how their home had been wrecked by the earthquake, as well as by the fire across the street and the dynamite. We groped around inside, by the fire light. Vail Bakewell tried to play on the pipe organ—but there was no sound. In the street a man came running up to us and presented me with a box of face powder—said he had no use for it and it might come handy!

Friday, April 20.—Fort Mason. 6 A.M. An army surgeon made an inspection of the camp this morning and found a sick child next to us, which he diagnosed as suffering from small-pox. Even this announcement did not create a panic. It seemed all in the day's doings.

1 P.M. We are at the little dock below the Fort waiting for a navy cutter to take us around to the Oakland ferry.

The fire is within two blocks of my house—everyone in my block had been told to leave. Our house has been ordered dynamited. The apathy of the last two days has given way. The firemen are frantic. If they don't stop the fire now the whole Western Addition will go—a policeman with a red face is running up and down in front of the house. A dead Italian lies in the middle of the street opposite my house. Members of his family sit around his body in a circle. I got so scared I couldn't swallow a glass of water. The heat on the balcony was intense—too hot to stay out there. The paint on the woodwork was blistering. Everyone was fire mad. My home will surely go.

Mary Edith Griswold was born in 1875 and raised in San Jose, California. In 1906 she was working as an assistant editor at Sunset *magazine in San Francisco when the 7.9-magnitude earthquake struck. Her story of the temblor and resulting fire, titled "Three Days Adrift" and published in* Sunset, *remains among the best firsthand accounts of the disaster. Griswold survived the quake and was married shortly afterward to Edwin Emerson Jr., foreign correspondent for* The Nation *and* Harper's Weekly, *among other publications, who had rushed cross-country to rescue her. The wedding—in the home of Fanny Stevenson, widow of Robert Louis Stevenson—was said to be the first under an actual roof in the quake-shattered city. Griswold later traveled widely with her husband before settling in New York City. She died in 1955 in San Jose.*

George Sterling

THE COOL, GREY CITY OF LOVE

Tho I die on a distant strand,
  And they give me a grave in that land,
Yet carry me back to my own city!
Carry me back to her grace and pity!
  For I think I could not rest
  Afar from her mighty breast.
  She is fairer than others are
    Whom they sing the beauty of.
  Her heart is a song and a star—
    My cool, grey city of love.

Tho they tear the rose from her brow,
  To her is ever my vow;
Ever to her I give my duty—
First in rapture and first in beauty,
  Wayward, passionate, brave,
  Glad of the life God gave.
  The sea-winds are her kiss,
    And the sea-gull is her dove;
  Cleanly and strong she is—
    My cool, grey city of love.

The winds of the Future wait
  At the iron walls of her Gate,
And the western ocean breaks in thunder,
And the western stars go slowly under,

And her gaze is ever West
In the dream of her young unrest.
Her sea is a voice that calls,
   And her star a voice above,
And her wind a voice on her walls—
   My cool, grey city of love.

Tho they stay her feet at the dance,
  In her is the far romance.
Under the rain of winter falling,
Vine and rose will await recalling.
  Tho the dark be cold and blind,
  Yet her sea-fog's touch is kind,
  And her mightier caress
   Is joy and the pain thereof;
  And great is thy tenderness,
   O cool, grey city of love!

George Sterling was born in 1869 in Sag Harbor, New York. He attended Saint Charles College in Maryland, then in 1890 traveled west to California to work for his uncle, a real estate developer. Sterling himself worked in real estate for some years, but his true love was literature. Inspired by other Bay Area writers—Jack London, Ambrose Bierce, and Joaquin Miller—Sterling began publishing poetry. His collections include The Testimony of the Suns *(A. M. Robertson, 1903) and* A Wine of Wizardry *(A. M. Robertson, 1909). In 1905 Sterling and his wife moved to Monterey Bay and helped establish the village of Carmel as a writers and artists colony. Other residents would include Jack London, Mary Austin, and photographer Arnold Genthe. Sterling's later years were unhappy, marred by divorce, the deaths of friends, and his own alcoholism. He moved from Carmel to San Francisco, where he lived his final years in a room at the Bohemian Club. He committed suicide in 1926.*

⚘ Gertrude Atherton

Selection from *Adventures of a Novelist*

M Y FATHER-IN-LAW, FAXON DEAN ATHERTON, lived at his country place, covering a square mile, some thirty miles "down the peninsula" from San Francisco, and between the village of Menlo Park and the station Fair Oaks—afterward renamed Atherton in memory of him. It was at least two-thirds covered with magnificent woods, left in their natural state save for roads cut through the heavy underbrush.

Born in Dedham, Massachusetts, of unmixed English descent, Mr. Atherton, in his early youth, had adventured as far as Chile in search of fortune. He made it in hardware. Not long after his arrival he married Dominga de Goñi, whose parents had fled from Spain in some political revolution, and six of his children, Alejandra, Frank, Elena, George, Isabel, and Faxon, were born in Valparaiso; the youngest, Florence, in San Francisco, whither he came with his family some time during the sixties. They lived on Rincon Hill until Mr. Atherton bought the country estate from the widow of Louis Arguello, the first Mexican Governor of California, and built a large comfortable house with two bath-rooms—few houses boasted more than one—and a wing for the servants. It was adequately but plainly furnished, and a fair sample of the country houses of that time. With but one exception that I know of, only those of recent and sudden fortunes were disposed to magnificence, and were scornfully criticized by the old régime. Style of any sort in the country was bad style. The place had been known familiarly as "Los Pulgas" (the fleas), but was rechristened more euphemistically (not more fittingly), Valparaiso Park.

The house stood in a clearing of the middle woods about half a mile from the entrance gates. There were fine lawns before it and the gardens were rich with imported flowers and ornamental trees; the only flowers indigenous to central California were sweet-briar, the golden poppy (now hideously known as escholtzia), blue-bells, wood violets, "baby-eyes," yellow and purple lupins—which grew everywhere, even on the sand-hills of San Francisco. But in Mr. Atherton's garden, as in many others, were every variety of rose, fuchsia, mignonette, morning glory, heliotrope, tulips, as well as magnolia trees, orange trees, bridal wreath, lilac and syringa. About the house was a continuous bed of Parma violets whose fragrance greeted one when passing the deer park. (The deer generally died, homesick for their redwood forests on the mountains.)

Mr. Atherton, with the true instinct of the patriarch, had intended to build a house on the estate for each of his children as they married. But at the time of my advent only one had risen. Alejandra Atherton, after a long reign as a belle, was now the wife of a New Yorker, Major Lawrence Rathbone, and lived on the south-east corner of the property in a very modern and beautiful house—designed by herself—but still carefully avoiding the palatial. Elena, now Mrs. Macondray, preferred to live in the city and had a house in the Western Addition. Isabel was married in Chile, to one of the Edwards, of banking fame. Of the boys only George had married and Florence was still a schoolgirl.

I seemed fated to have strong silent men presiding over my immediate destinies. Mr. Atherton rarely opened his mouth. He was a handsome old man with regular features, a short gray beard but shaven upper lip, and was taller than any of his sons. I remember him as always kind in an absent manner, but, although I suppose he did talk sometimes, I cannot recall a word that he may have uttered.*

Mrs. Atherton was exactly five feet in height and weighed two hundred pounds. Perhaps it was her breadth and width that made her impressive, or her enormous Spanish dignity that diverted attention from her negligible inches. Her skin was fair—she was very proud of her Castilian blood—but her hair had been a dark auburn-brown. Her features were undistinguished;

---

*Mr. Atherton had been in indifferent health for some time, but I was told that for years he corresponded with Daniel Webster, Louis Agassiz, Secretary Seward, and other distinguished men, many of whom had been entertained at Valparaiso Park. There were several trunks full of these letters in the attic at the time of his death. They probably had a certain value, but unfortunately Mrs. Atherton destroyed them.

fortunately all her children inherited, in varying length of nose, the regular features of their father. Her English was very broken, but she cherished the delusion that she had mastered the tongue of her husband. Frank and George were rather dark, but Faxon and Elena had reasonably fair skins, blue eyes and brown hair. Alejandra had the most magnificent blue eyes I have ever seen—Spanish eyes despite their color. Set in an olive skin they were all the more striking. She was still a beautiful woman, notwithstanding the hundred and eighty pounds she had prematurely accumulated; her height carried them off. Florence, then fifteen, had a brilliant complexion, dazzling teeth, brown hair with golden glints in it, and the long dark green eyes—*los ojos verdes*—famed in Spanish song. But she was then as thin as I was, which afforded me much satisfaction. My grandfather knew his world. They did not receive me with open arms, for no less demonstrative people ever lived, but they were philosophical, and they had escaped a great calamity; they were extremely "nice" to me, and I was given to understand immediately that I now had the honor of being one of them.

I do not think I have ever met a family so completely satisfied with themselves, with their condition, with life itself, as the Athertons. They were well born, well bred, had always known wealth—as wealth went in those days; they prided themselves upon having the shortest visiting list in San Francisco, and what they did or had or were was of an indisputable rightness. Everything else suffered by comparison. As none of her children was a pure blonde, Mrs. Atherton lamented my surface accessories, but consoled me with the hope that my hair would grow darker with the years, and, possibly, my skin also. As none of them cared for reading I was given to understand that reading was not the thing. Neither was impulsiveness, and Mrs. Atherton conceived it to be her holy mission to tone me down. She read me little abstract lectures, priding herself upon her subtlety. Intellect had no place in woman. Her whole duty was to be a good wife, mother, and housekeeper. If called to social position she must be careful to set a good example. I soon learned to listen amiably and think about something else.

I fancy she had hopes of making a true Atherton out of me, and I sometimes wonder she did not. I was very young, unformed in character, and it is extraordinary how the collective pressure of the religiously average can almost convince anyone subject to pangs of originality that they are right and he wrong. It is the bourgeois standard, of course, but one that has invaded all aristocracies—to say nothing of royalties. At certain of the older courts of Europe no one can be officially presented who has ever received money for a more or less corresponding value. That, of course, excludes artists of all denominations, even were one a Sophocles or a Velasquez. The attitude of my new family was precisely similar. Gentlemen engaged in business or followed one of the professions; but writers and painters, sculptors or musicians, were beyond the pale, not only in Menlo Park but in San Francisco generally, as no scion of a leading family had then taken to any of the arts. Therefore, necessarily, artists were common.

My mother-in-law had an even higher standard. "Ladies in Spain do not write," she said to me when I began to betray symptoms; and it was quite twelve years after I published my first novel before the painful subject that I wrote at all was mentioned by any of the family in my presence, although I was generally upon good terms with them. (Mrs. Rathbone was an exception, but that comes later.) I dedicated one of my first little books to Mrs. Atherton, and she thanked me politely and never referred to it again. I think she felt she had been visited with an undeserved notoriety.

I HAD NO COMPANIONS OF MY OWN AGE. Alejandra and Elena were but a few years younger than my mother. Florence was either away at school or had her intimate friends, Lizzie and Manuela Page, with her during the holidays. (Seas and peaks between fifteen and eighteen!) George, who was never any sort of companion, went to town every day with his father, who had set him up in the brokerage business.

It seems to me, looking back, that I must have reverted to my childhood for a year or two, although I had thought myself extremely grown-up and worldly-wise before. But then I had always been among people who more or less spoilt me, and encouraged my mental aspirations. It was not in the Atherton credo to spoil any one, although they regarded me as little more than an infant. "So child!" my mother-in-law would exclaim despairingly. She was horrified that I could not sew, and tried to teach me to embroider flannel petticoats for the impending Atherton, over which unknown quantity she was pleasurably excited. It would be the first child to inherit the name, and she insisted that it be born in the family mansion; our own house was building, but it would hardly be finished in time, and I doubt if I should have been permitted to move in if it had been.

Possibly my condition had something to do with my reversion. It is too much to say that I resented it, for I thought little about it. Babies, it seemed, opened the second chapter of the book of marriage, but it added to my bewilderment. I was thoroughly disoriented, and as there were no books to read in the house, my mind went to sleep. I forgot I had ever posed as intellectual, desired to be well read. Above all, to be different.

Well that it was so. To be different in that environment would have been a social offence.

Mrs. Macondray and her brood spent the summer at the "Big House." Mrs. Rathbone came over every afternoon. Neighbors dropped in. They sat on the wide verandah, sewing, embroidering, exchanging recipes, gossiping. I often wondered if life anywhere else in the whole wide world were as dull. Mrs. Atherton soon gave up trying to make a needlewoman out of me, so I merely sat among them, stifling yawns and listening vaguely. I had gone through many vicissitudes in my short life, but dullness had not been one of their attributes. By contrast they seemed highly dramatic. I doubt if any of my new friends would have recognized drama off the stage had it been paraded in front of her. But there was no prospect of drama here.

The meals were endless. Eight or ten courses. And conversation, unless there was company present, was entirely in Spanish, which I thought rather rude as I could not understand a word of it. Unfortunately this gave me a dislike for the language and I missed a great opportunity.

It is only just that a word should be said in regard to Mrs. Atherton's "table," for it was famous—among those invited to Valparaiso Park—as the best table in California. Her Chinese cook had come to her unexcelled in the usual American repertoire; she sent him to cook for three months in one of San Francisco's renowned French restaurants, and then herself taught him the dishes of her native Chile. It was the last that made her table famous, but I really liked only one of them: large green peppers, the outer skin parboiled off, the seeds removed, and then filled with cheese and fried in batter, the whole covered with browned cream. It was a dish to appeal to any palate, but I hated all the others at the time and the cook hated me because he was obliged to prepare my food in the simplest possible manner. On one occasion when I went out to the kitchen to take him a message from Mrs. Atherton he threw an iron saucepan at my head and missed me by an inch. I made a lively exit, but had sense enough to keep the adventure to myself.

If there was no drama in Menlo Park, sometimes there were mild sensations. Whether it was during that first summer or later—I spent many afternoons of my married life on that verandah—I have forgotten, but one topic of discussion was the impertinent invasion of Menlo Park—a term that embraced all that part of the county—by one of the Bonanza millionaires. For many years two men named Flood and O'Brien had kept a saloon in San Francisco. Then came the excitement of the Virginia City mines; they speculated and made millions. O'Brien preferred to live in the city, but Flood built himself a colossal white house on the Middlefield road, not far from the Rathbones, and contiguous to the estates of other members of the ancient aristocracy. It looked more like a house on a wedding cake than something to live in, and was uglier than anything in San Francisco. The county was both annoyed and agitated, and for weeks the leading topic on the verandah was whether or not the Floods should be called upon when they moved in. However, for business reasons, impressed upon them by their husbands, the women did call, and Mrs. Rathbone left her mother's card with her own.

I was present when they returned the call, and was stricken too dumb to take any part in the conversation. As this call marked their formal entrance into Menlo Park society, they had got themselves up for the occasion. Mrs. Flood wore a flowing dark blue silk wrapper, discreetly ruffled, and "Miss Jennie" a confection of tourquoise-green flannel trimmed with deep flounces of Valenciennes lace! We always wore the simplest of thin frocks in summer—generally white batiste or cross-barred muslin—but I doubt if we, in our ostentatious simplicities, made the initiates feel out of it. I fancy they went away after that stiff and nervous call with the pleasant feeling of superiority that only multi-millions can give.

An even more amusing episode had occurred several years before. Milton S. Latham had married the most beautiful of the "three Macs,"

Mollie McMullen, a lovely brunette, with large soft dark eyes, delicate features, and an expression of such sweetness that she retained much of her beauty and a semblance of youth when I last saw her at the age of seventy. Both were of the old régime, but she had been poor all her life and now wanted all that money could buy, including two trousseaux a year from Paris and a fine house. As he was many years older than she was he gratified her every whim. Although, as I have said, simplicity was *de rigueur* in the country, his house in Menlo Park was large and imposing, but in perfect taste. It was furnished magnificently and he had a chef, an English butler, a host of other servants, a vintage cellar, and entertained on the grand scale.

The Duke of Manchester was making a tour round the world and passed through California. He brought a letter to Mr. Latham, who left a card on him at once, at the Palace Hotel, and invited him to spend the following night at his country house. He also invited guests from San Francisco to meet him, as well as Mr. and Mrs. Atherton, the Rathbones, Selbys, and other county fashionables.

The duke arrived by a late train and was taken at once to his room. The company assembled in the great drawing-room, women in Paris gowns and jewels, men in their poor best.

The English butler announced in faltering accents: "His grace, the Duke of Manchester." All turned expectantly to the door. It was the first time any of them had seen a duke and they were agreeably fluttered.

And then the duke strode in, and they nearly fainted. He wore boots that reached his thighs and a red flannel shirt!

No doubt he too nearly fainted when he saw that glittering assemblage of gentlemen and ladies who would not have disgraced his own ancestral halls. Poor man, he was terribly mortified, and explained to his suave and smiling host that all he knew of California he had gleaned from the stories of Bret Harte, and had provided himself with what he believed to be the regulation Western costume, that all whom he met might feel quite at their ease! True, he had had misgivings when he saw the splendor of the house, but he had brought no other change and had hoped against hope that all would be right.

The company had recovered before he finished his embarrassed apology and concluded to take the matter as a huge joke, putting him at his ease at once. I believe there was never a more successful dinner given in Menlo Park. The duke invited them all to visit him in England and went on his way delighted with Californians.

Gertrude Atherton was born in San Francisco in 1857. In 1876 she married into the wealthy Atherton family, for whom the San Francisco Peninsula town is named. Her husband died at sea eleven years later. Atherton then devoted her energies to a literary career. Over the next forty years she published dozens of books, many of them set in the California of her youth; these include The Californians *(Macmillan, 1898) and* The Splendid Idle Forties *(Macmillan, 1902). Atherton moved to London in 1895 and later lived in Germany; some of her later works are set in England and Europe. In 1932, having returned to California, she published her autobiography,* The Adventures of a Novelist *(Liveright). She died in San Francisco in 1948.*

◈ *Herb Caen*

From *Only in San Francisco*
MIRACLE IN OCTOBER

T HIS PARTICULAR SATURDAY AWOKE LIKE A DAY that had a
good night's sleep.

The skies were a clear-eyed blue, and the Bay was as calm and
unruffled as a pond. Even harsh Alcatraz softened under the warm sun;
with a few white sailboats frolicking nearby, it looked like an island resort—
the Alcatraz-Hilton?—and by screwing your mind's eye to a telescope, you
could see prisoners stretched out for a sunbath.

Slowly, the city yawned, stretched, and came to life. Then it looked out at
the day through its many windows and emerged to revel in the soft, dreamy
magic of it all.

In late October, midsummer had come at last to Baghdad-by-the-Bay.

BY NOON, THE CITY WAS working hard at the job of enjoying Saturday's
warm miracle. The streets were full of convertibles that had blown their tops.
The girls were dressed in sheerest joy. Small boys shed their mothers and
their complexes and became just small boys again, heading Huckfinnishly
toward the nearest shores, to dangle their toes and fishing poles.

Downtown, delighted tourists in aloha shirts pointed fingers and
cameras in all directions. Old men and pigeons squinted at each other on
the grass of Union Square. In the stores, the salespeople agreed every fifteen
minutes that "it's much too nice a day to be working," and went on shirking.
Cabdrivers took off their coats and the city followed suit, suitless.

On Montgomery Street, even Jake Ehrlich, a midwintery sort of fellow, walked to lunch at Jack's with his hat in his hand. The sun beamed down to see such fun, and the cow jumped over the moon, including, presumably, Lunik II.

MIDSUMMER OCTOBER IN CHINATOWN. The smell of fish and poultry hanging powerfully in the heavy air. Girls in dark glasses and Bermuda shorts wandering along Grant Avenue, wrinkling their noses and staring through a dirty window at a huge dangling octopus that stared back with all its tentacles.

Chinatown was in a festive mood. A mighty politician had died, and his funeral was satisfyingly vast, tying up traffic for blocks and making the motorcycle cops sweat rings in their black shirts. After the procession had broken up, the musicians sauntered through the streets, still carrying their instruments and now and then tootling a loud blast for no reason at all except that the funeral was over and it was good to be alive on a summer day in October.

The Ferry Building shining like all the golden yesterdays at the foot of Commercial Street. Teak, jade, and junk in the windows. In the Italian Market, which is Chinese, a young man inserting an air hose into the necks of very dead ducks and blowing them up like footballs, which makes them easier to glaze for barbecued and Peking duck.

Three fire engines raced down Washington toward North Beach, the firemen hatless. Children screamed for joy as the hook'n' ladder raced past, and the tillerman, a blond hero with crew-cut hair, waved a hero's greetings to his admirers. Through an open window, you could hear a Chinese record, its voice echoing the fading sirens. Old Chinese ladies, their once-bound feet still tiny and misshapen, went on talking in the sunshine.

It was that kind of day, when firemen wave at children and a funeral calls for a celebration. The sun hung high over Hang Far Low, and Chinatown was full of life after death.

THE DAY DARKENED, THE BAY GLOWED in luminous beauty, but the mercury stayed up, refusing to let go of the sudden summer. Near midnight, the downtown streets of the city were still in their shirt sleeves. A Powell cable cranked its way down Nob Hill, cradled in the warm grip of passengers clinging to its sides. A few were drunk. At each stop, they hopped off, let the cable get a start down the hill, and then ran shouting after it to leap back on. The conductor grinned foolishly at them. It was a foolish night.

The big hotel lobbies were alive with cool young girls in their ball gowns, escorted by hot young men with damp foreheads. At the Roger Laphams' fiftieth wedding anniversary party in the St. Francis, the band played on and on, and the champagne swirled and bubbled like the Bay around a piling. Roger danced every dance with the pretty young girls and easily achieved the impossible: he enjoyed himself at his own party.

At 3 A.M., summer still ruled the night skies, and the lady in the window of Tiny's Waffle Shop was still making waffles.

SUNDAY GOT UP LATE AND GRAY-EYED, with a slight hangover. It groaned slightly in the voice of many foghorns and made a rustling sound, as though leafing through the Sunday papers. Sixty thousand jammed their way into Kezar Stadium—miles and miles of Park, and not a place to park—and yelled through the Grownups' Big Game. The sun, which had given of itself so lavishly the day before, made a few tired attempts to get up, pulled the pillows back over its head, and said, "Aw, the heck with it."

But it didn't matter. It had been a weekend to remember—a miniature season crammed with life and death, joy and tragedy—in the city that knows no seasons.

Herb Caen was born in Sacramento, California, in 1916 and began writing for the Sacramento Union *newspaper in 1932. In 1936 he moved to San Francisco to write for the* San Francisco Chronicle. *With a break for service in the U.S. Army Air Corps during World War II, Caen would write for the* Chronicle—*and, for a few years, its rival, the* San Francisco Examiner—*for the next six decades. Filled with gossip, humor, and wordplay (he is credited with coining the word "beatnik" in the 1950s), Caen's columns explained San Francisco to itself and—after the column was syndicated to the rest of the nation—to the outside world as well. Among his books are* Baghdad-by-the-Bay *(Doubleday, 1949),* Don't Call It Frisco *(Doubleday, 1953),* Only in San Francisco *(Doubleday, 1960), and* The Best of Herb Caen *(Chronicle Books, 1991). Caen won a special Pulitzer Prize in 1996. He died in 1997.*

Anne Lamott

From *Hard Laughter*
THE TOWN WHERE I LIVE

T HE CABIN BENEATH THE EUCALYPTUSES was encased in
fog when I awoke this morning, butt to butt with my ten-year-
old friend Megan, who was making waking-up noises. It was nine
o'clock and the cabin was still dark enough so that the piles, clumps, and
general squalor receded in the gray mildewy air. There were clothes on the
table, on the floor, on the top of the refrigerator. There was food on top of
the piles of clothes, sometimes on a plate or in a cup but not always—for
instance, there was a large bolus of partly chewed pineapple core on a purple wool bathrobe. There were books and magazines and newspapers hov-
ering about like unkempt relatives at a reunion. There was a T-shirt beside
the bed with which I had wiped up most of a half gallon of red wine, a big
ball of blond kinky hair culled from my hairbrush, which I am now down
to using once a week, and there was a decrepit, senile, incontinent alley cat
pacing across the room, glaring at nothing in particular. Not to mention
the pungent smell of his cat box. Megan had propped herself up on her
elbows, scanned the room groggily, and said, "You must be a saint to live in
a place like this."

She turned on the radio and picked up the cat. The cat has only one
tooth, on the bottom, to the left: at sixteen years old he eats his food like a
toothless old man gumming saltines. I would have his teeth fixed somehow
but he will probably not last long. Megan's seventy-eight-year-old great-
aunt was recently told by her dentist that her dentures were acceptable,
but that for twenty-three hundred dollars he would fit her with teeth that
would last her a lifetime. Megan held the cat in the rocking chair, beside the
Franklin stove, rocking slowly and drowsily: both of us would start talking

in about ten minutes. The cat smiled. A long strand of embroidery thread hung from his tooth.

"Farrrrrrr out," said someone on the radio doing an impersonation of John Denver, whose great moment, insofar as either Megan or I was concerned, was an interview in *Rolling Stone* in which he stated, "I think it is so far out that birds fly in the sky and fish swim in the sea."

"That guy's a feeb," Megan muttered. In the anteroom the cat peed on the outside of his box.

The disc jockey played a song called "My Feet Stink, My Head Aches and I Don't Love Jesus."

"*My* feet stink," Megan told me. "I've had this same pair of socks on for three days, and they weren't even clean to begin with."

"So don't tell *me* about it."

"Well, I can't very well go around all day with my feet stinking, can I?"

"You did it yesterday. You can wear a pair of mine."

"None of yours match," said Megan, holding one of her socks at a healthy distance. It looked like it had crumpled cardboard in it.

"But mine don't stink. So you can spray Lysol on yours, or you can borrow mine. And frankly, I think you're going to have to burn your pair." Megan waggled her sock at the cat, who rolled his eyes and looked appalled.

"O.K. I want to stay here and read until you do your housecleaning job. Then we could go to the beach or something. I can't believe *you* make money housecleaning."

I can't believe it either. I used to be an editor with a national magazine, and now I spend my days cleaning schmootz off the inside of refrigerators, and wiping up pubic hairs from the bottoms of bathtubs. There are few jobs available in the small town where I live, and I will not commute over the hill. My time is too important to me. My time is so important to me that I choose to spend it sucking up dust bunnies with upright Hoovers.

When I was dressed and about to leave, Megan looked up with feigned annoyance from one of the bookshelves. "If you didn't have so many books, I could probably find something to read."

"Good luck, toots. See you later."

"See you later," she said. In this town where I live, we rarely say "Goodbye." We say "See you later," or simply "S'later."

Megan likes me more than almost anyone else in the world likes me. She has a seemingly blind eye to my top ten personality defects, and laughs at almost everything I say. She likes me so much that I do not panic too much when in her company I feel an unheralded pimple emerging on my chin, threatening to alter my profile. We have a relationship so special, so easy, so lacking in the complications of most friendships—we have so much fun together—that sometimes at the beach dodging waves I look at her and think, Phew.

MY NEXT-DOOR NEIGHBORS live three hundred feet away and raise worms in big wooden boxes in their front yard. The father and both children look much like the weird children one ran into occasionally in grammar school—very, very tiny and vaguely Martian. I hide from this family most of the time. They invite me to their yard parties, and I never show up. They drop by the cabin to discuss better ways to raise worms, and I hide in the bathroom while they knock. The ten-year-old daughter, who is outgoing and sort of striking in a tiny weird Martian sort of way, once told me I should brush my hair more. The little boy, who is five years old and looks like Oscar Levant, once put my alley cat in one of the worm boxes. My cat was not amused. The mother is a stunning blond heiress who makes a tremendous effort to be liked, and succeeds in offending and alienating almost everyone with whom she comes in contact, except for her husband, who has as much spark and humor as a cattle tick. On my lucky days—of which this is one—none of them see me sneak past their house to the main road. There are many of these strange humanoids in the town where I live.

ON THE DIRT ROAD that runs above the ocean cliffs, I ran into Frank Morgan, a tawny octogenarian who lives alone nearby. He entertains his friends—and everyone in town is his friend—with a wide variety of birdcalls that all sound alike. Today he was walking with a vicious-looking businessman of about forty who was wearing a green-orange diamond-print leisure suit. I decided that this man was Frank's son, and that he had come to town to see if Frank was still coherent enough to live by himself. Well, I thought, I'll show him that Frank has all sorts of reasonable friends with whom he can carry on meaningful conversations.

"Hello, Frank," I said. "How you doing?"

Frank beamed at me, spread his arms, fluttered his eyes, and flapped his wings, emitting a loud, quavering birdcall.

ON THE MAIN ROAD of the mesa, a 1964 Chevelle Malibu station wagon pulled over. "Wanna ride?" called the driver.

"O.K.," I said, and got in. The driver was one of our town's innumerable Burn Outs. Most are in their twenties and look like either Charlie Manson or Janis Joplin. This Burn Out was wearing horn-rimmed glasses with no lenses (which he pushed up on his nose before he put the car in gear) and seagull feathers in his hair. He almost immediately drove us into a ditch.

"Thanks for the ride," I said, and walked the rest of the way. One treats the Burn Outs with a distant respect, as some of them are dangerous.

MY YOUNGER BROTHER AND I do not enjoy most of the Burn Outs. They are generally a nuisance, although on occasion they deliver performances of unabashed and cinematically enjoyable lunacy. When I feel benevolently toward the town, especially during our saturnalias, I am reminded of the gentle insanity of the inmates in *King of Hearts;* the rest of the time, the characters of *Marat/Sade* spring to mind. The Burn Outs are usually refugees from Napa State, the Langley Porter Neurological Institute, and Bellevue. The rest of us, and sometimes there is a fine line, are—in the words of my dream consultant—refugees from anonymity. The rest of us have better acts, better packaging. The Burn Outs do not have such good acts, and they do not fool anyone. They continually leap in front of us with empty or imaginary cameras, clicking away. They attack dogs at the Community Center dances. They stab one another with pool cues at the bar.

Sometimes they get taken away, but they usually come back.

MY YOUNGER BROTHER, who is seventeen, and, like the rest of us, rav-enously insecure, feels he must be kind and attentive to the Burn Outs or risk having his dog attacked with a pool cue. He was once picked up by the Burn Out in the 1964 Chevelle Malibu, and rode halfway over the moun-tain in silence, until the Burn Out shouted, "I have a can of beans at home with fifty-seven colors!"

"Fifty-seven," my brother said. "That's a lot of colors for one can of soup."

"You're damned right," said the Burn Out huffily, just before he eased the station wagon into a ditch.

Another time, my brother was picked up by a woman with a crew cut and a large eye drawn in the middle of her forehead with felt pens. She didn't say a word for a few minutes, and then the woman whispered, some-what hostilely, "Last night my cat threw up a hairball."

"Oh," my brother whispered back. "What is your cat's name?"

There is a Burn Out in this town who gets paid a thousand dollars a month to stay out of his parents' hometown, the last of the remittance men. His name is Moonboy, because he howls at the moon nightly, regardless of its visibility; whether it's waxing or waning he howls at or to it. Moonboy today walked toward me, on the road that leads from the town, with com-posure and solemnity, until he was attacked from the sky by his demons. He looked to the sky with terror and anger, flailed at the air around his head, and tore the attackers like leeches from his shoulders and back. When he had thrown them all to the ground, he continued his walk, head held high, and nodded stoically to me as we passed.

In this town there is also a group of people who are so hip, so high, so cheerful, so compassionate and concerned and loving and full of high consciousness, that hardly anyone (beside their own) can stand them. They travel in packs of goodwill and vapid conversation. Megan's father calls them the Cosmica Ramas. Megan and I avoid them as much as possible, as they are always trying to touch us. Last week we were sitting in front of the

Laundromat eating M&Ms when one of the largest female Cosmica Ramas approached us. Being a tall and large-boned woman, she boasts a composite weight and IQ of about one-ninety; her chosen name is Moss. She sat between Megan and me and began discussing the restorative properties of daily miso soup. Megan excused herself and went inside the Laundromat, giggling uncontrollably by the time she reached the doorway.

"So," I said politely, "what kind of miso do you use, the red or the brown?"

"Oh, sometimes I *mix* them!" she said happily. "I think it is *great fun.*"

WE ARE A BITTERLY POLITICAL TOWN, perhaps because so many people here are bored. We form factions on every conceivable issue, and frequently they are backbiting factions, such as the people who divided into camps on the issue of painting or not painting a white line down the middle of the main road downtown. Mostly we are afraid of losing the town to developers who would turn us from a mostly agrarian and artistic community of two thousand into another Carmel, but we have become confused and paranoid about the proper means to the proper end. We are mostly counterculture bleeding-heart-liberal types of every age, farmers, writers, teachers, carpenters, musicians, therapists, gardeners, laborers, poets, professionals, fishermen, seekers, Burn Outs, and children, with some geniuses, egomaniacs, lunatics, trust-fund radicals, Republicans and martyrs thrown in for flavor, and the flavor is often bitter. We have a few ex-convicts, a disproportionately high number of Ivy League graduates (my father is one; most are much younger), one Roman Polanski type who at thirty-four sleeps exclusively with girls under sixteen, one Rastafarian, half a dozen male homosexuals and no visible lesbians, hundreds of counterculture clotheshorses, many heirs and heiresses, a dozen addicts, our share of wife- and child-beaters, and no one ever starves to death. There are several dozen adults and innumerable children whom I like and/or admire, and many people I cannot stand, and Clement is the closest thing I have to a home, as ingrown and incestuous and irritating as it sometimes is.

My uncle Colin once said that in this town of almost unspeakable physical beauty, our boredom and conceit has bred the worst sort of self-righteous paranoia, and that our tensions along these lines are so rampant that our horses—and there are hundreds of horses, with which we see the world of the ridges and the waters, stunning natural luxuries that diminish much of our angst—are going to develop long, pointy teeth and attack us.

I CLEAN HOUSE THREE TIMES A WEEK. On Mondays I clean the house of an elderly and feisty environmentalist. On Wednesdays I clean the three-story house of a Prabhavananda disciple who makes his living speculating on land in this town. On Thursdays I clean the house of a trust-fund radical, whose major revolutionary act of the last two decades has been to hang the Symbionese Liberation Army's group picture on his bedroom wall. His family owns a chain of drugstores. Every week he tries to cheat me out of a few dollars, but so far he hasn't succeeded.

I hate cleaning house, especially on Thursdays. I hate it even more than I hate brain tumors and cancer and pimples. But I make four dollars an hour twelve hours a week, which gives me enough income to write the rest of the time, and I am buying writing time—it is as simple as that. I would not hate cleaning houses so much, I think, if the houses were not so clean to begin with. Two of the houses, the environmentalist's and the land speculator's, are impeccable to begin with, and the trust-fund radical's appears to have been sterilized, except for a particularly loathsome toilet. So I spend four hours a week in each house taking swipes at imaginary cobwebs, diligently vacuuming immaculate carpets, wiping, sweeping, scrubbing, deodorizing, and polishing already-clean houses. It is equivalent to corporate paper shuffling. It bores me and frustrates me and angers me. The occasional dust globs, the sporadic refrigerator messes, those random pubic hairs on bathtub floors—these I eradicate triumphantly, like a paper shuffler in the moment of glory when he or she discovers a typo in an otherwise immaculate report on Systematized Reciprocal Contingencies.

The trust-fund radical, who wears extremely tight pants and shouldn't, left me the key to his house and the written admonition that last week I neglected to clean the fingerprints off his toaster. I cleaned his bachelor's house, which cost $120,000 to build, in four hours. When I finished, I left him a note to the effect that he owed me sixteen dollars that I would collect when he got back. At the last minute, I cleaned his toaster with spit and a shirt he left in the bathroom.

He arrived as I closed the door behind me.

"Hello," I said.

"What do I owe you?" he asked.

"Same as usual. Sixteen dollars."

Reaching into his left pants pocket, he brought out a ten and a five.

"Could we make it fifteen?" he asked. "You've cleaned me out."

"Sure," I said. "I'll debit your account."

His pants were so tight that his other hand got stuck in his pocket when he withdrew it to shake my hand. We shook hands and he flinched and grabbed his hand as if I had crushed it. He chuckled heartily and said, "Say, that reminds me, I heard a news story on the radio this morning that I thought would crack you up—I love your sense of humor...." I put my hands in my jeans and looked expectant. "See, this old lady had a poodle, and the poodle got sopping wet in the rain one day, so the lady pops it into a microwave oven for about a minute ..." He couldn't continue for a few moments, as he tried unsuccessfully to contain his laughter. "... and she opens the door and the dog has burnt to a crisp. *Ha ha ha ha ha. It's charred!*"

I faked a short laugh—a fake laugh is one of the most obvious and disgusting sounds in the world; it feels awful to fake a laugh—and said, "Jeez!"

"Ha ha ha," he finished up. "I knew you'd like it."

There are any number of people—my friends—who could have told this story with the proper sense of black humor, of isn't-life-the-shits irony, and I would have laughed a bit sadly and then improvised something to the effect that dogs who fit into microwave ovens are usually yappy and hateful anyway, and we would have laughed to make everything all right. But the way the trust-fund radical told the story made me feel sorry for him, and I left liking him more than I had before, which still wasn't much but was tinged with compassion, and compassion, I think, is the hard and estimable one.

I USED TO CLEAN HOUSE for an arrogant but charming Gestalt thera-pist, until she moved out of town. Very few of us ever move out of town; the real world is very likely even more cruel and scary than it is in our town. The therapist moved because she was offered more money over the hill, and because she got tired of dealing with the parents of our teenagers, who as a whole are confident and undisciplined and sexually active. A father called her once when I was cleaning her house and said that his sixteen-year-old daughter had stolen three cars in two weeks. "I think she needs therapy," said the distraught father.

"I think she needs a car," said the therapist.

I WALKED TO THE CABIN after leaving the radical's house. I passed the lagoon, two sections of the Pacific beach, innumerable birds, dogs, horses and riders, amid the spectacular and overgrown foliage. Everywhere you look here you see a million trees, a million birds.

Megan was hanging upside down from one of the old cypresses in the grove that grow behind the cabin. There is something, for me, indescrib-ably lovely about the long, thin brown legs of a child: I was glad to find Me-gan hanging from my tree. I thought she might be gone when I returned.

"Hey, Megan," I said.

"Hey," she said. "I've got two new tricks." She was glad I was back. Her first trick involved a slow, limber backward flip from the branch. She land-ed on her feet and beamed. I smiled and nodded.

"And now for my next number," she said.

She climbed up the widespread trunk to her branch, and stood up, hold-ing a thin upper branch for balance. She moved one leg forward and farted, a quiet, ten-year-old child fart, and blushed.

"What was *that?*" I asked, grinning.

"That," she said with prim composure, "was my next number."

MEGAN AND I LEFT THE CABIN for the beach, holding hands and kicking rocks, exchanging details of the day. "What did you end up reading?" I asked.

"I just read a bunch of magazine articles. Mostly I hung out in the trees because the cat kept getting on my nerves." Her voice is soft and precise, medium high. "Everywhere I went, he'd follow me and stare. I read one pretty interesting article, though. Do you want to hear about it?"

"Of course I want to hear about it."

"Well, there's a drug called 'Pergonal' or something that makes women pregnant with four or five babies."

"A fertility drug?" I asked. "Does that ring a bell?"

"Yeah, a fertility drug. And you will never believe what it's made of." She looked at me. "Urine!"

"I don't believe it," I said, although I did.

"It's true. And you know who pees most of the urine?"

"Who?"

"You are *never* going to believe this." She looked at me sideways to see if she had my full attention. *"Italian nuns!"*

THE CATTLE IN THE MEADOWS alongside the road were so fat by this time of year that they were lying down, black and white spotted hulks amid the sparse grass and thick brush. Only two of the beasts were standing. A bull lumbered over to a confused-looking female and heavily lifted his front legs onto her back. The animal being humped—the humpee—rolled her eyes indifferently. They looked like two Dalmatian Volkswagens making love. The wrentits sang from the coyote bush. Megan wanted to stop and watch, so we sat on a cypress log alongside the field.

There are many three-legged dogs in the town where I live. A golden retriever with one front leg ran across the field in a well-choreographed limp toward his owner, a small boy named Zapata who lives in a tepee with his mother at the north end of the pasture, and whom my father's lover and roommate has in her third-grade class. Zapata was carrying his lumpy, angry Siamese cat named Gandhi toward the tepee, several hundred yards away from where Megan and I sat. He didn't see us.

Many of the children and animals in this town are named after East Indian heavies, herbs, recipes using soybeans, and imprisoned revolutionaries. There are children named Ram, Blueberry, Jesus, Tania, and Tahini, and many of the children in this town are a joy. There are dogs named Renaissance, Rosenberg, and Coriander. Zapata himself owns, besides Gandhi, a black and slightly retarded cat named Batman, a greenish collie named Liberace, a horse named Eldridge, and a rooster named Junior who twitches continually.

"Have you ever seen *The Glass Menagerie?*" Megan asked.

"Yeah," I said, watching the three-legged dog. "Why?"

Megan was silent for a moment. "Zapata's got a *spaz* menagerie," she said. "And I don't think it's fair that his mother is so nutsy."

"Neither do I."

"Usually if you point out that something isn't fair, an adult says"—her voice became nasal and patronizing—"'Now, no one ever said it would be fair.' It drives me crazy."

"Me too," I said.

"See, I can't even tell what's fair and what's not."

"That's one of the things that isn't fair," I said.

"'Now,'" she repeated in her adult voice, "'no one ever said it would be fair.'" We both laughed. "So what do you think?"

Megan was trying to pull a foxtail out of one of her back teeth: she puts foxtails in her mouth so that she can spit them at nonmoving objects—my back, for instance—but often they become lodged between her teeth. It is one of her recurring dilemmas.

"I don't know," I said. "One thing that I think is that there are a lot of good shows around here. You never even have to look for them. It's like a puppet show in this town."

"Here comes one now," said Megan as Zapata's mother, Aurora, stepped out of the tepee wearing six empty Tampax tubes on her fingers, in the way that children wear pitted olives on their fingers at holiday dinners. Aurora is a Burn Out. For Halloween last year she went to the Community Center dance dressed as a capillary, in a skintight red tube dress with lipstick above her eyelids and ketchup on her hands and neck. She has a strange sense of humor: nothing amuses her more than an especially poignant memorial service. She goes to the Laundromat for entertainment, where she tears the pleated paper cups that the management provides for detergent into animal shapes—a bat, a monkey, a snake. Once, I slammed my fingers in a washing-machine door, and Aurora laughed off and on through the entire wash cycle. Once, she called the fire department at three A.M. to report a terrifying flying object that had hovered outside the tepee all evening. When the fire chief arrived, she was crying and pointing at the luminous white orb in the mist, which upon careful scrutiny by the chief was determined to be the moon.

Megan was watching Aurora deliberately and sadly. "Some of the shows are sort of sad, aren't they?"

"Yeah," I said, "they are."

"That's what you like most about the town, isn't it? The shows, right?"

"I like you better than the shows. I like the waters and the lands around here better than the shows. I like some people better than the shows. But you're right, I do like them."

"So do I," she said. "But some of them are sad."

When Zapata reached Aurora in front of the tepee, she tousled his hair gently with the Tampax tubes still on her fingers, glared at the three-legged dog, and ushered Zapata inside, disappearing after him. The dog sat down outside and scratched the area where his front right leg would have been if he had one.

Anne Lamott was born in San Francisco in 1954 and grew up in Marin County, the setting of her first novel, Hard Laughter *(Farrar, Straus and Giroux, 1980). She studied at Goucher College in Maryland. Her other works include the novels* Rosie *(Viking, 1983) and* All New People *(Counterpoint, 1989) and several nonfiction books:* Operating Instructions: A Journal of My Son's First Year *(Pantheon Books, 1993),* Bird by Bird: Some Instructions on Writing and Life *(Pantheon Books, 1994),* Traveling Mercies: Some Thoughts on Faith *(Pantheon Books, 1999), and* Grace (Eventually): Thoughts on Faith *(Riverhead Books, 2007). She lives in Marin County.*

◟ Amy Tan

From *The Joy Luck Club*
RULES OF THE GAME

I WAS SIX WHEN MY MOTHER TAUGHT ME the art of invisible strength. It was a strategy for winning arguments, respect from others, and eventually, though neither of us knew it at the time, chess games.

"Bite back your tongue," scolded my mother when I cried loudly, yanking her hand toward the store that sold bags of salted plums. At home, she said, "Wise guy, he not go against wind. In Chinese we say, Come from South, blow with wind—poom!—North will follow. Strongest wind cannot be seen."

The next week I bit back my tongue as we entered the store with the forbidden candies. When my mother finished her shopping, she quietly plucked a small bag of plums from the rack and put it on the counter with the rest of the items.

MY MOTHER IMPARTED HER DAILY TRUTHS so she could help my older brothers and me rise above our circumstances. We lived in San Francisco's Chinatown. Like most of the other Chinese children who played in the back alleys of restaurants and curio shops, I didn't think we were poor. My bowl was always full, three five-course meals every day, beginning with a soup full of mysterious things I didn't want to know the names of.

We lived on Waverly Place, in a warm, clean, two-bedroom flat that sat above a small Chinese bakery specializing in steamed pastries and dim sum. In the early morning, when the alley was still quiet, I could smell fragrant red beans as they were cooked down to a pasty sweetness. By daybreak, our flat was heavy with the odor of fried sesame balls and sweet curried chicken crescents. From my bed, I would listen as my father got ready for work, then locked the door behind him, one-two-three clicks.

At the end of our two-block alley was a small sandlot playground with swings and slides well-shined down the middle with use. The play area was bordered by wood-slat benches where old-country people sat cracking roasted watermelon seeds with their golden teeth and scattering the husks to an impatient gathering of gurgling pigeons. The best playground, however, was the dark alley itself. It was crammed with daily mysteries and adventures. My brothers and I would peer into the medicinal herb shop, watching old Li dole out onto a stiff sheet of white paper the right amount of insect shells, saffron-colored seeds, and pungent leaves for his ailing customers. It was said that he once cured a woman dying of an ancestral curse that had eluded the best of American doctors. Next to the pharmacy was a printer who specialized in gold-embossed wedding invitations and festive red banners.

Farther down the street was Ping Yuen Fish Market. The front window displayed a tank crowded with doomed fish and turtles struggling to gain footing on the slimy green-tiled sides. A hand-written sign informed tourists, "Within this store, is all for food, not for pet." Inside, the butchers with their bloodstained white smocks deftly gutted the fish while customers cried out their orders and shouted, "Give me your freshest," to which the butchers always protested, "All are freshest." On less crowded market days, we would inspect the crates of live frogs and crabs which we were warned not to poke, boxes of dried cuttlefish, and row upon row of iced prawns, squid, and slippery fish. The sanddabs made me shiver each time; their eyes lay on one flattened side and reminded me of my mother's story of a careless girl who ran into a crowded street and was crushed by a cab. "Was smash flat," reported my mother.

At the corner of the alley was Hong Sing's, a four-table café with a recessed stairwell in front that led to a door marked "Tradesmen." My brothers and I believed the bad people emerged from this door at night. Tourists never went to Hong Sing's, since the menu was printed only in Chinese. A Caucasian man with a big camera once posed me and my playmates in front of the restaurant. He had us move to the side of the picture window so the photo would capture the roasted duck with its head dangling from a juice-covered rope. After he took the picture, I told him he should go into Hong Sing's and eat dinner. When he smiled and asked me what they served, I shouted, "Guts and duck's feet and octopus gizzards!" Then I ran off with my friends, shrieking with laughter as we scampered across the alley and hid in the entryway grotto of the China Gem Company, my heart pounding with hope that he would chase us.

My mother named me after the street that we lived on: Waverly Place Jong, my official name for important American documents. But my family called me Meimei, "Little Sister." I was the youngest, the only daughter. Each morning before school, my mother would twist and yank on my thick black hair until she had formed two tightly wound pigtails. One day, as she struggled to weave a hard-toothed comb through my disobedient hair, I had a sly thought.

I asked her, "Ma, what is Chinese torture?" My mother shook her head. A bobby pin was wedged between her lips. She wetted her palm and smoothed the hair above my ear, then pushed the pin in so that it nicked sharply against my scalp.

"Who say this word?" she asked without a trace of knowing how wicked I was being. I shrugged my shoulders and said, "Some boy in my class said Chinese people do Chinese torture."

"Chinese people do many things," she said simply. "Chinese people do business, do medicine, do painting. Not lazy like American people. We do torture. Best torture."

MY OLDER BROTHER VINCENT was the one who actually got the chess set. We had gone to the annual Christmas party held at the First Chinese Baptist Church at the end of the alley. The missionary ladies had put together a Santa bag of gifts donated by members of another church. None of the gifts had names on them. There were separate sacks for boys and girls of different ages.

One of the Chinese parishioners had donned a Santa Claus costume and a stiff paper beard with cotton balls glued to it. I think the only children who thought he was the real thing were too young to know that Santa Claus was not Chinese. When my turn came up, the Santa man asked me how old I was. I thought it was a trick question; I was seven according to the American formula and eight by the Chinese calendar. I said I was born on March 17, 1951. That seemed to satisfy him. He then solemnly asked if I had been a very, very good girl this year and did I believe in Jesus Christ and obey my parents. I knew the only answer to that. I nodded back with equal solemnity.

Having watched the other children opening their gifts, I already knew that the big gifts were not necessarily the nicest ones. One girl my age got a large coloring book of biblical characters, while a less greedy girl who selected a smaller box received a glass vial of lavender toilet water. The sound of the box was also important. A ten-year-old boy had chosen a box that jangled when he shook it. It was a tin globe of the world with a slit for inserting money. He must have thought it was full of dimes and nickels, because when he saw that it had just ten pennies, his face fell with such undisguised disappointment that his mother slapped the side of his head and led him out of the church hall, apologizing to the crowd for her son who had such bad manners he couldn't appreciate such a fine gift.

As I peered into the sack, I quickly fingered the remaining presents, testing their weight, imagining what they contained. I chose a heavy, compact one that was wrapped in shiny silver foil and a red satin ribbon. It was a twelve-pack of Life Savers and I spent the rest of the party arranging and rearranging the candy tubes in the order of my favorites. My brother Winston chose wisely as well. His present turned out to be a box of intricate plastic parts; the instructions on the box proclaimed that when they were properly assembled he would have an authentic miniature replica of a World War II submarine.

Vincent got the chess set, which would have been a very decent present to get at a church Christmas party, except it was obviously used and, as we discovered later, it was missing a black pawn and a white knight. My mother graciously thanked the unknown benefactor, saying, "Too good. Cost too much." At which point, an old lady with fine white, wispy hair nodded toward our family and said with a whistling whisper, "Merry, merry Christmas."

When we got home, my mother told Vincent to throw the chess set away. "She not want it. We not want it," she said, tossing her head stiffly to the side with a tight, proud smile. My brothers had deaf ears. They were already lining up the chess pieces and reading from the dog-eared instruction book.

I WATCHED VINCENT AND WINSTON play during Christmas week. The chess board seemed to hold elaborate secrets waiting to be untangled. The chessmen were more powerful than Old Li's magic herbs that cured ancestral curses. And my brothers wore such serious faces that I was sure something was at stake that was greater than avoiding the tradesmen's door to Hong Sing's.

"Let me! Let me!" I begged between games when one brother or the other would sit back with a deep sigh of relief and victory, the other annoyed, unable to let go of the outcome. Vincent at first refused to let me play, but when I offered my Life Savers as replacements for the buttons that filled in for the missing pieces, he relented. He chose the flavors: wild cherry for the black pawn and peppermint for the white knight. Winner could eat both.

As our mother sprinkled flour and rolled out small doughy circles for the steamed dumplings that would be our dinner that night, Vincent explained the rules, pointing to each piece. "You have sixteen pieces and so do I. One king and queen, two bishops, two knights, two castles, and eight pawns. The pawns can only move forward one step, except on the first move. Then they can move two. But they can only take men by moving crossways like this, except in the beginning, when you can move ahead and take another pawn."

"Why?" I asked as I moved my pawn. "Why can't they move more steps?"

"Because they're pawns," he said.

"But why do they go crossways to take other men. Why aren't there any women and children?"

"Why is the sky blue? Why must you always ask stupid questions?" asked Vincent. "This is a game. These are the rules. I didn't make them up. See.

Here. In the book." He jabbed a page with a pawn in his hand. "Pawn. P-A-W-N. Pawn. Read it yourself."

My mother patted the flour off her hands. "Let me see book," she said quietly. She scanned the pages quickly, not reading the foreign English symbols, seeming to search deliberately for nothing in particular.

"This American rules," she concluded at last. "Every time people come out from foreign country, must know rules. You not know, judge say, Too bad, go back. They not telling you why so you can use their way go forward. They say, Don't know why, you find out yourself. But they knowing all the time. Better you take it, find out why yourself." She tossed her head back with a satisfied smile.

I found out about all the whys later. I read the rules and looked up all the big words in a dictionary. I borrowed books from the Chinatown library. I studied each chess piece, trying to absorb the power each contained.

I learned about opening moves and why it's important to control the center early on; the shortest distance between two points is straight down the middle. I learned about the middle game and why tactics between two adversaries are like clashing ideas; the one who plays better has the clearest plans for both attacking and getting out of traps. I learned why it is essential in the endgame to have foresight, a mathematical understanding of all possible moves, and patience; all weaknesses and advantages become evident to a strong adversary and are obscured to a tiring opponent. I discovered that for the whole game one must gather invisible strengths and see the endgame before the game begins.

I also found out why I should never reveal "why" to others. A little knowledge withheld is a great advantage one should store for future use. That is the power of chess. It is a game of secrets in which one must show and never tell.

I loved the secrets I found within the sixty-four black and white squares. I carefully drew a handmade chessboard and pinned it to the wall next to my bed, where at night I would stare for hours at imaginary battles. Soon I no longer lost any games or Life Savers, but I lost my adversaries. Winston and Vincent decided they were more interested in roaming the streets after school in their Hopalong Cassidy cowboy hats.

ON A COLD SPRING AFTERNOON, while walking home from school, I detoured through the playground at the end of our alley. I saw a group of old men, two seated across a folding table playing a game of chess, others smoking pipes, eating peanuts, and watching. I ran home and grabbed Vincent's chess set, which was bound in a cardboard box with rubber bands. I also carefully selected two prized rolls of Life Savers. I came back to the park and approached a man who was observing the game.

"Want to play?" I asked him. His face widened with surprise and he grinned as he looked at the box under my arm.

"Little sister, been a long time since I play with dolls," he said, smiling benevolently. I quickly put the box down next to him on the bench and displayed my retort.

Lau Po, as he allowed me to call him, turned out to be a much better player than my brothers. I lost many games and many Life Savers. But over the weeks, with each diminishing roll of candies, I added new secrets. Lau Po gave me the names. The Double Attack from the East and West Shores. Throwing Stones on the Drowning Man. The Sudden Meeting of the Clan. The Surprise from the Sleeping Guard. The Humble Servant Who Kills the King. Sand in the Eyes of Advancing Forces. A Double Killing Without Blood.

There were also the fine points of chess etiquette. Keep captured men in neat rows, as well-tended prisoners. Never announce "Check" with vanity, lest someone with an unseen sword slit your throat. Never hurl pieces into the sandbox after you have lost a game, because then you must find them again, by yourself, after apologizing to all around you. By the end of the summer, Lau Po had taught me all he knew, and I had become a better chess player.

A small weekend crowd of Chinese people and tourists would gather as I played and defeated my opponents one by one. My mother would join the crowds during these outdoor exhibition games. She sat proudly on the bench, telling my admirers with proper Chinese humility, "Is luck."

A man who watched me play in the park suggested that my mother allow me to play in local chess tournaments. My mother smiled graciously, an answer that meant nothing. I desperately wanted to go, but I bit back my tongue. I knew she would not let me play among strangers. So as we walked home I said in a small voice that I didn't want to play in the local tournament. They would have American rules. If I lost, I would bring shame on my family.

"Is shame you fall down nobody push you," said my mother.

During my first tournament, my mother sat with me in the front row as I waited for my turn. I frequently bounced my legs to unstick them from the cold metal seat of the folding chair. When my name was called, I leapt up. My mother unwrapped something in her lap. It was her *chang*, a small tablet of red jade which held the sun's fire. "Is luck," she whispered, and tucked it into my dress pocket. I turned to my opponent, a fifteen-year-old boy from Oakland. He looked at me, wrinkling his nose.

As I began to play, the boy disappeared, the color ran out of the room, and I saw only my white pieces and his black ones waiting on the other side. A light wind began blowing past my ears. It whispered secrets only I could hear.

"Blow from the South," it murmured. "The wind leaves no trail." I saw a clear path, the traps to avoid. The crowd rustled. "Shhh! Shhh!" said the corners of the room. The wind blew stronger. "Throw sand from the East to distract him." The knight came forward ready for the sacrifice. The wind hissed, louder and louder. "Blow, blow, blow. He cannot see. He is blind now. Make him lean away from the wind so he is easier to knock down."

"Check," I said, as the wind roared with laughter. The wind died down to little puffs, my own breath.

MY MOTHER PLACED MY FIRST TROPHY next to a new plastic chess set that the neighborhood Tao society had given to me. As she wiped each piece with a soft cloth, she said, "Next time win more, lose less."

"Ma, it's not how many pieces you lose," I said. "Sometimes you need to lose pieces to get ahead."

"Better to lose less, see if you really need."

At the next tournament, I won again, but it was my mother who wore the triumphant grin.

"Lost eight piece this time. Last time was eleven. What I tell you? Better off lose less!" I was annoyed, but I couldn't say anything.

I attended more tournaments, each one farther away from home. I won all games, in all divisions. The Chinese bakery downstairs from our flat displayed my growing collection of trophies in its window, amidst the dust-covered cakes that were never picked up. The day after I won an important regional tournament, the window encased a fresh sheet cake with whipped-cream frosting and red script saying, "Congratulations, Waverly Jong, Chinatown Chess Champion." Soon after that, a flower shop, headstone engraver, and funeral parlor offered to sponsor me in national tournaments. That's when my mother decided I no longer had to do the dishes. Winston and Vincent had to do my chores.

"Why does she get to play and we do all the work," complained Vincent.

"Is new American rules," said my mother. "Meimei play, squeeze all her brains out for win chess. You play, worth squeeze towel."

By my ninth birthday, I was a national chess champion. I was still some 429 points away from grand-master status, but I was touted as the Great American Hope, a child prodigy and a girl to boot. They ran a photo of me in *Life* magazine next to a quote in which Bobby Fischer said, "There will never be a woman grand master." "Your move, Bobby," said the caption.

The day they took the magazine picture I wore neatly plaited braids clipped with plastic barrettes trimmed with rhinestones. I was playing in a large high school auditorium that echoed with phlegmy coughs and the squeaky rubber knobs of chair legs sliding across freshly waxed wooden floors. Seated across from me was an American man, about the same age as Lau Po, maybe fifty. I remember that his sweaty brow seemed to weep at my every move. He wore a dark, malodorous suit. One of his pockets was stuffed with a great white kerchief on which he wiped his palm before sweeping his hand over the chosen chess piece with great flourish.

In my crisp pink-and-white dress with scratchy lace at the neck, one of two my mother had sewn for these special occasions, I would clasp my hands under my chin, the delicate points of my elbows poised lightly on the table in the manner my mother had shown me for posing for the press. I would swing my patent leather shoes back and forth like an impatient child riding on a school bus. Then I would pause, suck in my lips, twirl my chosen piece in midair as if undecided, and then firmly plant it in its new threatening place, with a triumphant smile thrown back at my opponent for good measure.

⁓

I NO LONGER PLAYED IN THE ALLEY of Waverly Place. I never visited the playground where the pigeons and old men gathered. I went to school, then directly home to learn new chess secrets, cleverly concealed advantages, more escape routes.

But I found it difficult to concentrate at home. My mother had a habit of standing over me while I plotted out my games. I think she thought of herself as my protective ally. Her lips would be sealed tight, and after each move I made, a soft "Hmmmmph" would escape from her nose.

"Ma, I can't practice when you stand there like that," I said one day. She retreated to the kitchen and made loud noises with the pots and pans. When the crashing stopped, I could see out of the corner of my eye that she was standing in the doorway. "Hmmmph!" Only this one came out of her tight throat.

My parents made many concessions to allow me to practice. One time I complained that the bedroom I shared was so noisy that I couldn't think. Thereafter, my brothers slept in a bed in the living room facing the street. I said I couldn't finish my rice; my head didn't work right when my stomach was too full. I left the table with half-finished bowls and nobody complained. But there was one duty I couldn't avoid. I had to accompany my mother on Saturday market days when I had no tournament to play. My mother would proudly walk with me, visiting many shops, buying very little. "This my daughter Wave-ly Jong," she said to whoever looked her way.

One day, after we left a shop I said under my breath, "I wish you wouldn't do that, telling everybody I'm your daughter." My mother stopped walking. Crowds of people with heavy bags pushed past us on the sidewalk, bumping into first one shoulder, then another.

"Aiii-ya. So shame be with mother?" She grasped my hand even tighter as she glared at me.

I looked down. "It's not that, it's just so obvious. It's just so embarrassing."

"Embarrass you be my daughter?" Her voice was cracking with anger.

"That's not what I meant. That's not what I said."

"What you say?"

I knew it was a mistake to say anything more, but I heard my voice speaking. "Why do you have to use me to show off? If you want to show off, then why don't you learn to play chess."

My mother's eyes turned into dangerous black slits. She had no words for me, just sharp silence.

I felt the wind rushing around my hot ears. I jerked my hand out of my mother's tight grasp and spun around, knocking into an old woman. Her bag of groceries spilled to the ground.

"Aii-ya! Stupid girl!" my mother and the woman cried. Oranges and tin cans careened down the sidewalk. As my mother stooped to help the old woman pick up the escaping food, I took off.

I raced down the street, dashing between people, not looking back as my mother screamed shrilly, "Meimei! Meimei!" I fled down an alley, past dark curtained shops and merchants washing the grime off their windows. I sped into the sunlight, into a large street crowded with tourists examining trinkets and souvenirs. I ducked into another dark alley, down another street, up another alley. I ran until it hurt and I realized I had nowhere to go, that I was not running from anything. The alleys contained no escape routes.

My breath came out like angry smoke. It was cold. I sat down on an upturned plastic pail next to a stack of empty boxes, cupping my chin with my hands, thinking hard. I imagined my mother, first walking briskly down one street or another looking for me, then giving up and returning home to await my arrival. After two hours, I stood up on creaking legs and slowly walked home.

The alley was quiet and I could see the yellow lights shining from our flat like two tiger's eyes in the night. I climbed the sixteen steps to the door, advancing quietly up each so as not to make any warning sounds. I turned the knob; the door was locked. I heard a chair moving, quick steps, the locks turning—click! click! click!—and then the door opened.

"About time you got home," said Vincent. "Boy, are you in trouble."

He slid back to the dinner table. On a platter were the remains of a large fish, its fleshy head still connected to bones swimming upstream in vain escape. Standing there waiting for my punishment, I heard my mother speak in a dry voice.

"We not concerning this girl. This girl not have concerning for us."

Nobody looked at me. Bone chopsticks clinked against the insides of bowls being emptied into hungry mouths.

I walked into my room, closed the door, and lay down on my bed. The room was dark, the ceiling filled with shadows from the dinnertime lights of neighboring flats.

In my head, I saw a chessboard with sixty-four black and white squares. Opposite me was my opponent, two angry black slits. She wore a triumphant smile. "Strongest wind cannot be seen," she said.

Her black men advanced across the plane, slowly marching to each successive level as a single unit. My white pieces screamed as they scurried and fell off the board one by one. As her men drew closer to my edge, I felt myself growing light. I rose up into the air and flew out the window. Higher and higher, above the alley, over the tops of tiled roofs, where I was gathered up by the wind and pushed up toward the night sky until everything below me disappeared and I was alone.

I closed my eyes and pondered my next move.

Amy Tan was born in Oakland, California, in 1952, the daughter of Chinese immigrants. After the deaths of Tan's older brother and father, Tan's mother moved the family to Switzerland, where Tan graduated from high school. She returned to the United States to attend college, earning her B.A. and M.A. from San Jose State University and doing graduate work at University of California, Berkeley. She worked for a number of years as a technical writer and editor, writing fiction in her spare time. In 1989 she published The Joy Luck Club (Penguin). Based in part on Tan's mother's experiences in China and the United States, the book received excellent reviews, became a bestseller, and was made into a film in 1993. Later books include The Kitchen God's Wife (G. P. Putnam's Sons, 1991), The Bonesetter's Daughter (G. P. Putnam's Sons, 2001), and Saving Fish From Drowning (Putnam/Penguin, 2005).

Ron Hansen

MY COMMUNIST

I AM CONSCIOUS OF THE LACKS AT MY ENGLISH, which is my least language, so you will please correct my errors. My story is happening in California during 1982. But it is beginning far, far away in my country of Poland where I was born and growing up in Kraków and where I matriculated in philosophy at famous, six-hundred-year-old Jagiellonian University. In fall, 1975, I have begun four years of theology studies at Rome's Pontifical Athenaeum of Saint Thomas Aquinas, which is called "the Angelicum," and in 1979 I was ordained a priest for the diocese of Kraków by its former archbishop, Karol Wojtyla, who is then just a few months Pope John Paul II. We have much in common, such as homeland and schoolings, and as friends it is day of great happiness for us, my ordination.

My first parish is in difficult times. We are oppressed country and hard-working people who cannot afford government price increases of sometimes one hundred percent on meats, and waves of strikes for social justice and freedom from Soviet Union have begun at shipyards, railways, bakeries, dairy farms. Many priests such as me join the strikers and preside at outdoor Masses for many thousands of workers. A revolution which is called Solidarność is underway, and there is nearly a military invasion by Warsaw Pact countries to "save socialist Poland," but it is halted by interventions from the Pope and warnings from the United States. Even so, priests are kidnapped and murdered to scare and make sad the strikers. In fall, 1981, General Wojciech Jaruzelski becamed First Secretary of Polish Communist Party and it is December when he declares state of war in my country. Martial law there is put on us, and many thousands of solidarity activists without warnings they are being arrested like with Nazis in Occupation.

I can hear the question, "Why this histories?" I will answer the asking in a small while, and you will find out why is necessary.

Also in December it was a bad news that my cardinal archbishop finds out the name of Stefan Nowak, me, is on a list of party enemies, and I am invited to his excellency's residence. There I hear a communication from His Holiness himself that his young friend, Stefan, not even yet three years from his ordination, is to go to California as a missionary. A big surprise, belief me!

I disliked to leave home so soon after joining my first parish, and if I open my heart to you I will confess I was thinking my friends would consider me coward. To die like Christ for my faith is a dear wish since childhood when I am reading about oldtime martyrs, so I am prepared to stay. But also ever since seminary I have dreamed to work in countries where Catholics suffer without the sacraments. Initially my thinking is Africa, Latin America, or Russia, but California is also still missionary country. And obedience to the Pope is no question.

With one week spending in Chicago city, giving lectures about my country in parishes and visiting beautiful churches and museums, I board an aeroplane for its fly to San Francisco, first time to visit in my life, though I have seen it, naturally, in the cinema. I am met at San Francisco International by the wonderful old pastor of All Souls parish, whose family name when I first heard in Kraków was sounding very homely for a man from Poland. Smolarski is very typical name there. Monsignor Smolarski asks I address him Joseph and admits he does not know Polish language. A disappointment. I promise to teach him some sentences, and songs too, and Joseph promises to correct my broken English. My much in pieces English.

All Souls is not old, old parish like in Kraków or Warsaw, but from beginning of twenty century. Forty kilometers south of San Francisco, and in the number of two thousand people, maybe less, the church has only fourteen parishioners from Eastern Europe, and none who speak my dear-to-my-heart Polish. Immediately upon learning, my soul cries out, Why have I come to this far place? The first nights there are long for me. Hours and hours I pray. I write hundreds letters home. But I feel silenced and not as much useful. I have looked up the word: I am forlorn.

California, so big a state and rich in different beauties, I like very much with its weather always in a good mood and its people friendly because not cold or persecuted. The Mass is familiar even in English, though I am embarrassed by my "charming" accent and I am frustrated to be sounding unintelligent with homilies too like a child. At first many humiliations, as in Italy and first year theology.

And such wealth here is horrifying, really. I have a day off and all afternoon I walk through a gigantic proportion supermarket. I have arrived in America with one luggage. With how many shall I leave? The both sides of the building seem a distance of a kilometer as up and down the aisles I am wandering, seeing fruits and vegetables even in winter, so much different foods to be sold, such plenty, but not wanting to buy even a chocolate piece for thinking of how much people in my homeland must do without.

And that is when I first see him. In a gray trenchcoat, no kidding, and gray Homburg hat, holding a shopping basket in the vegetable aisle but watching me, for sure, the face maybe from cousin to Leonid Brezhnev, the pig eyes, the slicked black hair. Weighty. You would not think: A Californian! This is herring man, a favorite to vodka. He is like to have hammer and sickle tattooed on his chest. Here for what is this spy? A friend of mine was found in a northern forest with a bullet in his brains. Has this fellow gun in pocket? Little hidden camera? Wanting confrontation, I walk forward but he is too fast away. On a bin for green cabbage that is being rained on he has left behind his plastic basket and inside it are kielbasa, piroshki, and from delicatessen a carton of kutia, which is Polish Christmas pudding. My father would buy such for the holy days.

Is fat man waiting for me outside? I do not wish to be surprised in lonesome place, so I rush opposite to his going and push through a steel door. I find myself in storing house where a garage door is lifting high overhead as outside a fruits truck backs up, a horn beeping. I hurry out and jump from the dock, and I do not stop hurrying until he for sure cannot be behind me. I say nothing to Monsignor, for he is old man with conditions of heart.

On Sunday again I notice my spy, looking hard at Stefan in my long white alb and green stole and chasuble after the ten o'clock Mass, and the not yet thirty priest is smiling because a sweet girl of sixteen has taught herself enough Polish to say, "Good morning, Father Nowak," and it is not so bad, her accent. Of mine, she says I mispronounce the word "love" like "laugh." I glance across the street and my Communist is standing in a wide circle of shade, for the sun is miraculous even in March, and he is in many clothings and Homburg hat, his hands behind his back, just watching me. I am certainly not an amusement to him. I am some garbages, some striker's wreckage that must to be removed. I lift my right hand high. Half a hello is it, and half a salute. My spy holds onto his expression, like his face is inflexible, and then he strolls away.

I find less and less I am afraid as weeks go by and he is around now and then only. I have no idea his thoughts, if he wants me dead, if he is KGB and I am only his idle hours, his hobby, and his main jobs is military secrets. But I have decided for sure he is Polish, and it pleases that whenever he is watching me he is thinking of me in the same language that I am thinking of him. I do not care the words he uses.

We are now last week of March, and he sends in mailing four photographs of me and back of each he is labeled in Polish handwriting: "Nowak at local bookstore," "Nowak in front of All Soul's rectory," "Nowak at funeral on 20 March," "Nowak, home of Mrs. Kaniecki." Was this to harass me? Was he just getting rid of? The photos are nice of me. One I send to parents. Others I hang them in my office.

But I am thinking: I like my pastoral job very much. I have a fine rectory to live in, my first car ever, friendly priests who join us for drinks or nights at the cinema, invitations to dinners with families, the joy and honor of my vocation. And how much could my Communist have? A flat maybe with small television, food he cooks for himself and eats lonely, a hundred worries and secrets, and no god to pray to? Was I a priest to have luxuries while another has so little?

With April, quite suddenly he is not spying on me anymore. I find myself looking and looking, but he is like I invented him. Poland is still in a "state of war" and my mailings from homeland tell of jailings and intimidations, but I seem to be no longer of interest. I am surprised by the loss I experience. To "stew and fret" is good slang for my feelings. I miss him, this Pole. Has he been recalled to Europe, or is he ill with no one to help him? I pray it is not so.

On first day off, I decide to investigate. I have habit of visiting a fine bookstore in Palo Alto where I read for free—please to excuse me, lovely store owners—their French, German, and Italian newspapers so to find out more about Poland, which is not so well covered in America. Many Europeans must do the same, for sure. I go to very nice woman at bookstore counter and describe, "My old friend whom I have lost touches with." Smiling, she remembers a man also with my charming accent who fits exactly my describing. Oskar, his name. She thinks he lives not far, since he drinks espresso in nextdoors café as he reads journals each mornings. She has not seen this Oskar lately.

Let me tell you, are fourteen apartment buildings within few blocks of bookstore. It is quite a job for me until I figure to go to cheapest apartments first, for this is Soviet system, not CIA. The Spirit is leading me, for in third place I look I read his handwriting on the mailbox: "O. Sienkiewicz." In Poland a very typical name. Weird that I am so happy, as if I have forgotten evil and murderous regime.

Up an outside flight of stairs to Apartment C, with no signs of life inside. I ring the doorbell many time and shade my eyes to peek through kitchen window, seeing nothing but a heap of dishes. Oskar's bathroom window is frosted glass and like Venetian blinds, each cranked open an inch for California air. I look in through slit and find his foot in pajamas as he sits on the bathroom floor, and when I stand taller there are his hands in his lap, and then just a slice of his square head can I make out, tilted toward his right shoulder, some trickles of sickness around his mouth.

"Oskar Sienkiewicz!" I shout, and there is a flutter like he wants to waken. "Are you ill?" I ask in Polish.

He a little nods and answers in Polish, "I'm resting," and just the one sentence in mother's tongue puts me in happiest mood. I walk to the flat's front door, try the handle, and find it is unlocked, no problem. His flat inside is torn furnitures that Monsignor would call "shoddy." Loud on small television is noontime sex opera. On food tray beside a stuffed chair is feast for a hundred flies and a half-full bottle of famous Wyborowa vodka, its blade of grass still floating in it.

Oskar is on hands and knees on the bathroom floor when I get there. His stink is hard to take, for sure, but I help him stand and he lets me, then my hands he hits away. We speak in Polish from now on. With sarcasm, he asks, "Why aren't you praying?"

"Are you so certain I'm not?"

He falls into the bathroom wall and just there he stays for a while, like he is drunk. But he recites: "'But I say unto you which hear, Love your enemies, do good to them which hate you.'" With satisfaction he smiles. "I have the quote right, no?"

"If you meant the sermon on the mount."

His forehead he taps. "I'm smart." And then he slides a foot or so until I catch his hot with fever weight and heave him to the hallway and onto his bed, its sheets in riot and still wet with night sweatings. He sits there, his head down, his hands useless beside him. "We are not friends," he says, "but I am glad to see you."

"I have missed speaking Polish."

"A hard language for outsiders," he says. Oskar squints at me. "I am from Wambierzyce. Have you heard of it?"

"Naturally. It's in Lower Silesia. A shrine to Mary is there."

Oscar falls to his left. "I have to lie down," he says.

Lifting up his white feet, I ask, "Is there anything I can I do for you?"

His left forearm covers his eyes as he sighs and gives it some thought. And then he says, "Die."

"I could find a doctor for you. And medicines. Wash your clothes and dishes."

"Were you to die," he says, "that would make me happiest; that would be quite enough."

And that is when I tell him how even in such a terrible times it was to me pleasing to have him around. We shared thousand year history. Wawel Castle meant to him. Rynek Główny, he knew, is a market place. Mariacki Church. The scent of the Vistula river. Hiking in the Carpathians. We are feeling nostalgia for identical things, and for these reasons he could never be my enemy.

With irritation he stares at me. "I was a Catholic once," Oskar says. "But I grew up."

Why this is hilarious to me is not clear, but he is infected by my laughter. I find a spot on the foot of his bed for sitting and he glances at me from under his forearm before shifting his legs to give me more room. "I found the kielbasa you left behind. And the delicatessen carton of kutia," I say. "And I was sure you were a real Polander."

"Oh, say nothing of Christmas pudding! My belly aches for it even now."

"And roasted walnuts?"

Oskar groans.

"And the pastries from that shop by the Jagiellonian?"

"Stop it, Stefan, or I shall weep!"

And so I go on naming foods until we both are crying.

Ron Hansen was born in Omaha in 1947. He was educated at Creighton University, the University of Iowa's Writers Workshop, and Stanford University, where he received a Wallace Stegner Creative Writing Fellowship. His books include Desperadoes *(Alfred A. Knopf, 1979),* The Assassination of Jesse James by the Coward Robert Ford *(Alfred A. Knopf, 1983),* Marriette in Ecstasy *(HarperCollins, 1991);* Atticus *(HarperCollins, 1996), and* Exiles *(Farrar, Straus and Giroux, 2008). He has taught at Stanford University, the University of Arizona, and the University of California, Santa Cruz, and he is now the Gerard Manley Hopkins, S.J. Professor in the Arts and Humanities at Santa Clara University.*

Robert Hass

From *Time and Materials*

AFTER THE WINDS

My friend's older sister's third husband's daughter—
That's about as long as a line of verse should get—
Karmic debris? A field anthropologist's kinship map?
Just sailed by me on the Berkeley street. A student
Of complex mathematical systems, a pretty girl,
Ash-blond hair. I could have changed her diapers.
And that small frown might be her parents' lives.
Desire that hollows us out and hollows us out,
That kills us and kills us and raises us up and
Raises us up. Always laughable from the outside:
The English wit who complained of sex that the posture
Was ridiculous had not been struck down by the god
Or goddess to whose marble threshing floor offerings
Of grapes or olive boughs and flowers or branches
Laden with new fruit or bundles of heavy-headed wheat
Were brought as to any other mystery or power.
My friend sat on the back steps on a summer night
Sick with her dilemma, smoking long cigarettes
While bats veered in the dark and the scraping sound
Of a neighbor cleaning a grill with a wire brush
Ratcheted steadily across the backyard fence.
"He's the nicest man I could imagine," she had said,
"And I feel like I'm dying." Probably in her middle thirties
Then. Flea markets on Saturday mornings, family dinners
On Sunday, a family large enough so that there was always

A birthday, a maiden aunt from the old neighborhood
In San Francisco, or a brother-in-law, or some solemn child
Studying a new toy in silence on the couch.
Had not lived where, tearing, or like burnished leaves
In a vortex of wind, the part of you that might observe
The comedy of gasps and moans gives way, does not
Demur. Though she did laugh at herself. An erotic
Attachment one whole winter to the mouth
Of a particular television actor—she'd turn the TV on—
Watch him for a minute with a kind of sick yearning—
Shake her head—turn the TV off—go back to the translation
Of Van Gogh's letters which was her project that year—
Or do some ironing—that always seemed to calm her—
The sweet iron smell of steam and linen. "Honest to God,"
She'd say, an expression the elderly aunts might have used,
"For Pete's sake," she'd say, "get yourself together."
Hollow flute, or bell not struck, sending out a shimmering
Not-sound, in waves and waves, to the place where the stunned dead
In the not-beginning are gathered to the arms of the living
In the not-noon: the living who grieve, who rage against
And grieve the always solicited, always unattended dead
In the tiered plazas or lush meadows of their gathered
Absence. A man wants a woman that way. A person a person.
Down on all fours, ravenous and humbled. And later—
"Lovers, you remember the shoeshine boys in Quito
In the city market? Missing teeth, unlaced tennis shoes.
They approach you smiling. Their hands are scrofulous,
They have no rules, and they'll steal anything and so
Would you if you were they." The old capital has always
Just been sacked, the temple hangings burned, and peasants
In the ruins are roasting the royal swans in a small fire
Coaxed from the sticks of the tax assessor's Empire chair
Up against a broken wall. Lent: the saints' bodies
Dressed in purple sacks to be taken off at Easter.
For Magdalen, of course, the resurrection didn't mean

She'd got him back. It meant she'd lost him in another way.
It was the voice she loved, the body, not the god
Who, she had been told, ascended to his heaven,
There to disperse tenderness and pity on the earth.

Robert Hass was born in San Francisco in 1941. He earned a B.A. from St. Mary's College of California, then received a Ph.D. in English from Stanford University. His first book, Field Guide *(Yale University Press, 1973), won the Yale Series of Younger Poets Award. Later collections include* Praise *(Ecco Press, 1979),* Human Wishes *(Ecco Press, 1989),* Sun Under Wood *(Ecco Press, 1996), and* Time and Materials *(Ecco Press, 2007), which won the National Book Award. Other works include* Twentieth Century Pleasures: Prose on Poetry *(Ecco Press, 1984) and numerous translations of the work of Polish poet Czeslaw Milosz. In 1984 he was awarded a MacArthur Foundation grant; from 1995 to 1997 he served as poet laureate of the United States. He teaches at the University of California, Berkeley.*

SOUTHERN CALIFORNIA

✦ Helen Hunt Jackson

Selection from *Ramona*

I T WAS SHEEP-SHEARING TIME in Southern California, but sheep-shearing was late at the Señora Moreno's. The Fates had seemed to combine to put it off. In the first place, Felipe Moreno had been ill. He was the Señora's eldest son, and since his father's death had been at the head of his mother's house. Without him, nothing could be done on the ranch, the Señora thought. It had been always, "Ask Señor Felipe," "Go to Señor Felipe," "Señor Felipe will attend to it," ever since Felipe had had the dawning of a beard on his handsome face.

In truth, it was not Felipe, but the Señora, who really decided all questions from greatest to least, and managed everything on the place, from the sheep-pastures to the artichoke-patch; but nobody except the Señora herself knew this. An exceedingly clever woman for her day and generation was Señora Gonzaga Moreno,—as for that matter, exceedingly clever for any day and generation; but exceptionally clever for the day and generation to which she belonged. Her life, the mere surface of it, if it had been written, would have made a romance, to grow hot and cold over: sixty years of the best of old Spain, and the wildest of New Spain, Bay of Biscay, Gulf of Mexico, Pacific Ocean,—the waves of them all had tossed destinies for the Señora. The Holy Catholic Church had had its arms round her from first to last; and that was what had brought her safe through, she would have said, if she had ever said anything about herself, which she never did,—one of her many wisdoms. So quiet, so reserved, so gentle an exterior never was known to veil such an imperious and passionate nature, brimful of storm, always passing through stress; never thwarted, except at peril of those who did it; adored and hated by turns, and each at the hottest. A tremendous force, wherever she appeared, was Señora Moreno; but no stranger would suspect it, to see her gliding about, in her scanty black gown, with her rosary hanging at her side, her soft dark eyes cast down, and an expression of mingled melancholy and devotion on her face. She looked simply like a sad, spiritual-minded old lady, amiable and indolent, like her race, but sweeter and more thoughtful than their wont. Her voice heightened this mistaken impression. She was never heard to speak either loud or fast. There was at times even a curious hesitancy in her speech, which came near being a stammer, or suggested the measured care with which people speak who have been cured of stammering. It made her often appear as if she did not known her own mind; at which people sometimes took heart; when, if they had only known the truth, they would have known that the speech hesitated solely because the Señora knew her mind so exactly that she was finding it hard to make the words convey it as she desired, or in a way to best attain her ends.

About this very sheep-shearing there had been, between her and the head shepherd, Juan Canito, called Juan Can for short, and to distinguish him from Juan Jose, the upper herdsman of the cattle, some discussions which would have been hot and angry ones in any other hands than the Senora's.

Juan Canito wanted the shearing to begin, even though Señor Felipe were ill in bed, and though that lazy shepherd Luigo had not yet got back with the flock that had been driven up the coast for pasture. "There were plenty of sheep on the place to begin with," he said one morning,—"at least a thousand;" and by the time they were done, Luigo would surely be back with the rest; and as for Señor Felipe's being in bed, had not he, Juan Canito, stood at the packing-bag, and handled the wool, when Señor Felipe was a boy? Why could he not do it again? The Señora did not realize how time was going; there would be no shearers to be hired presently, since the Señora was determined to have none but Indians. Of course, if she would employ Mexicans, as all the other ranches in the valley did, it would be different; but she was resolved upon having Indians,—"God knows why," he interpolated surlily, under his breath.

"I do not quite understand you, Juan," interrupted Señora Moreno at the precise instant the last syllable of this disrespectful ejaculation had escaped Juan's lips; "speak a little louder. I fear I am growing deaf in my old age."

What gentle, suave, courteous tones! and the calm dark eyes rested on Juan Canito with a look to the fathoming of which he was as unequal as one of his own sheep would have been. He could not have told why he instantly and involuntarily said, "Beg your pardon, Señora."

"Oh, you need not ask my pardon, Juan," the Señora replied with exquisite gentleness; "it is not you who are to blame, if I am deaf. I have fancied for a year I did not hear quite as well as I once did. But about the Indians, Juan; did not Señor Felipe tell you that he had positively engaged the same band of shearers we had last autumn, Alessandro's band from Temecula? They will wait until we are ready for them. Señor Felipe will send a messenger for them. He thinks them the best shearers in the country. He will be well enough in a week or two, he thinks, and the poor sheep must bear their loads a few days longer. Are they looking well, do you think, Juan? Will the crop be a good one? General Moreno used to say that you could reckon up the wool-crop to a pound, while it was on the sheep's backs."

"Yes, Señora," answered the mollified Juan; "the poor beasts look wonderfully well considering the scant feed they have had all winter. We'll not come many pounds short of our last year's crop, if any. Though, to be sure, there is no telling in what case that—Luigo will bring his flock back."

The Señora smiled, in spite of herself, at the pause and gulp with which Juan had filled in the hiatus where he had longed to set a contemptuous epithet before Luigo's name.

This was another of the instances where the Señora's will and Juan Canito's had clashed and he did not dream of it, having set it all down as usual to the score of young Señor Felipe.

Encouraged by the Señora's smile, Juan proceeded: "Señor Felipe can see no fault in Luigo, because they were boys together; but I can tell him, he will rue it, one of these mornings, when he finds a flock of sheep worse than dead on his hands, and no thanks to anybody but Luigo. While I can have him under my eye, here in the valley, it is all very well; but he is no more fit to take responsibility of a flock, than one of the very lambs themselves. He'll drive them off their feet one day, and starve them the next; and I've known him to forget to give them water. When he's in his dreams, the Virgin only knows what he won't do."

During this brief and almost unprecedented outburst of Juan's the

Señora's countenance had been slowly growing stern. Juan had not seen it. His eyes had been turned away from her, looking down into the upturned eager face of his favorite collie, who was leaping and gambolling and barking at his feet.

"Down, Capitan, down!" he said in a fond tone, gently repulsing him; "thou makest such a noise the Señora can hear nothing but thy voice."

"I heard only too distinctly, Juan Canito," said the Señora in a sweet but icy tone. "It is not well for one servant to backbite another. It gives me great grief to hear such words; and I hope when Father Salvierderra comes, next month, you will not forget to confess this sin of which you have been guilty in thus seeking to injure a fellow-being. If Señor Felipe listens to you, the poor boy Luigo will be cast out homeless on the world some day; and what sort of a deed would that be, Juan Canito, for one Christian to do to another? I fear the Father will give you penance, when he hears what you have said."

"Señora, it is not to harm the lad," Juan began, every fibre of his faithful frame thrilling with a sense of the injustice of her reproach.

But the Señora had turned her back. Evidently she would hear no more from him then. He stood watching her as she walked away, at her usual slow pace, her head slightly bent forward, her rosary lifted in her left hand, and the fingers of the right hand mechanically slipping the beads.

"Prayers, always prayers!" thought Juan to himself, as his eyes followed her. "If they'll take one to heaven, the Señora'll go by the straight road, that's sure! I'm sorry I vexed her. But what's a man to do, if he's the interest of the place at heart, I'd like to know. Is he to stand by, and see a lot of idle mooning louts run away with everything? Ah, but it was an ill day for the estate when the General died,—an ill day! an ill day! And they may scold me as much as they please, and set me to confessing my sins to the Father; it's very well for them, they've got me to look after matters. Señor Felipe will do well enough when he's a man, maybe; but a boy like him! Bah!" And the old man stamped his foot with a not wholly unreasonable irritation, at the false position in which he felt himself put.

"Confess to Father Salvierderra, indeed!" he muttered aloud. "Ay, that will I. He's a man of sense, if he is a priest," —at which slip of the tongue the pious Juan hastily crossed himself,— "and I'll ask him to give me some good advice as to how I'm to manage between this young boy at the head of everything, and a doting mother who thinks he has the wisdom of a dozen grown men. The Father knew the place in the olden time. He knows it's no child's play to look after the estate even now, much smaller as it is! An ill day when the old General died, an ill day indeed, the saints rest his soul!" Saying this, Juan shrugged his shoulders, and whistling to Capitan, walked towards the sunny veranda of the south side of the kitchen wing of the house, where it had been for twenty odd years his habit to sit on the long bench and smoke his pipe of a morning. Before he had got half-way across the court-yard, however, a thought struck him. He halted so suddenly that Capitan, with the quick sensitiveness of his breed, thought so sudden a change of purpose could only come from something in connection with sheep; and, true to his instinct of duty, pricked up his ears, poised himself for a full run, and looked up in his master's face waiting for explanation and signal. But Juan did not observe him.

"Ha!" he said, "Father Salvierderra comes next month, does he? Let's see. To-day is the 25th. That's it. The sheep-shearing is not to come off till the Father gets here. Then each morning it will be mass in the chapel, and each night vespers; and the crowd will be here at least two days longer to feed, for the time they will lose by that and by the confessions. That's what Señor Felipe is up to. He's a pious lad. I recollect now, it was the same way two years ago. Well, well, it is a good thing for those poor Indian devils to get a bit of religion now and then; and it's like old times to see the chapel full of them kneeling, and more than can get in at the door; I doubt not it warms the Señora's heart to see them all there, as if they belonged to the house, as they used to: and now I know when it's to be, I have only to make my arrangements accordingly. It is always in the first week of the month the Father gets here. Yes; she said, 'Señor Felipe will be well enough in a week or two, he thinks.' Ha! ha! It will be nearer two; ten days or thereabouts. I'll begin the booths next week. A plague on that Luigo for not being back here. He's the best hand I have to cut the willow boughs for the roofs. He knows the difference between one year's growth and another's; I'll say that much for him, spite of the silly dreaming head he's got on his shoulders."

Juan was so pleased with his clearing up in his mind as to Señor Felipe's purpose about the time of the sheep-shearing, that it put him in good humor for the day,—good humor with everybody, and himself most of all. As he sat on the low bench, his head leaning back against the whitewashed wall, his long legs stretched out nearly across the whole width of the veranda, his pipe firm wedged in the extreme left corner of his mouth, his hands in his pockets, he was the picture of placid content. The troop of youngsters which still swarmed around the kitchen quarters of Señora Moreno's house, almost as numerous and inexplicable as in the grand old days of the General's time, ran back and forth across Juan's legs, fell down between them, and picked themselves up by help of clutches at his leather trousers, all unreproved by Juan, though loudly scolded and warned by their respective mothers from the kitchen.

"What's come to Juan Can to be so good-natured to-day?" saucily asked Margarita, the youngest and prettiest of the maids, popping her head out of a window, and twitching Juan's hair. He was so gray and wrinkled that the maids all felt at ease with him. He seemed to them as old as Methuselah; but he was not really so old as they thought, nor they so safe in their tricks. The old man had hot blood in his veins yet, as the under-shepherds could testify.

"The sight of your pretty face, Señorita Margarita," answered Juan quickly, cocking his eye at her, rising to his feet, and making a mock bow towards the window.

"He! he! Señorita, indeed!" chuckled Margarita's mother, old Marda the cook. "Señor Juan Canito is pleased to be merry at the doors of his betters;" and she flung a copper saucepan full of not over-clean water so deftly past Juan's head, that not a drop touched him, and yet he had the appearance of having been ducked. At which bit of sleight-of-hand the whole court-yard, young and old, babies, cocks, hens, and turkeys, all set up a shout and a cackle, and dispersed to the four corners of the yard as if scattered by a volley of bird-shot. Hearing the racket, the rest of the maids came running,—Anita and Maria, the twins, women forty years old, born on the place the year after General Moreno brought home his handsome young bride; their two daughters, Rosa and Anita the Little, as she was still called, though she outweighed her mother; old Juanita, the oldest woman in the household, of whom even the Señora was said not to know the exact age or history; and she, poor thing, could tell nothing, having been silly for ten years or more, good for nothing except to shell beans: that she did as fast and well as ever, and was never happy except she was at it. Luckily for her, beans are the one crop never omitted or stinted on a Mexican estate; and for sake of old Juanita they stored every year in the Moreno house, rooms full of beans in the pod (tons of them, one would think), enough to feed an army. But then, it was like a little army even now, the Señora's household; nobody ever knew exactly how many women were in the kitchen, or how many men in the fields. There were always women cousins, or brother's wives or widows or daughters, who had come to stay, or men cousins, or sister's husbands or sons, who were stopping on their way up or down the valley. When it came to the pay-roll, Señor Felipe knew to whom he paid wages; but who were fed and lodged under his roof, that was quite another thing. It could not enter into the head of a Mexican gentleman to make either count or account of that. It would be a disgraceful niggardly thought.

To the Señora it seemed as if there were no longer any people about the place. A beggarly handful, she would have said, hardly enough to do the work of the house, or of the estate, sadly as the latter had dwindled. In the General's day, it had been a free-handed boast of his that never less than fifty persons, men, women and children, were fed within his gates each day; how many more, he did not care, nor know. But that time had indeed gone, gone forever; and though a stranger, seeing the sudden rush and muster at door and window, which followed on old Marda's letting fly the water at Juan's head, would have thought, "Good heavens, do all those women, children, and babies belong in that one house!" the Señora's sole thought, as she at that moment went past the gate, was, "Poor things! how few there are left of them! I am afraid old Marda has to work too hard. I must spare Margarita more from the house to help her." And she sighed deeply, and unconsciously held her rosary nearer to her heart, as she went into the house and entered her son's bedroom. The picture she saw there was one to thrill any mother's heart; and as it met her eye, she paused on the threshold for a second,—only a second, however; and nothing could have astonished Felipe Moreno so much as to have been told that at the very moment when his mother's calm voice was saying to him, "Good morning, my son, I hope you have slept well, and are better," there was welling up in her heart a passionate ejaculation, "O my glorious son! The saints have sent me in him the face of his father! He is fit for a kingdom!"

The truth is, Felipe Moreno was not fit for a kingdom at all. If he had been, he would not have been so ruled by his mother without ever finding it out. But so far as mere physical beauty goes, there never was a king born, whose face, stature, and bearing would set off a crown or a throne, or any of the things of which the outside of royalty is made up, better than would Felipe Moreno's. And it was true, as the Señora said, whether the saints had anything to do with it or not, that he had the face of his father. So strong a likeness is seldom seen. When Felipe once, on the occasion of a grand celebration and procession, put on the gold-wrought velvet mantle, gayly embroidered short breeches fastened at the knee with red ribbons, and gold-and-silver-trimmed sombrero, which his father had worn twenty-five years before, the Señora fainted at her first look at him,—fainted and fell; and when she opened her eyes, and saw the same splendid, gayly arrayed, dark-bearded man, bending over her in distress, with words of endearment and alarm, she fainted again.

"Mother, mother mia," cried Felipe, "I will not wear them if it makes you feel like this! Let me take them off. I will not go to their cursed parade;" and he sprang to his feet, and began with trembling fingers to unbuckle the sword-belt.

"No, no, Felipe," faintly cried the Señora, from the ground. "It is my wish that you wear them;" and staggering to her feet, with a burst of tears, she rebuckled the old sword-belt, which her fingers had so many times— never unkissed—buckled, in the days when her husband had bade her farewell and gone forth to the uncertain fates of war. "Wear them!" she cried, with gathering fire in her tones, and her eyes dry of tears,—"wear them, and let the American hounds see what a Mexican officer and gentleman looked like before they had set their base, usurping feet on our necks!" And she followed him to the gate, and stood erect, bravely waving her handkerchief as he galloped off, till he was out of sight. Then with a changed face and a bent head she crept slowly to her room, locked herself in, fell on her knees before the Madonna at the head of her bed, and spent the greater part of the day praying that she might be forgiven, and that all heretics might be discomfited. From which part of these supplications she derived most comfort is easy to imagine.

Juan Canito had been right in his sudden surmise that it was for Father Salvierderra's coming that the sheep-shearing was being delayed, and not in consequence of Señor Felipe's illness, or by the non-appearance of Luigo and his flock of sheep. Juan would have chuckled to himself still more at his perspicacity, had he overheard the conversation going on between the Señora and her son, at the very time when he, half asleep on the veranda, was, as he would have called it, putting two and two together and convincing himself that old Juan was as smart as they were, and not to be kept in the dark by all their reticence and equivocation.

"Juan Canito is growing very impatient about the sheep-shearing." said the Señora. "I suppose you are still of the same mind about it, Felipe,—that it is better to wait till Father Salvierderra comes? As the only chance those Indians have of seeing him is here, it would seem a Christian duty to so arrange it, if it be possible; but Juan is very restive. He is getting old, and chafes a little, I fancy, under your control. He cannot forget that you were a boy on his knee. Now I, for my part, am like to forget that you were ever anything but a man for me to lean on."

Felipe turned his handsome face toward his mother with a beaming smile of filial affection and gratified manly vanity. "Indeed, my mother, if I can be sufficient for you to lean on, I will ask nothing more of the saints;" and he took his mother's thin and wasted little hands, both at once, in his own strong right hand, and carried them to his lips as a lover might have done. "You will spoil me, mother," he said, "you make me so proud."

"No, Felipe, it is I who am proud," promptly replied the mother; "and I do not call it being proud, only grateful to God for having given me a son wise enough to take his father's place, and guide and protect me through the few remaining years I have to live. I shall die content, seeing you at the head of the estate, and living as a Mexican gentleman should; that is, so far as now remains possible in this unfortunate country. But about the sheep-shearing, Felipe. Do you wish to have it begun before the Father is here? Of course, Alessandro is all ready with his band. It is but two days' journey for a messenger to bring him. Father Salvierderra cannot be here before the 10th of the month. He leaves Santa Barbara on the 1st, and he will walk all the way,—a good six days' journey, for he is old now and feeble; then he must stop in Ventura for a Sunday, and a day at the Ortega's ranch, and at the Lopez's,—there, there is a christening. Yes, the 10th is the very earliest that he can be here,—near two weeks from now. So far as your getting up is concerned, it might perhaps be next week. You will be nearly well by that time."

"Yes, indeed," laughed Felipe, stretching himself out in the bed and giving a kick to the bedclothes that made the high bedposts and the fringed canopy roof shake and creak; "I am well now, if it were not for this cursed weakness when I stand on my feet. I believe it would do me good to get out of doors."

In truth, Felipe had been hankering for the sheep-shearing himself. It was a brisk, busy, holiday sort of time to him, hard as he worked in it; and two weeks looked long to wait.

"It is always thus after a fever," said his mother. "The weakness lasts many weeks. I am not sure that you will be strong enough even in two weeks to do the packing; but, as Juan Can said this morning, he stood at the packing-bag when you were a boy, and there was no need of waiting for you for that!"

"He said that, did he!" exclaimed Felipe, wrathfully. "The old man is getting insolent. I'll tell him that nobody will pack the sacks but myself, while I am master here; and I will have the sheep-shearing when I please, and not before."

"I suppose it would not be wise to say that it is not to take place till the Father comes, would it?" asked the Señora, hesitatingly, as if the thing were evenly balanced in her mind. "The Father has not that hold on the younger men he used to have, and I have thought that even in Juan himself I have detected a remissness. The spirit of unbelief is spreading in the country since the Americans are running up and down everywhere seeking money, like dogs with their noses to the ground! It might vex Juan if he knew that you were waiting only for the Father. What do you think?"

"I think it is enough for him to know that the sheep-shearing waits for my pleasure," answered Felipe, still wrathful, "and that is the end of it." And so it was; and, moreover, precisely the end which Señora Moreno had had in her own mind from the beginning; but not even Juan Canito himself suspected its being solely her purpose, and not her son's. As for Felipe, if any person had suggested to him that it was his mother, and not he, who had decided that the sheep-shearing would be better deferred until the arrival of Father Salvierderra from Santa Barbara, and that nothing should be said on the ranch about this being the real reason of the postponing, Felipe would have stared in astonishment, and have thought that person either crazy or a fool.

To attain one's ends in this way is the consummate triumph of art. Never to appear as a factor in the situation; to be able to wield other men, as instruments, with the same direct and implicit response to will that one gets from a hand or a foot,—this is to triumph, indeed: to be as nearly controller and conqueror of Fates as fate permits. There have been men prominent in the world's affairs at one time and another, who have sought and studied such a power and have acquired it to a great degree. By it they have manipulated legislators, ambassadors, sovereigns; and have grasped, held, and played with the destinies of empires. But it is to be questioned whether even in these notable instances there has ever been such marvellous completeness of success as is sometimes seen in the case of a woman in whom the power is an instinct and not an attainment; a passion rather than a purpose. Between the two results, between the two processes, there is just that difference which is always to be seen between the stroke of talent and the stroke of genius.

Señora Moreno's was the stroke of genius.

Born Helen Maria Fiske in 1830, Helen Hunt Jackson was raised in Amherst, Massachusetts, where her childhood friends included poet Emily Dickinson. She was educated at the Ipswich Female Seminary in Massachusetts and the Abbott Institute in New York City. In 1852 she married U.S. Army Captain Edward Bissell Hunt, and she followed him to military postings around the United States. Her family life was shattered by tragedy; her husband died in a military accident, and she lost both of her sons to illness. After a period of mourning, she decided to pursue a career as a writer, publishing numerous short stories, travel sketches, and essays, generally under pseudonyms. In 1875 she married banker William Sharpless Jackson. At the same time, Helen Hunt Jackson had become increasingly interested in the American West, particularly the U.S. government's mistreatment of Native Americans. In 1881 she published a blistering attack on federal policy toward Native Americans titled A Century of Dishonor. *The book made her a national figure and led the Department of the Interior to commission her to investigate the conditions of the Mission Indians of Southern California. The government ignored her final report, and so Jackson decided to use her research as the basis for a novel,* Ramona, *which she published in 1884. Jackson intended her portrait of Southern California rancho life to be a call for social change, comparable to Harriet Beecher Stowe's* Uncle Tom's Cabin. *And although the book was enormously popular, its most powerful effect was to make Southern California a major tourist destination. Jackson died in San Francisco in 1885.*

✿ Charles Nordhoff

Selection from *California: For Health, Pleasure,
and Residence—A Book for Travellers and Settlers*

A FRIEND AND NEIGHBOR OF MY OWN, consumptive for some years, and struggling for his life in a winter residence for two years at Nice and Mentone, and during a third at Aiken, in South Carolina, came last October to Southern California.

He had been "losing ground," as he said, and his appearance showed, for two years, and last summer suffered so severely from night sweats, sleeplessness, continual coughing, and lack of appetite, that it was doubtful whether he would live through the winter anywhere; and it was rather in desperation than with much hope of a prolonged or comfortable life that he made ready for the journey across the continent with his family.

In January I was one day standing in the door-way of a hotel at Los Angeles, when I saw a wagon drive up; the driver jumped out, held out his hand to me, and sung out in a hearty voice, "How do you do?" It was my consumptive friend, but a changed man.

He had just driven sixty miles in two days, over a rough road, from San Bernardino; he walked with me several miles on the evening we met; he ate heartily and slept well, enjoyed his life, and coughed hardly at all. It was an amazing change to come about in three months, and in a man so ill as he had been.

"I shall never be a sound man, of course," he said to me when I spent some days with him, later, at San Bernardino; "but this climate has added ten years to my life; it has given me ease and comfort; and neither Nice, nor Mentone, nor Aiken are, in my opinion, to be compared with some parts of Southern California in point of climate for consumptives."

In Santa Barbara, San Diego, and San Bernardino, one may find abundant evidence corroborative of my friend's assertion. In each of these places I have met men and women who have been restored to health and strength by residence there; and though no one whom I met had had the wide experience of my friend in other winter resorts, I found not a few people of intelligence and means who bore the strongest testimony to the kindly and healing influences of the climate of Southern California.

I think I shall be doing a service, therefore, to many invalids if I give here some details concerning the places I have named, and some others, but little known as yet in the East, which are now accessible, and whose beneficial influences upon diseases of the throat and lungs are undoubtedly remarkable.

The whole of Southern California has a very mild and equable winter climate. Stockton, for instance, which lies at the head of the San Joaquin Valley, has a temperature all the year singularly like that of Naples, as is shown by observations kept for some years by one of the most eminent and careful physicians of the place. But local peculiarities cause in some places daily extremes which are not, I think, favorable for invalids; and in other points the winds are too severe for weakly persons. At Los Angeles, for instance, the days in January are warm and genial, but as soon as the sun sets the air becomes chilly, and quickly affects tender throats. San Diego, Santa Barbara, San Bernardino, with Stockton and Visalia, are the points most favorable for consumptives and persons subject to throat difficulties.

Of these, the friend of whom I spoke above found San Bernardino the most beneficial; and a physician, who had removed from an Eastern city to the new Riverside Colony near San Bernardino, told me that he lived nowhere so comfortably as there. He could not live in New York at all, being prostrated with severe throat disease; and he enjoyed, he told me, perfect health at Riverside.

Unfortunately, San Bernardino has but a poor hotel, and is not, as I write, well fitted to accommodate invalids. But I was told that comfortable board can be obtained in several private houses, and a new hotel is now building and will be opened before next fall. The sanitary advantages of the place are little known and not much thought of by its inhabitants. My friend, who has spent there a considerable part of this winter, and who, like a genuine valetudinarian, keeps a record of the temperature with both dry and wet bulb thermometer, reports to me that the air is dryer there than at points nearer the coast; and this greater dryness, which arises from its situation, about seventy-five miles from the sea, is probably its chief sanitary advantage. At the Riverside Colony there are yet but a few small houses, and no accommodations for visitors.

San Bernardino has a fine situation; it lies in a great plain, with picturesque mountains on three sides of it. Living is cheap; horses cost from $20 to $50 each; horse-keep is very cheap; the roads are generally good; and for those who do not ride, a wagon and a pair of horses will afford the means of pleasant excursions. Oranges are grown in old San Bernardino, which is where the old mission stood, and I have an idea that there, on higher ground, and nearer the mountains, the climate is perhaps a little better even than in the town.

To reach San Bernardino you take steamer at San Francisco for Los Angeles, which place you reach from San Pedro, its port, by a short railroad. The voyage, which lasts thirty-six hours, and is made all the way in sight of land, is usually pleasant. From Los Angeles you get to San Bernardino by stage, distance sixty miles—time ten hours. The Southern Pacific Railroad Company has just completed its surveys for a railroad to connect Los Angeles with San Bernardino; and when this line is completed the journey can be made in a few hours.

San Diego seems to me to possess the mildest and sunniest winter climate on the coast. It has the advantage of a large and excellent hotel, and very good shops, and the disadvantage of an almost entire absence of shade and trees. It has pleasant society, and within thirty miles very fine and varied scenery. If I were spending a winter in California for my health, I think I should go first to San Diego, and stay there the months of December and January. It is the most southern town in the State, and presumably warmer than either Santa Barbara or San Bernardino, though the difference is but slight. It affords some simple amusements, in fishing, shell-hunting, and boat-sailing; and here, as all over Southern California, horses are cheap; and to those who are fond of driving or riding, very fair roads are open. There is less rain here than in any other part of the State; and as the so-called winter in this State is a rainy season, San Diego has the advantage over other places of less mud in December and January. In fact, I doubt if it is ever muddy there.

Santa Barbara is on many accounts the pleasantest of all the places I have named; and it has an advantage in this, that one may there choose his climate within a distance of three or four miles of the town. It has a very peculiar situation. If you will examine a map of California, you will see that, while the general "trend" of the coast-line is from north-north-west to south-south-east, at Point Conception it makes a sharp and sudden turn, and runs to Rincon Point, below Santa Barbara, nearly due east and west. Thus Santa Barbara faces directly south.

But this is not the only advantage it gains from this turn in the coast-line. The harsh and foggy north and north-west winds, which make the coast north of Point Conception disagreeable, are entirely cut off from Santa Barbara by the high coast range, which comes almost to the very shore at Point Conception, and stretches along the coast, but two or three miles back from it, to San Buenaventura. Santa Barbara lies on a narrow strip of land, with the sea and some lovely islands to the south, and a picturesque mountain range between 3000 and 4000 feet high about one and a half miles back to the north.

The town and its vicinity gain thus a remarkably equable climate. I have before me a number of reports of temperature, and could overwhelm you, if I liked, with figures, tables, and statistics concerning the whole coast; but these records are almost altogether of a mean temperature for a week, month, or year. Now what an invalid suffers most from is not recorded in such tables: I mean the daily extremes. If the day is very warm, and the evening suddenly chilly and cold, that makes a bad climate for weakly persons. Both Santa Barbara and San Diego are remarkably free from such sudden and great changes, and I think there is no doubt that Santa Barbara has the most equable climate, in this sense as well as all others, on this coast. The coldest day in 1871 was the 22d of February, when the mercury stood at 42°.

There is a good hotel there, and another one is building; but neither of them stands in a pleasant situation, and both are near the shore, where the air is less dry than in the higher parts of the town. Persons who are very sensitive to damp will do well to find lodgings in the upper part of the town, or in what is called the "Montecito"—the little mountain—a suburb, two or three miles distant, and sheltered from the sea-breeze by an intervening range of low hills. Here it is somewhat warmer—indeed it is hot in the middle of the day, and the air is, I think, a little drier. In the Montecito there is also a hot sulphur spring which has some approved medicinal virtues; but I advise people to use it only on the orders of a physician.

Born in Prussia in 1830, Charles Nordhoff immigrated with his parents to the United States in 1835. He served in the U.S. Navy and later worked as a journalist. In the early 1870s he traveled through California, a journey that inspired the highly successful book California: For Health, Pleasure, and Residence *(Harper and Brothers, 1874); later books included works on politics and the sea, among them* The Communistic Societies of the United States *(Harper and Brothers, 1875). Nordhoff settled in California, first in Ventura County, where the town of Ojai was originally named for him, and later in Coronado. He died in 1901.*

✿ Walter Mosley

Selection from *Devil in a Blue Dress*

T HERE WAS STILL A LARGE STRETCH of farmland between Los Angeles and Santa Monica in those days. The Japanese farmers grew artichokes, lettuce, and strawberries along the sides of the road. That night the fields were dark under the slight moon and the air was chill but not cold.

I was unhappy about going to meet Mr. Albright because I wasn't used to going into white communities, like Santa Monica, to conduct business. The plant I worked at, Champion Aircraft, was in Santa Monica but I'd drive out there in the daytime, do my work, and go home. I never loitered anywhere except among my own people, in my own neighborhood.

But the idea that I'd give him the information he wanted, and that he'd give me enough money to pay the next month's mortgage, made me happy. I was dreaming about the day I'd be able to buy more houses, maybe even a duplex. I always wanted to own enough land that it would pay for itself out of the rent it generated.

When I arrived the merry-go-round and arcade were closing down. Small children and their parents were leaving and a group of young people were milling around, smoking cigarettes and acting tough the way young people do.

I went across the pier to the railing that looked down onto the beach. I figured that Mr. Albright would see me there as well as anyplace and that I was far enough away from the white kids that I could avoid any ugliness.

But that wasn't my week for avoiding anything bad.

A chubby girl in a tight-fitting skirt wandered away from her friends. She was younger than the rest of them, maybe seventeen, and it seemed like she was the only girl without a date. When she saw me she smiled and said,

"Hi." I answered and turned away to look out over the weakly lit shoreline north of Santa Monica. I was hoping that she'd leave and Albright would come and I'd be back in my house before midnight.

"It's pretty out here, huh?" Her voice came from behind me.

"Yeah. It's all right."

"I come from Des Moines, in Iowa. They don't have anything like the ocean back there. Are you from L.A.?"

"No. Texas." The back of my scalp was tingling.

"Do they have an ocean in Texas?"

"The Gulf, they have the Gulf."

"So you're used to it." She leaned on the rail next to me. "It still knocks me out whenever I see it. My name's Barbara. Barbara Moskowitz. That's a Jewish name."

"Ezekiel Rawlins," I whispered. I didn't want her so familiar as to use my nickname. When I glanced over my shoulder I noticed that a couple of the young men were looking around, like they'd lost someone.

"I think they're looking for you," I said.

"Who cares?" she answered. "My sister just brought me 'cause my parents made her. All she wants to do is make out with Herman and smoke cigarettes."

"It's still dangerous for a girl to be alone. Your parents are right to want you with somebody."

"Are you going to hurt me?" She stared into my face intently. I remember wondering what color her eyes were before I heard the shouting.

"Hey you! Black boy! What's happening here?" It was a pimply-faced boy. He couldn't have been more than twenty years and five and a half feet but he came up to me like a full-grown soldier. He wasn't afraid; a regular fool of a youth.

"What do you want?" I asked as politely as I could.

"You know what I mean," he said as he came within range of my grasp.

"Leave him alone, Herman!" Barbara yelled. "We were just talking!"

"You were, huh?" he said to me. "We don't need ya talking to our women."

I could have broken his neck. I could have put out his eyes or broken all of his fingers. But instead I held my breath.

Five of his friends were headed toward us. While they were coming on, not yet organized or together, I could have killed all of them too. What did they know about violence? I could have crushed their windpipes one by one and they couldn't have done a thing to stop me. They couldn't even run fast enough to escape me. I was still a killing machine.

"Hey!" the tallest one said. "What's wrong?"

"Nigger's trying to pick up Barbara."

"Yeah, an' she's just jailbait."

"Leave him alone!" Barbara shouted. "He was just saying where he was from."

I guess she was trying to help me, like a mother hugging her child when he's just broken his ribs.

"Barbara!" another girl shouted.

"Hey, man, what's wrong with you?" the big one asked in my face. He was wide-shouldered and a little taller than I; built like a football player. He had a broad, fleshy face. His eyes, nose, and mouth were like tiny islands on a great sea of white skin.

I noticed that a couple of the others had picked up sticks. They moved in around me, forcing me back against the rail.

"I don't want any problem, man," I said. I could smell the liquor on the tall one's breath.

"You already got a problem, boy."

"Listen, all she said was hi. That's all I said too." But I was thinking to myself, Why the hell do I have to answer to you?

Herman said, "He was tellin' her where he lived. She said so herself."

I was trying to remember how far down the beach was. By then I knew I had to get out of there before there were two or three dead bodies, one of them being mine.

"Excuse me," a man's voice called out.

There was a slight commotion behind the football player and then a Panama hat appeared there next to him.

"Excuse me," Mr. DeWitt Albright said again. He was smiling.

"What do you want?" the footballer said.

DeWitt just smiled and then he pulled the pistol, which looked somewhat like a rifle, from his coat. He leveled the barrel at the large boy's right eye and said, "I want to see your brains scattered all over your friends' clothes, son. I want you to die for me."

The large boy, who was wearing red swimming trunks, made a sound like he had swallowed his tongue. He moved his shoulder ever so slightly and DeWitt cocked back the hammer. It sounded like a bone breaking.

"I wouldn't move if I were you, son. I mean, if you were to breathe too heavily I'd just kill you. And if any of you other boys move I'll kill him and then I'll shoot off *all* your nuts."

The ocean was rumbling and the air had turned cold. The only human sound was from Barbara, who was sobbing in her sister's arms.

"I want you boys to meet my friend," DeWitt said. "Mr. Jones."

I didn't know what to do so I nodded.

"He's a friend'a mine," Mr. Albright continued. "And I'd be proud and happy if he was to lower himself to fuck my sister *and* my mother."

No one had anything to say to that.

"Now, Mr. Jones, I want to ask you something."

"Yes, sir, Mr., ah, Smith."

"Do you think that I should shoot out this nasty boy's eyeball?"

I let that question hang for a bit. Two of the younger boys had been weeping already but the wait caused the footballer to start crying.

"Well," I said, after fifteen seconds or so, "if he's not sorry for bullying me then I think you should kill him."

"I'm sorry," said the boy.

"You are?" Mr. Albright asked.

"Y-y-yes!"

"How sorry are you? I mean, are you sorry enough?"

"Yessir, I am."

"You're sorry enough?" When he asked that question he moved the muzzle of the gun close enough to touch the boy's tiny, flickering eyelid. "Don't twitch now, I want you to see the bullet coming. Now are you sorry enough?"

"Yessir!"

"Then prove it. I want you to show him. I want you to get! down on your knees and suck his peter. I want you to suck it good now …"

The boy started crying outright when Albright said that. I was pretty confident that he was just joking, in a sick kind of way, but my heart quailed along with the footballer.

"Down on your knees or you're dead, boy!"

The other boys had their eyes glued to the footballer as he went to his knees. They tore out running when Albright slammed the barrel of his pistol into the side of the boy's head.

"Get out of here!" Albright yelled. "And if you tell some cops I'll find every one of you."

We were alone in less than half a minute. I could hear the slamming of car doors and the revving of jalopy engines from the parking lot and the street.

"They got something to think about now," Albright said. He returned his long-barreled .44-caliber pistol to the holster inside his coat. The pier was abandoned; everything was dark and silent.

"I don't think that they'd dare call the cops on something like this but we should move on just in case," he said.

ALBRIGHT'S WHITE CADILLAC WAS PARKED in the lot down under the pier. He drove south down along the ocean. There were few electric lights from the coast, and just a sliver of moon, but the sea glittered with a million tiny glints. It looked like every shiny fish in the sea had come to the surface to mimic the stars that flickered in the sky. There was light everywhere and there was darkness everywhere too.

He switched on the radio and tuned in a big-band station that was playing "Two Lonely People," by Fats Waller. I remember because as soon as the music came on I started shivering. I wasn't afraid; I was angry, angry at the way he humiliated that boy. I didn't care about the boy's feelings, I cared that if Albright could do something like that to one of his own then I knew he could do the same, and much worse, to me. But if he wanted to shoot me he'd just have to do it because I wasn't going down on my knees for him or for anybody else.

I never doubted for a minute that Albright would have killed that boy.

"What you got, Easy?" he asked after a while.

"I got a name and an address. I got the last day she was seen and who she was with. I know the man she was seen with and I know what he does for a living." I was proud of knowledge when I was a young man. Joppy had told me just to take the money and to pretend I was looking for the girl, but once I had a piece of information I had to show it off.

"All that's worth the money."

"But I want to know something first."

"What's that?" Mr. Albright asked. He pulled the car onto a shoulder that overlooked the shimmering Pacific. The waves were really rolling that night, you could even hear them through the closed windows.

"I want to know that no harm is going to come to that girl, or anybody else."

"Do I look that much like God to you? Can I tell you what will happen tomorrow? I don't plan for the girl to be hurt. My friend thinks he's in love with her. He wants to buy her a gold ring and live happily ever after. But, you know, she might forget to buckle her shoes next week and fall down and break her neck, and if she does you can't hold me up for it. But whatever."

I knew that was the most I would get out of him. DeWitt made no promises but I believed that he meant no harm to the girl in the photograph.

"She was with a man named Frank Green, Tuesday last. They were at a bar called the Playroom."

"Where is she now?"

"Woman who told me said she thought that they were a team, Green and the girl, so she's probably with him."

"Where's that?" he asked. His smile and good manners were gone; this was business now—plain and simple.

"He's got an apartment at Skyler and Eighty-third. Place is called the Skyler Arms."

He took out the white pen and wallet and scribbled something on the notepad. Then he stared at me with those dead eyes while he tapped the steering wheel with the pen.

"What else?"

"Frank's a gangster," I said. That got DeWitt to smile again. "He's with hijackers. They take liquor and cigarettes; sell 'em all over southern California."

"Bad man?" DeWitt couldn't keep his smile down.

"Bad enough. He somethin' with a knife."

"You ever see him in action? I mean, you see him kill somebody?"

"I saw him cut a man in a bar once; loudmouth dude didn't know who Frank was."

DeWitt's eyes came to life for a moment; he leaned across the seat so far that I could feel his dry breath on my neck. "I want you to remember something, Easy. I want you to think about when Frank took his knife and stabbed that man."

I thought about it for a second and then I nodded to let him know that I was ready.

"Before he went at him, did he hesitate? Even for a second?"

I thought about the crowded bar down on Figueroa. The big man was talking to Frank's woman and when Frank walked up to him he put his hand against Frank's chest, getting ready to push him away, I suppose. Frank's eyes widened and he threw his head around as if to say to the crowd, "Look at what this fool is doin'! He deserve t'be dead, stupid as he acts!" Then the knife appeared in Frank's hand and the big man crumpled against the bar, trying to ward off the stroke with his big fleshy arms …

"Maybe just a second, not even that," I said.

Mr. DeWitt Albright laughed softly.

"Well," he said. "I guess I have to see what I shall see."

"Maybe you could get to the girl when he's out. Frank spends a lot of time on the road. I saw him the other night, at John's; he was dressed for hijacking, so he might be out of town for a couple of more days."

"That would be best," Albright answered. He leaned back across the seat. "No reason to be any messier than we have to, now. You got that photograph?"

"No," I lied. "Not on me. I left it at home."

He only looked at me for a second but I knew he didn't believe it. I don't know why I wanted to keep her picture. It's just that the way she looked out at me made me feel good.

"Well, maybe I'll pick it up after I find her; you know I like to make everything neat after a job … Here's another hundred and take this card too. All you have to do is go down to that address and you can pick up a job to tide you over until something else comes up."

He handed me a tight roll of bills and a card. I couldn't read the card in that dim light so I shoved it and the money in my pocket.

"I think I can get my old job back so I won't need the address."

"Hold on to it," he said, as he turned the ignition. "You did alright by me, getting this information, and I'm doing right by you. That's the way I do business, Easy; I always pay my debts."

THE DRIVE BACK WAS QUIET and brilliant with night lights. Benny Goodman was on the radio and DeWitt Albright hummed along as if he had grown up with big bands.

When we pulled up to my car, next to the pier, everything was as it had been when we left. When I opened the door to get out, Albright said, "Pleasure working with you, Easy." He extended his hand and when he had the snake grip on me again his look became quizzical and he said, "You know, I was wondering just one thing."

"What's that?"

"How come you let those boys get around you like that? You could have picked them off one by one before they got your back to the rails."

"I don't kill children," I said.

Albright laughed for the second time that night.

Then he let me go and said good-bye.

Walter Mosley was born in Los Angeles in 1952. He earned his B.A. from Johnson State College in Vermont in 1977, then settled in New York City. In 1990 he published the first of his novels about African-American private-eye Easy Rawlins, titled Devil in a Blue Dress. *The novel is set in the 1940s Los Angeles that Mosley's father encountered when he moved to California from Louisiana. Numerous other Rawlins novels have followed, including* Black Betty *(W. W. Norton, 1994),* Cinnamon Kiss *(Little, Brown and Company, 2005), and* Blonde Faith *(Little, Brown and Company, 2007). Mosley has also published science fiction and a young adult novel,* 47 *(Little, Brown and Company, 2005).*

Tobias Wolff

From *Our Story Begins: New and Selected Stories*
DESERT BREAKDOWN, 1968

KRYSTAL WAS ASLEEP WHEN THEY CROSSED the Colorado. Mark had promised to stop for some pictures, but when the moment came he looked over at her and drove on. Krystal's face was puffy from the heat blowing into the car. Her hair, cut short for summer, hung damp against her forehead. Only a few strands lifted in the breeze. She had her hands folded over her belly, which made her look even more pregnant than she was.

The tires sang on the metal grillwork of the bridge. The river stretched away on both sides, blue as the empty sky. Mark saw the shadow of the bridge on the water with the car running through the girders, and the glint of water under the grillwork. Then the tires went silent. *California,* Mark thought, and for a time he felt almost as good as he'd expected to feel.

That soon passed. He'd broken his word, and he was going to hear about it when Krystal woke up. He almost turned the car around. But he didn't want to have to stop, and hoist Hans up on his shoulders, and watch Krystal point that camera at him again. By now Krystal had hundreds of pictures of Mark, and of Mark with Hans on his shoulders, standing in front of canyons and waterfalls and monumental trees and the three automobiles they'd owned since coming stateside.

Mark did not photograph well. For some reason he always looked discouraged. But those pictures gave the wrong idea. An old platoon sergeant of Mark's had an expression he liked to use—"free, white, and twenty-one." Well, that was an exact description of Mark. Everything was in front of him. All he needed was an opening.

Two hawks wheeled overhead, their shadows immense on the baking sand. A spinning funnel of dust moved across the road and disappeared behind a billboard. The billboard had a picture of Eugene McCarthy on it. McCarthy's hair was blowing around his head. He was grinning. The slogan below read A BREATH OF FRESH AIR. You could tell this was California because in Arizona a McCarthy billboard would last about five minutes. This one did have some bullet holes in it, but in Arizona someone would have burned it down or blown it up. The people there were just incredibly backward.

In the distance the mountains were bare and blue. Mark passed exit signs for a town called Blythe. He considered stopping for gas, but there was still half a tank and he didn't want to risk waking Krystal or Hans. He drove on into the desert.

They would make Los Angeles by dinnertime. Mark had an army buddy there who'd offered to put them up for as long as they wanted to stay. There was plenty of room, his buddy said. He was house-sitting for his parents while they made up their minds whether to get divorced or not.

Mark was sure he'd find something interesting in Los Angeles. Something in the entertainment field. He had been in plays all through high school and could sing pretty well. But his big talent was impersonation. He could mimic anybody. In Germany he'd mimicked a southern fellow in his company so accurately that after a couple of weeks of it the boy asked to be transferred to another unit. Mark knew he'd gone overboard. He laid off and in the end the boy withdrew his request for transfer.

His best impersonation was his father, Dutch. Sometimes, just for fun, Mark called his mother and talked to her in Dutch's slow, heavy voice, rolling every word along on treads, like a tank. She always fell for it. Mark would go on until he got bored, then say something like, "By the way, Dottie, we're bankrupt." Then she'd catch on and laugh. Unlike Dutch, she had a sense of humor.

A truck hurtled past. The sound of the engine woke Hans, but Mark reached into the back and rubbed the satin edge of the baby blanket against his cheek. Hans put his thumb in his mouth. Then he stuck his rear end in the air and went back to sleep.

The road shimmered. It seemed to float above the desert floor. Mark sang along with the radio, which he'd been turning up as the signal grew weaker. Suddenly it blared. He turned it down, but too late. Hans woke up again and started fussing. Mark rubbed his cheek with the blanket. Hans pushed Mark's arm away and said, "No!" It was the only word he knew. Mark glanced back at him. He'd been sleeping on a toy car whose wheels had left four red dents on the side of his face. Mark stroked his cheek. "Pretty soon," he said, "pretty soon, Hansy," not meaning anything in particular but wanting to sound upbeat.

Krystal was awake now, too. For a moment she didn't move or say anything. Then she shook her head rapidly from side to side. "So hot," she said. She held up the locket-watch around her neck and looked at Mark. He kept his eyes on the road. "Back from the dead," he said. "Boy, you were really out."

"The pictures," she said. "Mark, the pictures."

"There wasn't any place to stop," he said.

"But you promised."

Mark looked at her, then back at the road. "I'm sorry," he said. "There'll be other rivers."

"I wanted that one," Krystal said, and turned away. Mark could tell that she was close to tears. It made him feel tired. "All right," he said. "Do you want me to go back?" He slowed the car to prove he meant it. "If that's what you want just say the word."

She shook her head.

Mark sped up.

Hans began to kick the back of the seat. Mark didn't say anything. At least it was keeping Hans busy and quiet. "Hey, gang," Mark said. "Listen up. I've got ten big ones that say we'll be diving into Rick's pool by six o'clock." Hans gave the seat a kick that he felt clear through to his ribs. "Ten big ones," he said. "Any takers?" He looked over at Krystal and saw that her lips were trembling. He patted the seat beside him. She hesitated, then slid over and leaned against him, as he knew she would. Krystal wasn't one to hold a grudge. He put his arm around her shoulder.

"So much desert," she said.

"It's something, all right."

"No trees," she said. "At home I could never imagine."

Hans stopped kicking. Then he grabbed Mark's ears. Krystal laughed and pulled him over the seat onto her lap. He immediately arched his back and slid down to the floor, where he began tugging at the gear shift.

"I have to stop," Krystal said. She patted her belly. "This one likes to sit just so, here, on my bladder."

Mark nodded. Krystal knew the English words for what Dottie had always been content to call her plumbing, and when she was pregnant she liked to describe in pretty close detail what went on in there. It made Mark queasy.

"Next chance we get," he said. "We're low on gas anyway."

MARK TURNED OFF AT AN EXIT with one sign that said GAS. There was no mention of a town. The road went north over bleached hardpan crazed with fissures. It seemed to be leading them toward a distant, solitary mountain that looked to Mark like a colossal sinking ship. Phantom water glistened in the desert. Rabbits darted back and forth across the road. Finally they came to the gas station, an unpainted cement-block building with some pickup trucks parked in front.

There were four men sitting on a bench in the shade of the building. They watched the car pull up.

"Cowboys," Krystal said. "Look, Hans, cowboys!"

Hans stood on Krystal's legs and looked out the window.

Krystal still thought everyone who wore a cowboy hat was a cowboy. Mark had tried to explain that it was a style, but she refused to understand. He stopped at a pump and turned off the engine.

The men stared at them, their faces dark under the wide brims of their hats. They looked as if they'd been there forever. One of them got up from the bench and walked over. He was tall and carried a paunch that seemed out of place on his bony frame. He bent down and looked inside the car. He had little black eyes with no eyebrows. His face was red, as if he were angry about something.

"Regular, please," Mark said. "All she'll take."

The man stared openly at Krystal's belly. He straightened up and walked away, past the men on the bench, up to the open door of the building. He stuck his head inside and yelled. Then he sat on the bench again. The man next to him looked down and mumbled something. The others laughed.

Somebody else in a cowboy hat came out of the building and went around to the back of the car.

"Mark," Krystal said.

"I know," Mark said. "The bathroom." When he got out of the car the heat took him by surprise; he could feel it coming down like rain.

The person pumping gas said, "You need oil or anything?" and that was when Mark realized it was a woman. She was looking down at the nozzle, so he couldn't see her face, only the top of her hat. Her hands were black with grease. "My wife would like to use your bathroom," he said.

She nodded. When the tank was full she thumped on the roof of the car. "Okay," she said, and walked back to the building.

Krystal opened the door and swung her legs out, then rocked forward and pushed herself up into the light. She stood for a moment, blinking. The four men looked at her. So did Mark. He made allowances for the fact that Krystal was pregnant, but she was still too heavy. Her bare arms were flushed from the heat. So was her face. She looked like one of those stein-slinging waitresses in the *Biergarten* where they used to drink. He wished these men could have seen how she looked wearing that black dress of hers, with her hair long, when they'd first started going out together.

Krystal shaded her eyes with one hand. With the other she pulled her blouse away from where it stuck to her skin. "More desert," she said. She lifted Hans out of the car and carried him toward the building, but he kicked free and ran over to the bench. He stood there in front of the men, naked except for his diaper.

"Come here," Krystal said. When he didn't obey she started after him, then looked at the men and stopped.

Mark went over. "Let's go, Hansy," he said, picking him up, feeling a sudden tenderness that vanished when the boy began to struggle.

The woman took Krystal and Hans inside the building, then came out and stood by the pile of scrap lumber beside the door. "Hans," she said. "That's a funny name for a little boy."

"It was her father's name," Mark said, and so it was. The original Hans had died shortly before the baby was born. Otherwise Mark never would have agreed. Even Germans didn't name their kids Hans anymore.

One of the men flicked a cigarette butt toward Mark's car. It fell just short and lay there, smoldering. Mark took it as a judgment on the car. It was a good one, a 1958 Bonneville he'd bought two weeks ago when the Ford started belching smoke, but a previous owner had put a lot of extra chrome on it and right now it was gleaming every which way. It looked foolish next to these dented pickups with their gun racks and dull, blistering paint. Mark wished he'd tanked up in Blythe.

Krystal came outside again, carrying Hans. She had brushed her hair and looked better.

Mark smiled at her. "All set?"

She nodded. "Thank you," she said to the woman.

Mark would have liked to use the bathroom too, but he wanted to get out of there. He started for the car, Krystal behind him. She laughed deep in her throat. "You should have seen," she said. "They have a motorcycle in their bedroom." Krystal probably thought she was whispering, but to Mark every word was like a shout. He didn't say anything. He adjusted the visor while Krystal settled Hans on the backseat. "Wait," she told Mark, and got out of the car again. She had the camera.

"Krystal," Mark said.

She aimed the camera at the four men. When she snapped the shutter their heads jerked up. Krystal advanced the film, then aimed the camera again.

"Krystal, get in!"

"Yes," Krystal said, but she was still aiming, braced on the open door of the car, her knees bent slightly. She snapped another picture and slid onto the seat. "Good," she said. "Cowboys for Reiner."

Reiner was Krystal's brother. He had once driven sixty miles to see *Shane.*

Mark didn't dare look over at the bench. He put the key in the ignition and glanced up and down the road. He turned the key. Nothing happened.

Mark waited for a moment. Then he tried again. Still nothing. The ignition went *tick tick tick tick,* and that was all. Mark turned it off and the three of them sat there. Even Hans was quiet. Mark felt the men watching him. That was why he didn't lower his head to the wheel. He stared straight ahead, furious at the tears stinging his eyes, blurring the line of the horizon, the shape of the building, the dark forms of the trucks, and the figure coming toward them over the white earth.

It was the woman. She bent down. "Okay," she said. "What's the trouble?" The smell of whiskey filled the car.

FOR ALMOST HALF AN HOUR the woman messed with the engine. She had Mark turn the key while she watched, then turn it some more while she did various things under the hood. At last she decided that the trouble was in the alternator. She couldn't fix it and had no parts on hand. Mark would have to get one in Indio or Blythe or maybe as far away as Palm Springs. It wasn't going to be easy, finding an alternator for a ten-year-old car. But she said she'd call around for him.

Mark waited in the car. He tried to act as if everything were all right, but when Krystal looked at him she made a sympathetic noise and squeezed his arm. Hans was asleep in her lap. "Everything will be fine," she said.

Mark nodded.

The woman came back toward the car, and Mark got out to meet her.

"Aren't you the lucky one," she said, handing him a piece of paper with an address written on it. "There wasn't anything in Indio," she said, "but this fellow in Blythe can fix you up. I'll need two dollars for the calls."

Mark opened his wallet and gave her the money. He had sixty-five dollars left, all that remained of his army severance pay. "How much will the alternator cost?" he asked.

She closed the hood of the car. "Fifty-six dollars, I think it was."

"Jesus," Mark said.

"You're lucky they had one."

"I suppose so," Mark said. "It just seems like a lot of money. Can you jump-start me?"

"If you've got cables. Mine are lent out."

"I don't have any," Mark said. He squinted against the sun. Though he hadn't looked directly at the men on the bench, he knew they'd been watching him and was sure they had heard everything. He was also sure they had jumper cables. People who drove trucks always carried stuff like that. But if they didn't want to help, he wasn't going to ask.

"I suppose I could walk up to the highway and hitch a ride," Mark said, more loudly than he meant to.

"I guess you could," the woman said.

Mark looked back at Krystal. "Is it okay if my wife stays here?"

"I guess she'll have to," the woman said. She took off her hat and wiped her brow with the back of her sleeve. Her hair was pure yellow, gathered in a loose bun that glowed in the light. Her eyes were a strangely pale blue. She put her hat back on and told Mark how to get to the parts store. She made him repeat the directions. Then he went back to the car.

Krystal looked straight ahead and bit her lip while Mark explained the situation. "Here?" she said. "You are going to leave us here?"

Hans was awake again. He had pulled the volume knob off the radio and was banging it on the dashboard.

"Just for a couple hours," Mark said, though he knew it would take longer.

Krystal wouldn't look at him.

"There's no choice," he said.

The woman had been standing next to Mark. She moved him aside and opened the door. "You come with me," she said. "You and the little one." She held out her arms. Hans went to her immediately and peered over her shoulder at the men on the bench. Krystal hesitated, then got out of the car, ignoring Mark's hand when he reached down to help her.

"It won't take long," he said. He smiled at Hans. "Pretty soon, Hansy," he said, and turned and began to walk toward the road.

THE WOMAN WENT INSIDE WITH HANS. Krystal stood beside the car and watched Mark move farther and farther away, until the line of his body started to waver in the heat and then vanished altogether. It was like seeing someone slip below the surface of a lake.

The men stared at Krystal as she walked to the building. She felt heavy, and vaguely ashamed.

The woman had all the shades pulled down. It was like evening inside:

dim, peaceful, cool. Krystal could make out the shapes of things but not their colors. There were two rooms. One had a bed and a motorcycle. The second, a bigger room, had a sofa and chairs on one side and on the other a refrigerator and stove and table.

Krystal sat at the table with Hans in her lap while the woman poured Pepsi from a large bottle into three tumblers full of ice. She had taken her hat off, and the weak light shining from the open door of the refrigerator made a halo around her face and hair. Usually Krystal measured herself against other women, but this one she watched with innocent, almost animal curiosity.

The woman took a smaller bottle off the top of the refrigerator. She wiggled it by the neck. "You wouldn't want any of this," she said. Krystal shook her head. The woman poured some of the liquor into her glass and pushed the other two glasses across the table. Hans took a drink, then started making motorboat noises.

"That boy," the woman said.

"His name is Hans."

"Not this one," the woman said. "The other one."

"Oh, Mark," Krystal said. "Mark is my husband."

The woman nodded and took a drink. She leaned back in her chair. "Where are you people headed?"

Krystal told her about Los Angeles, about Mark finding work in the entertainment field. The woman smiled, and Krystal wondered if she had expressed herself correctly. In school she had done well in English, and the American boys she talked to always complimented her, but during those two months with Mark's parents in Phoenix she had lost her confidence. Dutch and Dottie always looked bewildered when she spoke, and she herself understood almost nothing of what was said around her, though she pretended that she did.

The woman kept smiling, but there was a tightness to her mouth that made the smile look painful somehow. She took another drink.

"What does he do?" she asked.

Krystal tried to think how to explain what Mark did. When she first saw him, he had been sitting on the floor at a party and everyone around him was laughing. She had laughed too, though she didn't know why. It was a gift he had. But it was difficult to put into words. "Mark is a singer," she said.

"A singer," the woman said. She closed her eyes and leaned her head back and began to sing. Hans stopped fidgeting and watched her.

When the woman was through, Krystal said, "Good, good," and nodded, though she hadn't been able to follow the song and hated the style, which sounded to her like yodeling.

"My husband always liked to hear me sing," the woman said. "I suppose I could've been a singer if I'd wanted." She finished her drink and looked at the empty glass.

From outside Krystal heard the voices of the men on the bench, low and steady. One of them laughed.

"We had Del Ray to sing at our prom," the woman said.

The door banged. The man who'd stared at Krystal's belly stomped into the kitchen and stared at her again. He turned and started pulling bottles of Pepsi out of the refrigerator. "Webb, what do you think?" the woman said. "This girl's husband's a singer." She reached out and ran one hand up and down his back. "We'll need something for supper," she said, "unless you want rabbit again."

He kicked the refrigerator door shut with his foot and started out of the kitchen, bottles clinking. Hans slid to the floor and ran after him.

"Hans," Krystal said.

The man stopped and looked down at him. "That's right," he said. "You come with me."

It was the first time Krystal had heard him speak. His voice was thin and dry. He went back outside with Hans behind him.

THE SHOES MARK HAD ON WERE OLD AND LOOSE, comfortable in the car, but his feet started to burn after a few minutes of walking in them. His eyes burned too, from sweat and the bright sun shining into his face.

For a while he sang songs, but after a couple of numbers his throat cracked with dryness and he gave it up. Anyway, it made him feel stupid singing about Camelot in this desert, stupid and a little afraid because his voice sounded so small. He walked on.

The road was sticky underfoot, and his shoes made little sucking noises at every step. He considered walking beside the road instead of on it but he was afraid a snake would bite him.

Though he wanted to stay cheerful, he kept thinking that now they'd never get to Los Angeles in time for dinner. They'd pull in late like they always did, stuff spilling out of the car, Mark humping the whole mess inside while Krystal stood by looking dazed in the glare of the headlights, Hans draped over her shoulder. Mark's buddy would be in his bathrobe. They'd try to joke but Mark would be too preoccupied. After they made up a bed for Krystal and put the crib together for Hans, which would take forever because half the screws were missing, Mark and his buddy would go down to the kitchen, drink a beer, and try to talk, but they'd end up yawning in each other's faces. Then they would go to bed.

Mark could see the whole thing. Whatever they did, it always turned out like this. Nothing ever worked.

A truck went past in the wrong direction. The two men inside were wearing cowboy hats. They glanced at Mark, then looked straight ahead again. He stopped and watched the truck disappear into the heat.

He turned and kept walking. Broken glass glittered along the roadside.

If Mark lived here and happened to be driving down this road and saw some person walking all by himself, he'd stop and ask if anything was wrong. He believed in helping people.

But he didn't need them. He could manage, just as he'd manage without Dutch and Dottie. He would do it alone, and someday they'd wish they had helped. He would be in some place like Las Vegas, performing at one of the big clubs. Then, at the end of his booking, he'd fly Dutch and Dottie out for his last big show—the finale. He'd fly them first class and put them up in the best hotel, the Sands or whatever, and get them front-row seats. And when the show was over, all the people going crazy, whistling and stamping on the floor and everything, he would call Dutch and Dottie up on the stage. He'd stand between them, holding their hands, and then, when all the clapping and yelling trailed off and everybody was quiet, smiling at him from the tables, he would raise Dutch and Dottie's hands above his head and say, "Folks, I just wanted you to meet my parents and tell you what they did for me." Here he'd stop for a second and get this really serious look on his face. "It's impossible to tell you what they did for me," he would say, pausing for effect, "because they didn't do *anything* for me! They didn't do *squat.*" Then he would drop their hands and jump off the stage, leaving them there.

Mark walked faster, leaning forward, eyes narrowed against the light. His hands flicked back and forth as he walked.

No, he wouldn't do that. People might take it wrong. A stunt like that could ruin his career. He'd do something even better. He'd stand up there and tell the whole world that without the encouragement and support the two of them had given him, the faith and love, et cetera, he would've thrown in the towel a long time ago.

And the great part was, *it wouldn't be true!* Because Dutch and Dottie wouldn't do a thing for him unless he stayed in Phoenix and got a "real job," like selling houses. But nobody would know that except Dutch and Dottie. They would stand up on the stage listening to all those lies, and the more he complimented them the more they'd see the kind of parents they could have been but weren't, and the more ashamed they would feel, and the more grateful to Mark for not exposing them.

He could hear a faint rushing sound in the hot air, a sound like applause. He walked faster still. He hardly felt the burning of his feet. The rushing sound grew louder, and Mark looked up. Ahead of him, no more than a hundred yards off, he saw the highway—not the road itself, but a long convoy of trucks moving across the desert, floating westward through a blue haze of exhaust.

THE WOMAN TOLD KRYSTAL that her name was Hope.

"Hope," Krystal said. "How lovely."

They were in the bedroom. Hope was working on the motorcycle. Krystal lay on the bed, propped up with pillows, watching Hope's long fingers move here and there over the machine, then back to the sweating glass at her side. Hans was outside with the men.

Hope took a drink. She swirled the ice around and said, "I don't know, Krystal."

Krystal felt the baby move inside her. She folded her hands across her belly and waited for the bump to come again.

All the lights were off except for a lamp on the floor beside Hope. There were engine parts scattered around her, and the air smelled of oil. She picked up a part and looked at it, then began to wipe it down with a cloth. "I told you we had Del Ray to our prom," she said. "I don't know if you ever heard of Del Ray where you came from, but us girls were flat crazy about him. I had a Del Ray pillow I slept on. Then he showed up and it turned out he was only about yay high." Hope held her hand a few inches above the floor. "Personally," she said, "I wouldn't look twice at a man that couldn't stand up for me if it came to the point. No offense," she added.

Krystal didn't understand what Hope had said, so she smiled.

"You take Webb," Hope said. "Webb would kill for me. He almost did, once. He beat a man that bad."

Krystal understood this. She felt sure it was true. She ran her tongue over her dry lips. "Who?" she asked. "Who did he beat?"

Hope looked up from the part she was cleaning. "My husband."

Krystal waited, uncertain whether she had heard this correctly.

"Webb and me were on a tear," Hope said. "When we weren't together, which was most of the time, we were always checking up on each other. Webb used to drive past my house at all hours and follow me everywhere. Sometimes he'd follow me places with his wife in the car next to him." She laughed. "It was a situation."

The baby was pressing against Krystal's spine. She shifted slightly.

Hope looked up at her. "It's a long story."

"Tell me."

Hope got up and went out to the kitchen. Krystal heard the crack of an ice tray. It was pleasant to lie here in this dark, cool room.

Hope came back and settled on the floor. "Don't get me going," she said. She took a drink. "It happened at the movie theater. We were coming out and Webb saw my husband put his arm around me and just completely lost his senses. I can tell you we did some fancy footwork after that. My husband had six brothers, and two of them in the police. We got out of there and I mean we *got*. Nothing but the clothes we had on. Never gone back since. Never will, either."

"Never," Krystal said. She admired the sound of the word. It was like Beethoven shaking his fist at the heavens.

Hope picked up the rag again. But she didn't do anything with it. She leaned against the wall, out of the little circle of light the lamp made.

"Did you have children?" Krystal asked.

Hope nodded. She held up two fingers.

"It must have been hard, not to see them."

"They'll do all right," Hope said. "They're both boys." She ran her fingers over the floor, found the part she'd been cleaning, and without looking at it began to wipe it down again.

"I couldn't leave Hans," Krystal said.

"Sure you could," Hope said. She sat there with her hands in her lap. Her breathing got deep and slow, and Krystal, peering through the gloom, saw that her eyes were closed. She was asleep, or just dreaming—maybe of that man out there.

The air conditioner went off abruptly. Krystal lay in the dark and listened to the sounds it had covered, the rasping of insects, the low voices of the men. The baby was quiet now. Krystal closed her eyes. She felt herself drifting, and as she drifted she remembered Hans. *Hans,* she thought. Then she slept.

MARK HAD ASSUMED THAT WHEN he reached the highway someone would immediately pick him up. But car after car went by, and the few drivers who looked at him scowled as if they were mad at him for needing a ride and putting them on the spot.

Mark's face burned, and his throat was so dry it hurt to swallow.

Twice he had to leave the road to stand in the shade of a billboard. Cars passed him by for more than an hour, cars from Wisconsin and Utah and Georgia and just about everywhere. Mark felt like the whole country had turned its back on him. The thought came to him that he could die out here.

Finally a car stopped. It was a hearse. Mark hesitated, then ran toward it.

There were three people in the front seat, a man between two women.

The space in the back was full of electrical equipment. Mark pushed some wires aside and sat cross-legged on the floor. The breeze from the air conditioner felt like a stream of cold water running over him.

The driver pulled back onto the road.

"Welcome to the stiffmobile," said the man in the middle. He turned around. His head was shaved except for one bristling stripe of hair down the center. It was the first Mohawk haircut Mark had ever seen on an actual person. The man's eyebrows were the same carroty color as his hair. Freckles covered his entire face and even the shaved parts of his skull.

"Stiffmobile, cliffmobile," said the woman driving. "Riffmobile."

"Bet you thought you'd be riding with a cold one," the man said.

Mark shrugged. "I'd rather ride with a cold one than a hot one."

The man laughed and pounded on the back of the seat.

The women also laughed. The one not driving turned around and smiled at Mark. She had a round, soft-looking face. Her lips were full. She wore a small gold ring in one side of her nose. "Hi," she said.

"Speaking of cold ones," the man said, "there's a case of 'em right behind you."

Mark fished a can of beer out of the cooler and took a long swallow, head back, eyes closed. When he opened his eyes again the man was watching him. They introduced themselves, all but the woman driving. She never looked at Mark or spoke, except to herself. The man with the Mohawk was Barney. The girl with the earring in her nose was Nance. They joked back and forth, and Mark discovered that Nance had a terrific sense of humor. She picked up on almost everything he said. After a while the ring stopped bothering him.

When Barney heard that Mark had been in the army he shook his head. "Pass on that," he said. "No bang-bang for Barney. I can't stand the sight of my own brains."

"Brains," the driver said. "Cranes, lanes, stains."

"Be cool," Barney told her. He turned back to Mark. "So what was it like over there?"

Mark realized that Barney meant Vietnam. Mark had not been to Vietnam. He'd had orders to go, but they got canceled just before he was supposed to ship out and were never reissued, he didn't know why. It was too complicated to explain, so he just said, "Pretty bad," and left it at that.

The mention of Vietnam broke the good feeling between them. They drank their beers and looked at the desert passing by. Then Barney crumpled his can and threw it out the window. Hot air blew into Mark's face. He remembered what it was like out there, and felt glad to be right where he was.

"I could get behind another beer," Nance said.

"Right," Barney said. He turned around and told Mark to pop some more frosties. While Mark was getting the cans out of the cooler Barney watched him, playing his fingers over the top of the seat as if it were a keyboard. "So what's in Blythe?" he said.

"Smythe," the driver said. "Smythe's in Blythe."

"Smooth out," Nance said to her.

"I need a part," Mark said. He handed out the beers. "An alternator. My car's on the fritz."

"Where's your car?" Barney said.

Mark jerked his thumb over his shoulder. "Back there. I don't know the name of the place. It's just this gas station off the highway."

Nance was watching him intently. "Hey," she said. "What if you didn't stop smiling? What if you just kept smiling and never stopped?"

Barney looked at her, then back at Mark. "To me," he said, "there are places you go and places you don't go. You don't go to Rochester. You don't go to Blythe."

"You definitely don't go to Blythe," Nance said.

"Right," Barney said. Then he listed some of the places where, in his opinion, you do go. They were going to one of them now, San Lucas, up in the mountains above Santa Fe. They were part of a film crew shooting a Western there. They'd shot another movie in the same place a year ago, and this was the sequel. Barney was a soundman. Nance did makeup. They didn't say anything about the driver.

"This place is unbelievable," Barney said. He paused and shook his head. Mark was waiting for him to describe San Lucas, but he just shook his head again and said, "It's just completely unbelievable."

"Really," Nance said.

It turned out that the star of the picture was Nita Damon. This was a real coincidence, because Mark had seen Nita Damon about six months ago in a show in Germany, a Bob Hope visit-with-the-troops kind of thing.

"That's amazing," Nance said. She and Barney looked at each other.

"You should scratch Blythe," Barney said.

Mark grinned.

Nance was staring at him. "*Marco*," she said. "You're not a Mark, you're a Marco."

"You should sign on with us," Barney said. "Ride the stiffmobile express."

"You should," Nance said. "San Lucas is just incredible."

"Partyville," Barney said.

"Jesus," Mark said. "No. I couldn't."

"Sure you could," Barney said. "Lincoln freed the slaves, didn't he? Get your car later."

Mark was laughing. "Come on," he said. "What would I do up there?"

Barney said, "You mean like work?"

Mark nodded.

"No problem," Barney said. He told Mark that there was always something to do. People didn't show up, people quit, people got sick—there was always a call out for warm bodies. Once you found a tasty spot, you just settled in.

"You mean I'd be working on the movie? On the film crew?"

"Absitively," Barney said. "I guarantee."

"Jesus," Mark said. He looked at Barney, then at Nance. "I don't know," he said.

"That's all right," Barney said. "I know."

"Barney knows," Nance said.

"What have you got to lose?" Barney said.

Mark didn't say anything.

Barney watched him. "Marco," he said. "Don't tell me—you've got a little something else back there besides the car, right?" When Mark didn't answer, he laughed. "That was then," he said. "The old days. Gone with the wind."

"I have to think," Mark said.

"Okay, think," Barney said. "You've got till Blythe." He turned around. "Don't disappoint me."

Nance gave him a long, serious look. Then she turned around too. The top of her head was just visible over the high seat back.

The desert went past the window, always the same. The road had an oily look. Mark felt rushed, a little wild.

His first idea was to get the directions to San Lucas, then drive up with Krystal and Hans after the car was fixed. But then he wouldn't have enough money left for the gas, let alone food and motels and a place to live once they got there. He'd miss his chance.

Because that's what this was—a chance.

There was no point in fooling himself. He could go to Los Angeles and walk the streets for months, maybe years, without ever getting anywhere. He could stand outside closed doors and suck up to nobodies and sit in plastic chairs half his life without ever coming close to where he was right now, on his way to a guaranteed job in Partyville.

Los Angeles wasn't going to work. Mark could see that. He'd borrow money from his friend and start hustling and he wouldn't get the time of day from anyone, because he was hungry and nobody ever had time for hungry people. Hungry people got written off. It was like Dutch said—them that has, gets.

He'd run himself ragged and his money would disappear, the way all his other money had disappeared. Krystal would get worried and sad. After a couple of weeks Mark and his buddy wouldn't have anything to say to each other, and his buddy would grow tired of living with a guy he didn't really know that well and a yelling kid and a sad, pregnant woman. He'd tell Mark some lie to get rid of them—his girl was moving in, his parents had decided to stay together after all. By then Mark would be broke again. Krystal would have a fit and probably go into labor.

And when that happened? What then?

Mark knew what. Crawl home to Dutch and Dottie.

No. No sir. The only way he was going back to Phoenix was in a coffin.

The driver started talking to herself, and Barney rapped her on top of the head with his knuckles. "Do you want me to drive?" he said. It sounded like a threat. She quieted down. "All right," he said. Without looking back he said, "Five miles to Blythe."

Mark looked out the window. He couldn't get it out of his mind that here he had exactly what he needed. A chance to show what he was made of. He'd have fun, sure, but he'd also be at work on time in the morning. He would do what he was told and do it right. He would keep his eyes open and his mouth shut, and after a while people would notice him. He wouldn't push too hard, but now and then he might do a song at one of the parties, or impersonate some of the actors. He could just hear Nita Damon laughing and saying, *Stop it, Mark! Stop it!*

What he could do, Mark thought, was to call Krystal and arrange to meet up with her at his buddy's house in a month or two, after they'd shot the film. Mark would have something going then. He'd be on his way. But that wouldn't work either. He didn't know how to call her. She had no money. And she wouldn't agree.

Mark wasn't going to fool himself. If he left Krystal and Hans back there, she would never forgive him. If he left them, he'd be leaving them for good.

I can't do that, he thought. But he knew this wasn't true. He could leave them. People left each other, and got left, every day. It was a terrible thing. But it happened and people survived as they survived even worse things. Krystal and Hans would survive, too. When she understood what had happened she would call Dutch, who'd hit the roof, of course, and then, in the end, come through for them. He didn't have any choice. And in four or five years what happened today would be no more than a bad memory.

Krystal would do well for herself. Men liked her. Even Dutch liked her, though he'd been dead set against the marriage. Someday, sooner than later, she'd meet a good man who could take care of her. She and Hans and the new baby would be able to go to sleep at night without wondering what would happen to them when they woke up. They didn't need Mark. Without him they would have a better life than if he and Krystal had stayed together.

This was a new thought for Mark, and it made him feel a little aggrieved to see how unimportant he really was to Krystal. Before now he had always assumed that their coming together had been ordained, and that in marrying Krystal he had fulfilled some need of the universe. But if they could live without each other, and do even better without each other, then this wasn't true and had never been true.

They did not need each other. There was no particular reason for them to be together. So what was this all about? If he couldn't make her happy, what was the point? They were dragging each other down like two people who couldn't swim. If they were lucky, they might keep at it long enough to grow old in the same house.

It wasn't right. She deserved better, and so did he.

Mark felt that he had been deceived. Not by Krystal, she would never do that, but by everyone who had ever been married and knew the truth about it and never let on. The truth was, when you got married you had to give up one thing after another. It never ended. You had to give up your life—the special one you'd been meant to have—and stumble along where neither of you had ever thought of going or wanted to go. And you never knew what was really happening. You gave up your life and didn't even know it.

"Blythe," Barney said.

Mark looked at the town, what he could see of it from the road. Lines of heat quivered above the rooftops.

"Blythe," Barney said again. "Going, going, gone."

KRYSTAL WOKE AND BOLTED UPRIGHT, blinking in the gloom. "Hans," she whispered.

"He's outside," Hope said. She was standing over the lamp, feeding shells into a shotgun. Her shadow swayed back and forth against the wall. "I'm going to get us some dinner," she said. "You just lie here and rest up. The boy will be fine." She finished loading the gun and pushed a few more shells into the pockets of her jeans.

Krystal lay on the bed, restless and thirsty but feeling too heavy to rise. The men had a radio on. A whiny song was playing, like the one Hope had sung in the kitchen. Krystal had not heard any good music for months now, since the day she left home. A warm day in early spring—sunlight flickering through the trees along the road. Trees. Streams swollen with snowmelt.

"Ah, God," Krystal said.

She pushed herself up and lifted the window shade and looked out at the desert, the mountains. And there was Hope, walking into the desert with her shotgun. The light was softer than before, still white but not so sharp. The tops of the mountains were touched with pink.

Krystal stared out the window. How could anyone live in such a place? There was nothing, nothing at all. Through all those days in Phoenix, Krystal had felt a great emptiness around her where she would count for no more than a rock or a spiny tree; now she was in the middle of it. She thought she might cry, but gave the idea up. It didn't interest her.

She closed her eyes and leaned her forehead against the glass.

I will say a poem, Krystal thought, *and when I am finished he will be here.* At first silently, because she had been trying to speak only English, then in a whisper, she recited a poem of Heine's the nuns had made her learn so long ago at school, the only poem she remembered. She repeated it, then opened her eyes. Mark was not there. As if she had really believed he would be there, Krystal kicked the wall with her bare foot. The pain made clear what she had been pretending not to know: that he had never really been there and never would be there in any way that mattered.

The window was warm against Krystal's forehead. She watched Hope move farther and farther away, then stop and raise her gun. A moment later Krystal heard the boom, and felt the glass shudder against her skin.

MARK WAS SORE FROM SITTING CROSS-LEGGED on the bare floorboards. He stretched out his legs and listened to the driver talk to herself, straining to get the point of the things she said. There was sometimes rhyme but never any reason to her words. Every possibility of meaning trailed off into nonsense.

The hearse was moving at great speed, really racing. The driver passed every car they came upon. She changed lanes without purpose. Mark tried to find a break between her words to say something, just a note of caution, something about how tough the police were around here. The car was going faster and faster. He hoped that Barney would tell her to shut up and slow down, maybe even take over himself for a while, but he wasn't saying anything and neither was Nance. She had disappeared completely and all Mark could see of Barney were the bristles of his hair.

"Hey," Mark said. "What's the hurry?"

The driver seemed not to hear him. She passed another car and went on yakking to herself. She was gripping the steering wheel so tightly that her knuckles had turned white.

"Better slow down," Mark said.

"Butter sold owl," she said.

Mark leaned over the top of the seat to check out the speedometer, and Nance looked up from what she was doing to Barney down there. Her eyes met Mark's, and she held his gaze as she kept at it, languorously, luxuriously. Mark rocked back on his heels as if he'd been struck. "Stop the car," he said.

"Star the cop," the driver said. "Stop the war."

"Stop the car," Mark said again.

"Hey," Barney said. "What's the problem?" His voice was sleepy, remote.

"I want out," Mark said.

"No, you don't," Barney said. "You already decided, remember? Just be Marco." Mark heard Nance whispering. Then Barney said, "Hey—Marco. Come on up here. You're with us now."

"Stop the car," Mark said. He reached over the seat and began to rap on the driver's head, softly at first, then hard. He could hear the knocking of his knuckles against her skull. She came to a squealing stop right in the road. Mark looked back. There was a car bearing down on them. It swerved into the other lane and went past with its horn wailing.

"Okay, *Mark,*" Barney said. "Ciao. You blew it."

Mark scrambled over equipment and cords and let himself out the back. When he closed the tailgate the driver pulled away, fast. Mark crossed the road and watched the hearse until it disappeared. The road was empty. He turned and walked back toward Blythe.

A few minutes later an old man stopped for him. He took a liking to Mark and drove him directly to the parts store. They were just closing up, but after Mark explained his situation the boss let him inside and found the alternator for him. With tax, the price came to seventy-one dollars.

"I thought it was fifty-six," Mark said.

"Seventy-one," the man said.

Mark stared at the alternator. "I've only got sixty-five."

"I'm sorry," the man said. He put his hands on the counter and waited.

"Look," Mark said, "I just got back from Vietnam. Me and my wife are on our way to Los Angeles. Once we get there I can send you the rest. I'll put it in the mail tomorrow morning, I swear."

The man looked at him.

Mark could see that he was hesitating. "I've got a job waiting."

"What kind of job?"

"I'm a soundman," Mark said.

"Soundman. I'm sorry," he said. "I know you think you'll send the money."

Mark argued for a while but without heat, because he knew that the man was right; he wouldn't send the money. He gave up and went back outside. The parts store adjoined a salvage yard filled with crumpled cars. Down the street was a gas station and a U-Haul depot. As Mark walked toward the gas station a black dog appeared on the other side of the salvage-yard fence and kept pace with him, silently baring his fangs whenever Mark glanced in his direction.

He was hot and tired. He could smell himself. He remembered the coolness of the hearse and thought, *I blew it.*

There was a pay phone outside the gas station. Mark got a handful of change and shut himself in. He wanted to call his buddy in Los Angeles and figure something out, but he'd left the address book in the car and it turned out that the number was unlisted. He tried explaining things to the operator but she refused to listen. Finally she hung up on him.

He looked across the shimmering asphalt toward the salvage yard. The dog was still at the fence, watching him. The only thing he could do, Mark decided, was to keep calling Los Angeles information until he got a human being on the other end. There had to be somebody sympathetic out there.

But first he was going to call Phoenix and give Dutch and Dottie a little something to sleep on. He would put on his official voice and tell them that he was Sergeant Smith—no, *Smythe,* Sergeant Smythe of the highway patrol, calling to report an accident. A head-on collision just outside of Palm Springs. It was his duty, he was sorry to say—here his voice would crack—that there were no survivors. No, ma'am, not one. Yes, ma'am, he was sure. He'd been at the scene. The one good thing he could tell her was that nobody had suffered. It was over just like *that,* and here Mark would snap his fingers into the receiver.

He closed his eyes and listened to the phone ring through the cool, quiet house. He saw Dottie where she sat in her avocado kitchen, drinking coffee and making a list, saw her rise and gather her cigarettes and lighter and ashtray. He heard her shoes tapping on the tile floor as she came toward the phone.

But it was Dutch who answered. "Strick here," he said.

Mark took a breath.

"Hello," Dutch said.

"It's me," Mark said. "Dad, it's me—Mark."

KRYSTAL WAS WASHING HER FACE when she heard the gun go off again. She paused, water running through her fingers, then finished up and left the bedroom. She wanted to find Hans. He should have been changed long before now, and it was almost time for him to eat. She missed him.

Stepping carefully through the parts on the floor, she went into the main room. It was almost completely dark. Krystal turned the overhead light on and stood there with her hand against the wall.

Everything was red. The carpet was red. The chairs and the couch were red. The lamp shades were red and had little red tassels hanging down from them. The pillows on the couch were shaped like hearts and covered in a satiny material that looked wet under the light, so that for a moment they had the appearance of real organs.

Krystal stared at the room. In a novel she had once come upon the expression "love nest," and had thought of light-washed walls, tall pines reaching to the balcony outside. But this, she thought, looking at the room, this was a love nest. It was horrible, horrible.

Krystal moved over to the door and opened it a crack. Someone was lying on the front seat of the car, his bare feet sticking out the window, his boots on the ground below with yellow socks hanging from the tops. She could not see the men on the bench but one of them was saying something, the same word again and again. Krystal couldn't make it out.

Then she heard Hans repeat the word, and the men laughed.

She opened the door wider. Still standing inside, she said, "Hans, come here." She waited. She heard someone whisper. "Hans," she said.

He came to the door. There was dirt all over his face but he looked happy. "Come in," she said.

Hans looked over his shoulder, then back at Krystal.

"Come, Hans," she said.

He stood there. "Bitch," he said.

Krystal took a step backward. "No," she said. "No, no, no. Don't say that. Come, sweet boy." She held out her arms.

"Bitch," he said again.

"Oh!" Krystal said. She pushed the door open and walked up to Hans and slapped him across the face. She slapped him hard. He sat down and looked up at her. She had never done that before. Krystal took a flat board from the pile of scrap near the door. The three men on the bench were watching her from under their hats. "Who did that?" she said. "Who taught him that word?" When they didn't answer she started toward the bench, reviling them in German. They stood and backed away from her. Hans began to cry. Krystal turned on him. "Be quiet!" she said. He whimpered once and was still.

Krystal turned back to the men. "Who taught him that word?"

"It wasn't me," Webb said.

The other men just stood there.

"Shame," Krystal said. She looked at them, then walked over to the car. She kicked the boots aside. Holding the board with both hands, she swung it as hard as she could across the bare feet sticking out of the window. The man inside screamed.

"Get out," Krystal said. "Out, out, out!"

He scrambled out the other door and squinted at her over the top of the car. Without his big hat he looked like a grumpy baby, face all red and puffy. She hefted the board and he started dancing over the hot sand toward the building, his hair flapping up and down like a wing. He stopped in the shade and looked back, still shifting from foot to foot. He kept his eyes on Krystal. So did Hans, sitting by the door. So did the men near the bench. They were all watching to see what she would do next.

So, Krystal thought. She flung the board away, and one of the men flinched. Krystal almost laughed. *How angry I must look,* she thought, *how angry I am,* and then her anger left her. She tried to keep it, but it was gone the moment she knew it was there.

She shaded her eyes and looked around her. The distant mountains cast long shadows into the desert. The desert was empty and still. Nothing moved but Hope, walking toward them with the gun slung at her back, barrel poking over her shoulder. As she drew near, Krystal waved, and Hope raised her arms. A rabbit hung from each hand, swinging by its ears.

Tobias Wolff was born in 1945 in Birmingham, Alabama. After serving in the U.S. Army, he graduated from Oxford University, worked as a reporter for the Washington Post, *and was a Wallace Stegner Fellow in Creative Writing at Stanford University. His books include the short story collection* In the Garden of the North American Martyrs *(Ecco Press, 1981),* The Barracks Thief *(Ecco Press, 1984),* This Boy's Life: A Memoir *(Harper, 1989),* Old School *(Alfred A. Knopf, 2003), and* Our Story Begins: New and Selected Stories *(Alfred A. Knopf, 2008). He has taught at Arizona State and Syracuse universities and is currently a professor of English at Stanford University.*

Virginia Hamilton Adair

From *Ants on the Melon*
MOJAVE EVENING

Sundown when the wind turns off
we walk over tessellated sand
to Johnstones' ranch.
They have a well.
They shut the dog indoors
and hose-fill old pans
to water the wild things.
On the cooling earth we sit back
so silent the dreams come.
Is this a conference of shadows
father coyote and his family
around the water pans?
And not far enough to mean fear
only decorum
the periscope ears of three
no five rabbits. Waiting.
A narrow moon steals up.
All shadows are brothers.
Now when the tall ears
bob toward the water circle
we know the coyotes are off
into silver spaces
their eyes coming out to hunt
with the other stars.

Virginia Hamilton Adair was born in the Bronx in 1913 and grew up in Montclair, New Jersey. In 1920 she graduated from Mount Holyoke College in Massachusetts—where she twice won college poetry prizes—and then earned an M.A. from Radcliffe College. In 1936 she married historian Douglas Adair II; they had three children. The family moved to Claremont, California, in 1955; from 1957 to 1980 Adair taught classes in poetry at nearby Cal Poly, Pomona. During this time Adair wrote poetry almost daily, even after losing her sight in her eighties. Her first collection, Ants on the Melon, was published in 1996, when she was eighty-three, and it earned considerable acclaim; the book was followed by Beliefs and Blasphemies (Random House) in 1998 and Living on Fire (Random House) in 2000. Adair died in 2004.

Tom McNeal

WINTER IN LOS ANGELES

LREADY MARCY HAS A BAD FEELING about what she has
done and what she's about to do. She is awake, but pretending
not to be, when Randall rises an hour before dawn. It's autumn
in Nebraska, already cold. Randall's getting ready to go hunting, and for
once in his life he's being quiet about it. He sounds almost like a prowler, in
fact—the slow, cautious way he moves through the dark trailer-home, setting out his coat and gear, wrapping up sandwiches, feeling in the closet for
a gun. When he steps outside, he sets the front door softly to behind him.
There is a clinking sound as he eases open the metal kennel gate, and the
tinkling of collars as the dogs cross the yard and bound into the truck. The
truck door opens and closes, the engine starts and idles.

Marcy lies in bed and listens as the truck door opens again, and then
the front door to their trailer. Randall moves slowly along the dark, narrow hallway toward their bedroom—under his boots, the trailer trembles
slightly on its piers—then stops at the open door. Marcy is turned from
him, but she can feel him there staring in. Finally he comes near and touches his hand to her neck. She doesn't move. When he speaks, his voice is gen-
tler than usual. "Guess you know I'm sorry I hit you," he says. "I lay there
in bed all night trying to figure out how I could've done that." A moment
passes. "Marcy?"

She still doesn't move.

His voice is low and serious. "Well, I just want to say that I love you, no
matter what. Even if I wanted to, that's something I couldn't ever change."

Marcy opens the one good eye and turns over in bed without speaking.
They try to see each other in the darkness, but she can only guess at what is
in his face. It is a little while in fact before she can see that he's brought one

of his long guns into the room with him. "What's that for?" she says. Her voice is sleepier, softer than she wants it.

"It's the wrong gun. I'm putting it back for something else." He forces a little laugh. "Shoulda turned on the light, I guess." She doesn't say anything. With three fingers she's carefully exploring the edges of the bad eye. He says, "If you want, Marcy, I won't go. I'll call Leo and tell him…." This is a sticking point for Randall—lying is something he prides himself in not doing. "I'll tell him we both feel punk and I need to lay low."

"No," Marcy says, "it's nice to offer, but it wouldn't help that much."

"Truth is, I'd rather stay," he says and stands waiting. The silence lengthens. In the darkness his face seems like a sad, ghostly mask of his face. At last he says, "Okay then, Marcy, Sugar. I'm going now."

He does. He goes, Randall and his dogs.

After he leaves, Marcy dresses and moves in a daze back and forth from the trailer to the car, not thinking, just taking what she can and piling it into the trunk and back seat. She keeps at it until the sky begins to lighten. Not too far off, a tractor cranks and starts. From somewhere the metallic sound of pigs rooting a creep feeder carries in the still cold air. Across the street, in another trailer, a light goes on. Marcy puts on her dark glasses. She doesn't write a note. She doesn't consider what more she ought to take. She gets into the old Mercury Cougar and slowly drives away from her home and hometown, her parents and her husband.

She drives east out of Goodnight, through Rushville and Gordon, toward Valentine, where, beyond her range of acquaintances, she will swing south, and then, when she hits I-80, turn the Mercury west, toward California.

Once she settles into the drive, a low-grade melancholy overtakes her. Old sights put her in mind of Randall, and old songs, so while she drives she listens instead to call-in shows, people with terrible sounding lives talking to announcers who in Marcy's opinion believe they have all the answers even though they pretend not to. Every now and then Marcy glances at the radio and says, "Well, that's one theory." Her favorite thing to say to a caller is "Join the club, Lady." But, once, when a woman doctor leaves a caller speechless by saying, "Look, Elaine, desires affect decisions and decisions have consequences and you have to take responsibility for those consequences," Marcy, on I-80 out of Cheyenne, can see nothing but the caved-in look of Randall's face when he comes home and finds her gone. What would he do? What in the world would he do? He would swallow it whole, she knew that. He would tell no one. Would answer not one question from one friend. He would swallow it whole and bear it alone. He would become one of those thin still men with gray eyes and stubbled beards and stained coats whose insides are not right, whose sadness makes a perfect nesting place for cancers.

It takes two days, driving like this, to make the desert. Late at night, she crests the Cajon pass and drops into the San Bernardino Valley, a vast blackness dotted with what seems like a million million shimmering lights. Marcy, in that jangly state of hope that sometimes comes from travel alone across wide-open spaces, sees each dot not as a light but as a person, a single person, suddenly come to life and made bright and brand-new. That is one moment. In the next, she wishes more than anything that Randall were here, too, so they could both start new.

ON HER FIRST MORNING IN LA, Marcy drives along Sunset Boulevard, past places she's only heard of—Frederick's, Grauman's, The Roxy, The Whiskey. To her surprise, there are frightening people everywhere. When a muscular man in black leather pants, no shirt, and lemon yellow hair glances at her license plate, steps out of the crosswalk and, leaning into her window, drawls, "Miss Nebraska, I'd like you to meet Mr. Peanut," Marcy winds up the window and doesn't lower it again until the street turns residential.

Farther on, in a normal-seeming commercial section of town, Marcy goes into the first realty she likes the looks of. It's a big, oddly formal office with thick gray carpet and, on each of the many white desks, a small vase of bright flowers that Marcy's never seen in Nebraska. She asks about rentals and gets passed around. The men in the office wear blazers and ties. The women go for skirt suits, a nice look, Marcy thinks, though it's hard to tell exactly because she doesn't want to take off her dark glasses.

One man in the office seems to change the way everyone else acts. He is a stiff, frail-seeming man in wire-rimmed spectacles, white shirt, and bur-gundy bow tie—the man, Marcy realizes, who is the source of the office's formality. A trim secretary follows behind as he goes through the office desk to desk, chatting briefly with different agents. Each stiffens slightly at his approach. "A rental, sir," the agent helping Marcy tells the man, and they pass on, the frail man, his secretary, and her perfume.

"Whew!" Marcy says in a low voice of the perfume, and in the same low voice the agent, still clacking away at his computer, says, "It's not that Mr. Realty likes it potent. It's that Mr. Realty's got no sense of smell."

Marcy laughs. In a funny, happy way, this is what, without ever having put a finger on it, she had wanted from Los Angeles. This fancy office. The muttering help. The frail, feared executive. Marcy keeps her eye on him. He's talking on the telephone while filling his briefcase with papers. When he looks her way, Marcy does something that surprises her. She tilts her head and combs her fingers through her long hair, a method of flirtation she developed in high school but which, here and now, seems suddenly klutzy. The man snaps closed his briefcase, hands the phone to his secre-tary, moves through the office in stiff strides, past Marcy and her agent. But he stops, turns back.

"Look, Miss," he says, "I know of a place that's not listed, a nicely old-fashioned studio. May I ask if you smoke?"

Marcy, looking up at him, knows this is the moment when anyone with an ounce of politeness would take off her sunglasses, but she doesn't. "No," she says.

"Pets?"

"Nope."

"Drugs?"

Marcy stifles a laugh. "Hardly."

The man asks a few more questions. His glasses are coke-bottle thick and, behind them, his eyes are hard to read. Quiet? he asks. Responsible? Employed, or soon will be? Marcy smiles and says yes to each.

For a moment she can almost hear him thinking her over. "Okay," he says, "why don't I just run you up there and show you the place."

The car they drive away in is white, enormous, and deeply quiet. "This is like driving in a new refrigerator," Marcy says, going for a joke, but the man merely responds by turning down the air conditioning. "Two stops to make," he says, almost to himself. With one hand he unsnaps the briefcase lying on the leather seat between them and brings out a roll of chocolate toffees. Before partaking himself, he offers one to Marcy, who wants to accept, but doesn't.

The first stop is at a place called Prestige Motors on Melrose Avenue. The man leaves Marcy in the car while he goes inside, where the salesmen treat him a lot like the people in the real estate office had. They smooth their clothes and work their faces into smiles. It's funny to watch. Also funny to watch is the way the man walks. He is so stiff that Marcy imagines that someone has just wound him up and pointed him her way. When he gets back in, she says, "That where you bought this car?"

He stares at the car agency. "This car is a little newer than those."

The man accelerates the car smoothly into traffic, and Marcy says, "You left me and your keys in the car."

He says nothing, makes a lane change, turns up a narrowing canyon road.

"I could've stolen this big, fancy, newer car of yours."

"It's part of my tenant screening process." A tiny smile seems to form on his lips. "You irrefutably passed." For the first time, Marcy senses something playful in the man's formality. And he has the right voice for it. Besides his brains and expensive clothes, it's the voice, Marcy decides, that's gotten this man up in the world. It is a clear, pure voice that goes into your ear in a ticklish way. Marcy gives him another look. Forty to forty-two, she decides. Marcy has just turned twenty-three.

Their second stop is at the man's home, perched on a cliff out among tall, slender, smooth-barked trees. Marcy waits in the car. As the realtor approaches his house, a male gardener very slightly picks up the pace of his clipping, but a woman in gardening clothes merely pushes back her dark red hair with the back of a hand and says something before she resumes puttering with the potted flowers along the walk. Marcy picks up the tube of toffees. *Callard & Bowser*, it says on the foiled outer wrap, *Made in Great Britain*. Inside, each toffee is neatly wrapped in wax paper. She slips one into her mouth, fiddles with the radio, then the car windows. They slide quietly down, and the car fills up with a pleasant menthol smell from the outside air. She asks about it when the man returns.

"Eucalyptus." He points to the tall trees.

The man drives slowly, the road spiraling upward. He starts to set the toffees back into his briefcase, but pauses to hold the roll out to Marcy. "Another?" he says, and she says, "Nope, one was fine."

A turn in the road affords a sudden, sweeping view of the city. The car slows just a little. "That's the way it used to be," he says. "You could see Catalina Island almost every day. It was a wide-open world then." He looks off into the haze. "One day, when I was ten or eleven, I walked into the Sav-On drugstore at Ventura and Laurel Canyon and found myself standing at the candy counter not far from a man who seemed dimly familiar. I was nearsighted even then, so without much awareness I was even doing it, I began edging closer and closer to this man, squinting up at him until I was so close I could smell his heavy tobacco smell. At the exact moment that I realized that he was in fact Bela Lugosi, he curled his lip and issued a hissing sound that scared the pea-wadding out of me." A small, self-mocking chuckle slips from the realtor. "I hastily retired. But as I was climbing onto my bicycle, a clerk caught up to me with a box of Callard & Bowser Toffee. There was also a note, which I still possess, that said, 'With this gift Mr. Bela Lugosi wishes to commemorate the pleasant occasion of your acquaintance.'"

The realtor glances at Marcy. "This reminds me that we haven't been formally introduced." He keeps his left hand on the wheel, short-arms his right toward her. "I'm Harmon Martin."

That was what the sign had said in front of the realty: *Harmon Martin's Mr. Realty.* Marcy decides to slip a small one by him. "Marcy Marlene Lockhardt," she says, "but everybody calls me Lena." Lockhardt is her maiden name and nobody in her lifetime has called her Lena.

Harmon Martin releases her hand. "Lena then," he says. More tall eucalyptus trees pass by, more snug bungalows. "So where are you from, Lena?"

Marcy considers lying about this, too, but worries that the man might've seen the plate on her Mercury. "Nebraska." She expects him maybe to ask what part of Nebraska, but he doesn't.

"I've been a lot of places," the man says, "but I've never been to Nebraska. In fact, I think of Nebraska as a kind of English-speaking foreign country. All that *swaggering* and *roping and branding.*"

"They don't brand so much anymore," Marcy says. "Mostly they just tag their ears."

"Darn," Harmon Martin says softly. "No more hiss and sizzle."

"Not so much anyway," Marcy says.

They fall silent. Marcy leans out the window, stares up at the slender, smooth white trees, takes into her lungs this new, mentholated air.

After a while she says to the man, "Your wife's pretty."

He looks at her in surprise. "Yes, she is." Then, "How did you know she was my wife and not, let us say, a fetching Hollywood Hills gardener?"

Because she wasn't like all the others. She treated Harmon Martin like just another human being. "I could just tell," Marcy says, and as they drive along a fact presents itself like a utensil she has no use for, namely that if a woman wanted to get to Harmon Martin, the way to do it was to force him to imagine everything, and allow him to touch nothing.

MARCY LOVES THE STUDIO. It has hardwood floors, white walls and, beyond the parted French doors, an enamelled deck with solid siding. "For total privacy," Harmon Martin says in an abstracted voice, as if he's saying one thing and thinking another. She asks about rent, is shocked at how high the figure is. "You're kidding," she says.

"I know. It's a very good deal. The owner could get quite a lot more, but won't advertise. She's afraid of the riffraff." He gazes down the canyon toward the freeway. "You'll get a nice view at night."

She stares out.

"This a Los Angeles address or Hollywood or what?"

"You're in the city of LA, but the mailing address is Hollywood." He glances at her. "Have you by any chance heard of Tom Hulce?"

"*Amadeus.*"

Harmon Martin seems pleased. "Yes. A good young actor, I'd say. He lived here nearly two years, until his salaries grew. He has a reputation, but he left the place neat as a pin."

Marcy knows she shouldn't take the apartment, but says she will. She takes out her folded cash, counts out the first two months' rent, and presents it to Harmon Martin, who, moving close as if to take it, instead reaches forward and gently slides off Marcy's sunglasses. In the change in his face, she sees what he sees: a swollen eye almost the color of eggplant with a yellowish subsurface. He slides the glasses back and steps away. "Who's the party responsible for this?"

Marcy answers quickly, as if there is only one answer. "A guy." She looks away. "My husband actually."

Harmon Martin makes a smile so small that Marcy wonders if she imagines it. "This isn't, I hope, an accepted form of husbandry out there in the hinterlands."

"No," Marcy says, pinkening a little, she isn't sure why. She also isn't sure what Harmon Martin is up to. He still hasn't taken the money.

"So is this imbecile husband going to be a problem?" he asks.

Marcy feels funny, letting this man call Randall an imbecile, which Randall is not, but she shakes her head certainly. "No," she says, "no problem whatsoever."

MARCY'S NEW NEIGHBORHOOD, a curving line of smooth-plaster cottages nestled into the hillside, is as different from Nebraska as different could be. She has painted the mailbox blue and nearly finished stencilling *L. Lockhardt* in yellow when a dog arrives, a small, bowlegged Doberman mix with a frisbee in his mouth. He drops it at her feet and looks up expectantly. She throws it, it wobbles off, the dog retrieves it. They do this several times. The dog's focus on the frisbee is absolute. Marcy can make him shake or nod his head by either waving the frisbee side to side or up and down. She kneels down, holds the frisbee overhead, and in a low voice says, "Will I find a job in television?"

The dog nods a slow yes.

"Will Randall find me?"

No.

"Will I find someone?"

An even more definite yes. Marcy laughs.

"Am I the fairest in the land?"

Yes.

Marcy laughs and tosses the frisbee a few more times, until it gets too slobbery to throw. The dog takes no offense. He merely picks up his toy and trots away, looking surprisingly businesslike. He knows what he wants and how to get it. He visits strangers, drops this plastic disc at their feet, and gives them the chance to make him happy. It seems so simple.

A FEW DAYS LATER, Marcy sits in the sun on the private deck hugging her knees. She's come to LA with the idea of working in television, but the truth is, except for a friend's cousin who is an assistant director on *The New Price is Right*, and who, it turns out, left yesterday for Berlin, Marcy knows no one in LA. She thumbs through a *Variety* with her right eye closed. Something is still wrong with that eye. The shiner has healed, but the eye floats, feels unhinged. It weeps and blurs her vision.

She puts down the paper and doesn't know how many minutes have gone by when she realizes that, in this space of time, however long it's been, all she's done is look at her feet. There is so much *time* here. In Goodnight, there were tons of ways to keep yourself busy, but here it is like a vacation, except with all the fun drained away because there's no stop to it.

Somewhere a dog barks, but not the frisbee dog—she knows his bark by now. It is seventy-nine degrees, mid-November. Marcy lies back on her towel, closes her eyes, and tilts her face to meet the angle of the sun. What she wants is something in the television or movie business, not in acting or anything big. Just something that helps keep things going day to day.

She tells Harmon Martin this the next time he telephones, which he does fairly often. Just checking in on the newest leaseholder, he will say dryly. "Sure you wouldn't like to shoot a little higher?" he says today.

"Naw. I like to shoot at things I have a chance of hitting."

Harmon Martin makes a little humming sound, then says he'll do some asking around, see what he can turn up.

THANKSGIVING DAY, MARCY CALLS HOME and is swarmed over by questions. "Where are you?" her mother asks. "Are you okay? Do you have enough money? What're you doing? Are you coming home?"

"Not for a while yet," Marcy says, "but I'm fine, Mom. I am."

"But where—"

"Someplace warmer," Marcy says. "Has he been asking, do you know?"

"Not that I know of. His friend Leo was asking around for a while, but I don't know if that was on his own or for Randall."

Marcy doesn't know what to say. "Is Dad okay then?" she asks finally.

"He'll be better now, knowing you're okay. Provided you are."

"I am, Mom. I really am."

After a little silence, her mother says, "We heard he hit you."

Marcy doesn't say anything.

"Why would he want to do that?"

"He had it in his head that I was running around, Mom."

"But you weren't."

"Nope. But I couldn't convince him, he had it so much in his head."

This much is true, but the larger truth is that Marcy had concluded she'd married the wrong man. She didn't want to spend her life with an ingrown man who wouldn't be happy until she was ingrown, too. Marcy wanted out. And she needed Randall to give her a good enough reason to go, so she invented and told him a story instinctively shaped to organize his anger. At the moment Randall struck her, he was more surprised than she was. Marcy knows this. And for this entrapment of Randall's pitiful worst self, Marcy is beginning to believe, she can never be forgiven.

Marcy in a soft voice says, "So do you think Randall's doing okay?"

"I wouldn't know. He doesn't call and he hardly speaks when spoken to. He still goes to work, I guess, but he stays mostly now in Scotts Bluff. People say he's hardly been at the trailer. It's a mess, they say."

A silence, then Marcy says, "I'll call soon, okay? I love you, and tell Dad I love him, too."

Later that day, Marcy cooks herself Thanksgiving dinner for one—a Cornish game hen, fresh peas, and a yam—then sits looking at it. She takes a few bites, wraps the rest in foil for the dog, and goes outside, but he's no-where to be found. She climbs a winding set of public stairs to the top of a knoll where a public lawn is maintained, and where the dog lies sleeping. He stretches, wags his nubby tail. "Happy Thanksgiving," Marcy says as he greedily bolts the food. Marcy is gazing down at the city when—a slight shock—she realizes that from here there is a narrow line of downward sight to Harmon Martin's house. She stands looking into the brightly lighted kitchen where guests are milling. She can pick out Harmon Martin from among the men—he is mixing drinks, measuring things very carefully—but she can't be certain which of the women is his wife. From a distance, all of them look elegant, handsome, and happy.

HARMON MARTIN HAS LINED UP THREE job interviews for Marcy, all on the same day. "Trial by fire," he says. "But my advice is not to commit to anything. Say you have another offer pending, that you will tell them something definite within seventy-two hours."

"Three days."

"But you might say hours." His little smile. "In order to create the im-pression that your time units are small, compressed, and important."

The interviews are a nightmare. Marcy wears a simple beige-and-black dress that she hoped would seem elegant, but, she realizes, is made to be overlooked in. The men who interview her wear more color than she does. They ask questions like, What unique talents can you bring to this job? Marcy sweats, stammers, and introduces to the room the kind of awkward-ness that infects others. At the final interview, the man breaks a long, hor-rible silence by picking up her application and reading through it. "What's KDUH?" he says finally.

"It's Channel 4 in northwest Nebraska." She daubs at her eye to keep the liquid in its pink sag from spilling down her cheek. "For about six months I read the weekend news."

"What's the ENG capacity there?" the man says and then, when he sees her confusion, says, "The electronic newsgathering capacity."

"Oh, I really don't know. I guess I should, but all I did was read the news." She pulls out another tissue from her purse.

Later, when Harmon Martin telephones to find out how the interviews went, Marcy says, "Not that great." She thinks about it and says, "Thinking about it makes me kind of tired."

"You might be wrong. You might be pleasantly surprised. But it doesn't matter. Those fellows were flyweights, they couldn't carry your bags. So let's say we keep looking until we find just the right fit."

The right fit, Marcy thinks. Fitting in. When she realizes she might begin to cry, she makes a quick excuse and says goodbye.

ANOTHER SUNNY DAY. Where she has come from, weather dictates activities and affects moods, and Marcy misses the little indicators. The smell of burning leaves, the creak of frozen porchboards, Randall carrying the fresh smell of winter with him into a warm room. But December in southern California is relentlessly green, leafy, and bright. There is only the changing angle of the sun as it streams onto the deck, where Marcy spends her afternoons reading and tanning.

Marcy has been offered a job. She can work as a cocktail waitress at a country-western place called The Palomino. Harmon Martin had nothing to do with this. Marcy saw the ad, called up, drove out to the valley. A woman looked her over the way a man would and said, "The one position is filled. But there's another in mid-January. Can you wait that long?"

Marcy said yes she could, but in truth she's not so sure about the job. The money would be good, and she wouldn't mind the get-up, but it seems so different out here. In Goodnight, she knew how to say no to men because she knew who they were and they knew who she was.

A crow glides past Marcy's deck. Marcy blinks, realizes she's been thinking of Randall. Of the tons of things she knows she shouldn't do, the one she knows she shouldn't do most of all is think about Randall, but she can't always help it. Usually she hopes Randall is with somebody, but today, a bad sign, she hopes he isn't. She sits down and writes Randall a long rushing letter full of explanation and questions and soft thoughts. Without reading it over, she seals it and means to walk it down the canyon to the mailbox before the last pickup, but when she opens the door, Harmon Martin is standing there about to knock. He hasn't saved her, not in any real sense, but when she awakens the next morning with the letter still in her purse, she will allow herself to think of it in almost that way.

Harmon Martin has come to the door because he has news. "Something quite remarkable." His little, self-knowing smile forms. "An interview, in January."

"Who with?" she says, but he merely winks. He's brought makings for what he calls "a celebratory gimlet." He mixes it precisely, savors his first sip. "Well," he says, seating himself. "I put in a word with a colleague. The colleague put in a word for me." He takes his handkerchief from his suit pocket, fogs and cleans his thick glasses, holds them to the light, gives them a finishing touch. He slides them on, looks beamingly at Marcy. "You have an interview on Tuesday, January 17th, 10:00 A.M., with Universal, for the position of personal secretary to Steven Spielberg."

Marcy stands frozen for a moment. "This isn't some kind of joke?"

"That's correct," Harmon Martin says. "It is not."

Marcy gives him a quick kiss on the cheek before walking about the apartment in a state of real agitation. "You did it," she says, as much to herself as to him and then, beside herself, she whoops, *"Hot chaw!"*—a phrase that makes Harmon Martin actually chuckle, a phrase that Marcy has never used before, a phrase that until now had been exclusively Randall's. She dances up to Harmon Martin, slips off his glasses, puts them on herself, keeps dancing. She takes his hand and, against his protests, pulls him up to dance. He moves mechanically for a minute or so, then retreats back to his chair. It's an endearing surprise, this rich man's embarrassment. When his blushing recedes, he makes a little smile. "I'm not much of a dancer," he says. "If I'd thought it was pertinent, I'd have told you sooner."

ON CHRISTMAS MORNING, Marcy dials her old number in Nebraska, imagines the telephone on the coffee table in the living room of the trailer as it rings and rings. Finally she gives up and tries her parents' number. Her father answers on the second ring. *"Ha!"* he says when she says hello.

"I *knew* it was you. It's the sixth time it's rung today, but this time I said to your mother, 'This one's her,' and, sure enough, here you are."

They talk amiably for a while, her father relying mostly on local crime stories to avoid touchy subjects. After telling about the stolen tractor discovered hidden in Raymond Fales's haymow, he says, "Okay, okay, I better give the phone to your mother before she turns blue."

"Hi, Polkadot," her mother says and, following a rush of questions, she takes a breath and says, "I was hoping you'd be home by now."

"I think I'm here to stay, Mom. The people are nice to me and I'm beginning to like it." Then, "Did you get my presents okay?"

Marcy has sent presents anonymously through a mail-order catalogue, a doe and fawn in a snow-globe for her mother and a set of nesting presidents for her father, who'd always taken pride in his ability to tick off all of them in order. To Randall she'd sent a pair of flannel boxer shorts in a duck-hunting pattern and a plaid electric blanket. She mentions this and her mother says, "I don't know that he'll receive those kindly."

"Why is that?" Marcy says. She can tell her mother is thinking something over. "What?"

"Oh, a story," her mother says.

"About him and somebody else?"

"No, but how would you feel about that?"

"Fine. I want him to be happy, is all I want."

"Well, I don't think he's so happy.'"

"What makes you say so?"

Another pause, then, "Well, the story, according to Flossie Boyles, is that about two weeks ago Randall took all your clothes out onto the carport by the trailer and heaped them up and burned them. Then he swept the ashes into a neat pile and put them in a Tupperware container and, the story goes, he consumes a teaspoon at a time by spreading it over his meals."

Marcy feels actually sickened. "Mom?"

"What, Polkadot?"

But Marcy catches herself. The story she was about to tell would've just played into her mother's hands. "I love you," she says, "and just tell Dad it's warm here and the people are nice to me and I miss him."

What she had thought to describe to her mother was the recurring dream she'd been having. In it, she brings Randall to the edge of a bluff overlooking the beach. They are both younger, in high school, happy, unsteady with laughter, trying to catch with their mouths black jelly beans they lob into the air. From the overhanging bluff face there is a steep, red-dirt channel, made by erosion, that is like a long chute down to the beach. There is sheer happiness in Randall's face when Marcy brings him to it. He plunges down at once, on the seat of his pants, whooping at first, but the moment he turns a corner, beyond Marcy's view, his voice stops and there are loud sickening thuds as his body bumps its way down the rocky slope. Marcy runs for the stairs, but cannot go down to look.

THE FIRST WEEK OF JANUARY, Marcy browses department stores for the right thing to wear to her interview (no luck) and reads everything about Steven Spielberg she can lay her hands on (the East Hampton inside-out barn in *Architectural Digest,* the money to Harvard for an extraterrestrial scanner in *Physics Today,* the rumors about Kate Capshaw in *People).* "Steven is boyish," says Richard Dreyfuss in *Life,* "and financially canny, but the word that really nails him is adventurous." In the background of one photograph, Marcy finds his secretary. She is dark-haired, too. Like his first wife. Like Amy Irving. Like Kate Capshaw.

The next morning Marcy spends seventy-five dollars on tinting her hair. "That color," she says to the hairdresser and points to a photograph of Kate Capshaw she's torn out of a magazine.

This is the first of two changes Marcy makes. The other is a molded leather eye patch she finds in a costume shop. It stops the double vision and the weeping, but she's not so sure about it. The first time she wears it outside the house, she turns away when a car passes. She whistles and before long the little bowlegged Doberman trots smartly around the corner carrying a new red frisbee. He drops it at her feet. She picks it up, holds it close to her head. "Shall I wear the eye patch?"

Yes.

No.

She tosses the frisbee into the empty street. It skips off the pavement and floats over the hillside. The dog leaps out into the air, disappears over the side. For a moment, time stands still, then the dog reappears, grinning around his red frisbee.

Whether she'll wear the eye patch, Marcy decides, will depend on the outfit she buys for the interview, but the days go by without finding the right thing. Finally, the day before the interview, she begins to cry in the dressing room of Bullocks Wilshire. Everything that looks good on the rack looks horrible on her. She takes off what she has on, goes to the most stylish saleswoman on the floor, and says, "I'm looking for something for a job interview at Universal, nice, but with a sense of adventure."

WHEN MARCY ARRIVES FOR THE INTERVIEW, she is directed to a large, tightly quiet room where about a dozen applicants are already waiting. Most of the women are wearing tasteful coat dresses in navy or cream, expensive but not too expensive. Marcy's outfit, she realizes, is just foolish. A semi-safari look, the saleswoman had called it. A khaki skirt, a Chinese peasant coat worn open to a tight, stretchy top in an orange color the saleswoman called quince. With suede flats, long, dangly, costume-gold earrings, and a brimless red hat, the total was $625, more money than Marcy had, so she opened an instant charge account.

"I heard the job was as an aid to Steven Spielberg," Marcy says to the woman closest to her.

Several of the women glance toward her. One of them, before turning just slightly away, says, "I hope you're right, Sweet Pea."

At a little past noon, Marcy is given a brief interview by a man—it goes fine—and then is shown into a round, windowless room where she is left alone. The walls are meant to be funny, Marcy guesses, but they scare her a little. White Roman columns have been painted on every wall and door, with dark vines trailing from one to the other. Walking among the columns is an odd cast of creatures—browsing zebras, penguins with parasols, grim-faced businessmen in bowler hats. Two black chairs and a white, glass-topped table are the only furniture in the room. Sitting on top of the table are a typewriter, a loud windup clock, a telephone, and a shrink-wrapped leather book. She is staring at the telephone when it rings. Marcy answers and a woman's voice says, "Miss Lockhardt, kindly check Mr. Spielberg's daybook, confirm for Lafcadio's and with Miss Wittenburg at CBS, cancel everything between 1:15 and 3:25, and if Mr. Wallace, White, or Wilson calls, advise them that Mr. Spielberg will be out of the office until tomorrow."

Marcy does these things, politely and, as far as she knows, correctly.

Shortly thereafter, as if of its own, a door Marcy hadn't seen swings open, cleanly sweeping out most of a Roman column. A woman rides into the room on a wave of confidence and energy, gives her name as Connie DeVrie, and, after a glance at Marcy's outfit, says, "What a *dramatic* coat!"

Connie DeVrie is wearing a dark, executive-looking skirt suit.

"First a five-minute typing test," she says and sets the clock.

The text concerns itself with the stress capacities of concrete. Moments after Marcy starts typing, the telephone rings. At the instant that Marcy picks it up, Connie DeVrie suspends time on the test. "Mr. Spielberg's office," Marcy says as briskly as she can.

A woman says, "Mr. Wade's office for Mr. Spielberg please."

Marcy, uncertain, says, "Your name again?" and the woman at the other end hangs up without a word. Connie DeVrie starts time running again and Marcy tries to concentrate on the typing. There are numbers and fractions everywhere. Marcy's fingers move unsurely over the top row of the keyboard. The last minute of the test, she tries to think up something worth saying to excuse her performance, but can't. She fights off the impulse to cry.

There are other tests, too, not quite as horrible, but almost.

When they're all completed, Connie DeVrie disappears through the swinging door, tests in hand. From the inner sanctum beyond the wall, Marcy can hear rich male laughter, and then laughter from men and women together, until finally the wall swings open again, but not completely. Connie DeVrie uses it like a shield, around which only her head appears. She says she'll call Marcy when all the interviews are completed and then, before Marcy can say a word, Connie DeVrie closes the door that wasn't a door.

WHEN SHE RETURNS TO HER BUNGALOW, the dog is asleep on her stoop. The door is also ajar. Through the window she can see Harmon Martin in shirt sleeves, wearing an apron, standing at the kitchen sink washing spinach leaves one by one. Marcy, stepping inside, asks how he got in.

"Key," he says, with enough unconcern to annoy Marcy. He doesn't look at her. He nods toward the sinkful of carrot peelings. "You know if you keep eating nothing but carrots, you will actually turn yellow."

She thinks of telling him that the reason Howard Hawks wanted Lauren Bacall for *To Have and Have Not* was her yellow complexion, which looked good on film—it's the kind of story that interests Harmon Martin—but he turns and is brought up short.

"Good grief," he says.

He's never before seen the eye patch, the peasant coat, the quince-colored top. Marcy's shoulders drop. "I know, I know," she says.

He lays down the spinach leaves. "Look, Lena," he says, "I knew you were very attractive, but I didn't know you could be so … fetching."

Marcy wonders if he's joking.

"I spoke to my colleague. He said the interview didn't work out so well. I was going to make you dinner as a way of … *condoling*, but, just for the record, whoever turned you down ought to have his head examined."

Marcy stares at him. "You're not joking, are you?"

"We're going out, Lena Lockhardt. I'm taking you out. That much you owe me."

They go to a place called Sports. She orders crab and a flaming dessert. She enjoys every bite. "I'll pay my half," she says while he's sipping coffee. He smiles. Half, rounded off, is seventy-two dollars.

She pays it. She pays it so that after he drives her home, she can give him a quick kiss, say goodnight, and feel virtuous even while experiencing the strange pleasure of watching his appetite grow.

LAST NIGHT MARCY WORKED her first shift at The Palomino. Joe Ely played, she made a couple of mistakes on drink orders, but still took home over ninety dollars. Except for a couple of unfunny remarks, it was okay, so this morning, a Saturday, Marcy feels just fine. She has gone out to sit in the sun on the deck, but as the sky clouds over she puts on a T-shirt and, a while later, sweat pants. When she hears Harmon Martin's peculiar knock on the door, she sings out, "It's unlocked! I'm out on the deck!"

He sets a grocery bag on the drainboard, slides open the door to the deck. "I've been wondering if you got mauled last night?"

She laughs. "No real bruises."

Harmon Martin regards her, then goes to the deck rail and looks out.

"Rain," she says. "Or would be if this was Nebraska."

He stares off. "It's coming up from the gulf. It's the kind that can really open up."

It's quiet except for the drone of an airplane. For the first time, Marcy wonders where Harmon Martin's wife thinks he is.

"Did I mention the hotel project we've begun in St. Martin?" he says, still looking off. "It's quite reckless, four hundred rooms, on the Dutch side." He turns around. "I have to go over there this week."

"How nice," Marcy says. It *does* sound nice, actually.

"Yes, well, I've been thinking," Harmon Martin says. "Do you remember the car dealership I went into the day I showed you this place?"

"The place with the old cars."

"*Vintage* cars, we call them, but yes. I own that agency. We sell pre-'68 Rollses, Mercedes, Porsches, Bentleys, and Bugattis that we bring over from Europe. We restore them to mint condition, guarantee them, and sell them as investment-quality classics, which they are."

Since when, Marcy wonders, does Harmon Martin fill her in on his work? "That's interesting," she says.

"There are three salesmen, but one will soon be leaving."

Marcy doesn't say anything.

He says, "What got me thinking were those clothes you wore the other night, the Asian coat and red top. Tasteful, but somewhat … *sportive*." He smiles his subdued smile. "I think you'd be, as they say, a selling fool."

On the freeway below, loose lines of traffic flow smoothly along.

Gently he says, "Six figures is not out of the question."

Marcy tries to keep her voice calm. "I don't know beans about cars."

"I'd be happy to teach you—history, horsepower, appreciation potential, that kind of thing." He snugs his glasses to the bridge of his nose. "Which is why I mention St. Martin. I'll have meetings, but there will be dead times. We could put them to use. Probably we'd just start with Mercedes and Bentleys for now, and work on the rest later on."

Marcy feels lightheaded. She needs to say something. "I never thought I was coming out to Hollywood to sell used cars," she says.

"*Vintage,*" he says, with his smile.

Then Harmon Martin half-closes his eyes, a few moments pass, and his lids slowly open. "Look, Lena," he says. "In a way it *is* part of the business. Take the day before yesterday. Alec Baldwin came in and used his American Express for a Porsche roadster, the '58 Super Speedster, eighteen thousand dollars. Last week Randy Quaid purchased a three-wheel Morgan. We sell to anybody, but it's amazing how many of the buyers are recognizable. Julie Newmar bought a '31 Bentley, and before he died Steve McQueen bought his 356 from us." Harmon Martin spreads his hands, looks at them, spreads them wider. His voice grows almost melodious. "Both of John Wayne's sons. Dwight Yoakam. Rita Moreno." It is a surprise and not a surprise, this new use of his fine, pure voice. Far away a car horn sounds. Harmon Martin slows his pace. "Fernando Lamas," he croons. "Whit Bissell ... Strother Martin ... John Cassavetes." Marcy grins dreamily. "Sterling Holloway ... Elizabeth Ashley ... Lou Diamond Phillips ..." One after another, the names, the dreamy, beautiful, expensive names, hover close by, floating, then on the updraft rise overhead.

"We'll need to leave by 4 P.M. Tuesday," Harmon Martin says. "You can pack light. We're building on the Dutch side, but staying on the French, where dress is informal, especially on the beach."

Slowly and with real effort Marcy brings the room back into focus. She has to say no, thanks but no thanks, and she has to say it now. Thanks but no thanks. Say it.

Harmon Martin is at the door, looking as lightheaded as Marcy feels, and then he is gone.

THE STORM TAKES HOLD THAT NIGHT and doesn't let go. The weatherman Marcy watches is called Dr. George by the cheery co-anchors. Dr. George runs a clip of two women in rain-drenched bikinis roller-skating in Santa Monica, then shoves his face muggingly into the camera and says that what we have here, folks, is a good old-fashioned gully whumper. Marcy spends the day reading and watching TV, eating popcorn and thinking of spending similar days when snow floated idly down in Nebraska. She puts on her swimming suit and stands on a stool to look at herself in the mirror. She tries it with the top off and actually laughs. If Harmon Martin thinks she'd go out on a public beach like that, he can think again. She wishes he would call so she could remember how his voice made her feel while he was saying those names, but he doesn't. By Sunday afternoon, whenever she looks at a clock, Marcy converts it to Nebraska time. That evening, for the first time since the storm moved in, she thinks of the dog. She opens the front door, calls into the sheets of slanting rain, but her voice is swallowed in the gurgling throat of the storm. Through the night she imagines hearing the dog scratching at the door, but when she shines a flashlight out, he isn't there. There is only the splash of water.

The storm is supposed to let up Tuesday morning, but doesn't. Marcy packs her suitcase in hopes that her feelings will catch up with her actions. She packs perfume, lingerie, diaphragm. But Harmon Martin's knock on the door makes her do something surprising. She slides the packed suitcase under the bed and opens another one on top, empty.

Harmon Martin shakes out his umbrella at the door and enters uncertainly. He doesn't seem completely surprised when Marcy leads him to the empty suitcase. "I'm not going," she says. He frets and coaxes, growing smaller by the minute. Beneath his linen jacket, he wears a pale pink long-sleeved shirt that seems to Marcy unpleasantly showy. While he walks stiffly about the room, he fusses with the pale pink cuffs, tugging them down on his too-thin wrists. When finally he sits down and pleads, Marcy says, "No. Once and for all, no."

Moments later, clouds outside part to a startling blue and the entire room lightens. Harmon Martin writes something down. "This is my home number. I'll be there another hour, in case you change your mind." He taps his glasses. "If my wife answers, just say, 'About the leak in the studio on Ione, tell Harmon never mind it's been fixed.'"

After he leaves, Marcy goes outside and is surprised that his car is actually gone. The sun glares down; vapor rises from the wet asphalt. Everywhere on the ground there are worms, and snails, and soaked newspapers. People begin popping out of houses. From a distance, a dog barks, *her* dog, his sharp clear anxious barking. Marcy follows the sound down the hillside streets, along Ione, down finally to Cahuenga. In the traffic, the barking is lost, or perhaps it's stopped. Marcy keeps walking, farther from her studio, farther from Harmon Martin's house, taking deep breaths of the new clean air. In Goodnight, after a storm like this, there would be careful appraisal of crops and stock, but here there is nothing but a general sense of freedom after long constraint. Joggers appear. Bicycles whiz by. Music carries from open car windows.

The clearing, however, is a false one. The skies again turn dark, car windows slide up, fat raindrops spatter, and the sweep of windshield wipers begins again. Marcy, coatless, keeps walking, following the flood control channel, watching the water pour by, branches and bottles and plastic containers all rushing along on the fierce current.

It is from a bridge spanning the channel that she sees the dog. He is down below, to the right, in a muddy lot within the fence enclosing the channel, an area used to park orange government trucks, where neither the dog nor the group of boys surrounding him should be. The boys are bickering over whose turn it is to throw the frisbee next. When finally one of them throws it, the dog seems to skate above the mud, and to rise out of it for the long moment needed to pluck the frisbee from the air. Marcy can hear the boys' shrill voices. *"Whoa!* Check it out! This canine can *fly!"*

The cars splash past Marcy on the bridge, but the pedestrians and bicyclists have disappeared. The rain turns hard and finally the boys notice it, too. They hunch their shoulders, look up at the sky, and move toward their bikes. One, however, lags back and, as he sees the others mount their bikes, this last boy picks up the frisbee for one last throw.

What is this like? Like watching one of those TV nature shows and knowing that the snow rabbit or the lame gnu is going to get it and not turning the channel. Marcy wants to call out to the dog, to retrieve him from danger, but she doesn't. She stands mute as the boy turns toward the storm channel and without a moment's hesitation flicks the frisbee toward it. The dog races after the frisbee, pitches forward when the level ground gives way beneath him, then tumbles and skids down the concrete bank into the rushing current. His neck stretches up out of the water for a moment before he is swept away.

Marcy feels suddenly boneless. There are so many ways to act cowardly. There are just so many ways to do it. She could've yelled at that boy and saved the dog. She could've done that little bit. And she could've given Harmon Martin, a married man, nothing whatsoever to think about. And she could've told Randall that for reasons she didn't get and couldn't explain, she had to change her life or go crazy. She could've done that instead of telling him lies and making him hit her, making him feel and look to all of Goodnight like a brute. She could've done these things, if she were only not such a coward, and then besides saving that dog's life and saving Randall and Harmon Martin a lot of trouble, her life would now have more of the decency she always meant it to have. It was like that boy who threw the frisbee. That boy knew what that poor dog would do. Probably that boy would grow into someone worthless, and then the dog wouldn't matter. But it would matter if that boy somehow began to turn into somebody decent. Then his carelessness with that trusting dog would nibble away at him and he would learn that, no matter who said what to you, it was the kind of sin that only you who committed it could forgive yourself for, except that you never could unless you began scaling back your ideas of what makes a wrongful act. Marcy begins to walk. Water streams from her hair into her face. Her pant legs and sweater soak up the rain and grow heavy. She walks and walks, along Cahuenga, up the canyon toward Ione, past Harmon Martin's house, soaked through, not thinking, just walking in her own watery world.

Marcy is at her gate when it dawns on her that the green Dodge pickup she has just passed seems familiar. Marcy turns and stares in disbelief. It is Randall's truck. The shadowy form slouched behind the steering wheel must then be Randall. Marcy moves toward him. In the truck bed there is a dark, wet canvas tarp roped over odd shapes that suggest furniture. Scattered on the dashboard are a seed cap, a road map, a box of Good & Plentys. A feeling of relief and perhaps even affection swells within Marcy. What kept you? she thinks of calling out when he rolls down the window, but he doesn't. He doesn't move at all, an indication, she guesses, of sullenness or mean satisfaction, and all at once Marcy has no real idea what she is feeling, what she will say. But she doesn't have to say anything. Behind the fogged windshield, behind the streaming rivulets of water, in a tightly closed cab that Marcy doesn't actually have to smell to know its wintry mingling of licorice and boot leather, coffee and flannel, Randall is fast asleep.

Tom McNeal graduated from the University of California, Berkeley, and was a Wallace Stegner Fellow and Jones Lecturer at Stanford University. His short fiction has been included in Best American Short Stories, The O. Henry Prize Collection, *and* The Pushcart Prize Collection. *"What Happened to Tully," which first appeared in the* Atlantic Monthly, *was made into the 2000 movie* Tully. *His 1998 novel* Goodnight, Nebraska *won the California Book Award for first fiction. He and his wife, Laura Rhoton McNeal, are the authors of four young adult novels,* Crooked *(Random House, 2002),* Zipped *(Alfred A. Knopf, 2003),* Crushed *(Alfred A. Knopf, 2007), and* The Decoding of Lana Morris *(Alfred A. Knopf, 2007). McNeal lives near San Diego.*

Jenny Price

Selection from *Thirteen Ways of Seeing Nature in L.A.*

PART ONE: THE FIRST SIX WAYS
AND A TRIP TO THE RIVER

PROLOGUE: FROM WALDEN TO L.A.

THERE ARE MANY PLACES IN L.A. you can go to think about the city, and my own favorite has become the Los Angeles River, which looks like an outsize concrete sewer and is most famous for being forgotten. The L.A. River flows fifty-one miles through the heart of L.A. County. It is enjoying herculean efforts to revitalize it, and yet commuters who have driven over it five days a week for ten years cannot tell you where it is. Along the river, the midpoint lies roughly at the confluence with the Arroyo Seco, near Dodger Stadium downtown. L.A. was founded near here in 1781: this area offers the most reliable aboveground supply of freshwater in the L.A. basin. It's a miserable spot now, a trash-strewn wasteland of empty lots, steel fences, and railroad tracks beneath a tangle of freeway overpasses: it looks like a Blade Runner set that a crew disassembled and then put back together wrong. It's not the most scenic spot to visit the river but may be the finest place on the river to think about L.A.

Like so many writers who come to Los Angeles—and I moved here seven years ago—I have succumbed inevitably to the siren call to write about the city. The long-established procedure has been to explore why one loves it or hates it, or both, and to proclaim loudly in the process that L.A. is the American dream or the American nightmare. The tradition tempts writers with a combination of navel-gazing and arm-waving that proves impossible to resist for too long.

Of course, I am a nature writer—a unique brand of writer that has felt no compulsion whatsoever to write about L.A. and even less to live here. Though you could toss an apple core into the bushes in Missoula, Montana, and hit a nature writer, I have found four practitioners so far among the ten million people in L.A. County, and one, my friend Bill Fox, fled to Portland for a couple of years. "Is there nature in L.A.?" people typically respond when I say I write about nature in this town. But I have ended up here happily, and Bill has just returned, exactly because L.A. has become the finest place in America to think and write about nature.

More urgently, L.A. is the ideal place to tackle the problem of how to write about nature. In the past twenty-five years, the venerable American literature of nature writing has become distressingly marginal. Even my nature-loving and environmentalist friends tell me they never read it. Earnest, pious, and quite allergic to irony: none of these trademark qualities plays well in 2006. But to me, the core trouble is that nature writers have given us endless paeans to the wonders of wildness since Thoreau fled to Walden Pond, but need to tell us far more about our everyday lives in the places we actually live. Perhaps you're not worrying about the failures of this literary genre as a serious problem. But in my own arm-waving manifesto about L.A. and America, I will proclaim that the crisis in nature writing is one of our most pressing national cultural catastrophes.

I love L.A. more than I hate it. I wasn't supposed to. A nature lover from suburban St. Louis, I have enjoyed a fierce and enduring attachment to the wilds of the Southern Rockies. I was supposed to love Boulder, Colorado, where I settled after graduate school in the hope that it might be the perfect place—and it's a town that every day adores itself in the mirror and confirms its perfection. But by pondering all the ways of seeing nature in L.A., I can explain why I have decided that I love L.A. instead—and why the L.A. River (site of the famous chase scenes in Grease and Terminator 2) has become my favorite place in L.A., and "Enjoy the beauty of another culture while learning more about wastewater treatment and reuse" my working motto as a nature writer. Also why so many of the best-known interpreters of L.A. as the American dream and nightmare, from Nathanael West to Raymond Chandler to Joan Didion to Mike Davis, have written obsessively about nature. Why perhaps the most quoted lines in all the fabled L.A. literature are Chandler's passage on the gale-force autumn winds:

> It was one of those hot dry Santa Anas…. On nights like that every booze party ends in a fight. Meek little wives feel the edge of the carving knife and study their husbands' necks. Anything can happen.

And why we need to rewrite entirely the stories we tell about nature, and why L.A. is the best place to do it.

⌒

ONE WAY OF SEEING NATURE IN L.A.:
AS NONEXISTENT

"IS THERE NATURE IN L.A.?" The question sometimes betrays sarcasm, but sometimes not. L.A., after all, has long been decried as the Anti-Nature: it's the American megalopolis with brown air, fouled beaches, pavement to the horizon, and a concrete river. It's sort of the Death Star to American nature lovers—the place from where the destruction of nature emanates—which is why woodsy towns like Missoula and Boulder hail themselves as the anti-L.A.

And this is the reigning nature story we tell about L.A.: There is no nature here.

⌒

A SECOND WAY:
AS THE WILD THINGS

BUT THIS STORY HEWS to a historically powerful definition of nature as only the wild things, which we destroy and banish when we build cities. This way to define nature—the great American nature story, and the heart and soul of nature writing—has become so firmly entrenched that seeing nature in other ways has been next to impossible.

Still, even by this inadequate definition, L.A. sports a great deal of nature: the extensive beaches, mountains, and canyons that have always brought people here. A few nature-writing anthologies include a single rogue piece about finding wildness inside a city. If L.A. symbolizes "the end of nature" (to use Bill McKibben's dangerously catchy phrase), it actually has more than enough real fodder for such tales, if you want to write about the sunset on Broad Beach in Malibu or the hawks soaring in Temescal Canyon or the dolphins leaping just offshore or how your heart soars like a hawk or leaps like a dolphin as you watch the sun set offshore from atop the trail in Temescal Canyon.

But there are so many more kinds of nature stories to tell here. I head for L.A.'s wild spots when I can, and delight in hawks, dolphins, and sunsets as much as the next nature lover. I have a special soft spot for ducks. But the anthologies ignore about 90 percent of the nature in L.A. and all the other places we live, as well as most of people's encounters with nature on Earth. What the crisis of nature writing amounts to, in a few words, is that Thoreau really, really needs to Get on the Bus.

And my own list of favorite representative topics for a more comprehensive, on the bus nature writing in Los Angeles would have to include mango body whips, the social geography of air, Zu-Zu the murdered Chihuahua, and Mapleton Drive near Bel Air. And, of course, the L.A. River, where all the possible kinds of nature stories in L.A. converge.

A THIRD WAY:
AS THE RESOURCES WE USE

THE MANGO BODY WHIP story begins like this: soon after I moved to L.A., a woman who ran into my car while it was parked on the USC campus left a note on the back of a receipt for a mango body whip, which she'd purchased at SkinMarket at the Beverly Center mall. What's a mango body whip? I didn't know. Skin product? More perverse? I made a trip to the Center, and found out that it's a mango-infused thick and buttery skin cream.

Nature stories abound in such an encounter. Begin with the mangoes. Follow them, and you can tell an intricate set of stories as farm workers harvest mangoes in rural Mexico, and drivers truck them into the L.A. area and into the SkinMarket factory in Simi Valley—just over the L.A. County line—where workers use industrial technologies to turn them into skin butter, and distributors transport them to upscale malls like the Beverly Center, and shoppers cart them away to bathrooms in adjacent Beverly Hills and West Hollywood and to other places throughout the country.

Mango body whip stories, in other words, look for and follow the nature we use, and watch it move in and out of the city, to track specifically how we transform natural resources into the mountains of stuff with which we literally build cities and sustain our urban lives. These tales might track nature through cars. They could be about soap or magazines. They can look for the nature in refrigerators, sushi, dog food, TVs, linguine, baseball caps, closet organizers, digital cameras, bracelets, concert halls, laptop computers, bicycles. If you tell stories that follow nature through our material lives, you will see a lot of L.A.—the city's warehouses, factories, commercial strips, and cultural centers, and its residential neighborhoods, some of which have a great deal more stuff than others.

A FOURTH WAY:
AS DIFFERENT TO DIFFERENT PEOPLE

WHICH BRINGS ME TO THE SOCIAL GEOGRAPHY of air. The air in L.A., if polluted, is not equally polluted everywhere. The coastal and mountain areas, which tend to be the wealthiest, enjoy the cleanest air on average. On the inland flats, the poorest, least white, and most industrial neighborhoods in L.A. suffer the worst air, along with alarming asthma rates. Another way to put it is that the Angelenos who work in and live near the factories that manufacture mango body whips breathe far more polluted air than the residents who are most likely to be the body whip devotees. I live on Venice Beach, near Ozone Avenue—named without irony in the clean-air early 1900s, but still one of the safest places to breathe in L.A. County. Twenty miles inland, the Southeast L.A. area—the most industrialized urban area in the U.S., with many of L.A.'s lowest-income and most heavily Latino neighborhoods—occupies 1 percent of the county by acreage but generates 18 percent of the toxic air emissions.

While mango body whip stories follow nature as resources through L.A., geography of air tales narrate who encounters what nature where. These tales begin with "who." They ask, importantly, who benefits most and who suffers the worst consequences as who uses and transforms nature. But they also ask who eats what foods and who doesn't, and who plants what in their gardens, and who lives nearest and farthest away from a city's parks, and who hunts and fishes or watches birds, and who chooses parrots or pit bulls or rabbits or goldfish as pets. This brand of tale asks how different people encounter nature differently.

Nature writing has ignored these third and fourth ways of seeing. It has been a literary universe in which we visit and contemplate wild nature, but seldom use and transform nature: when the mango becomes a mango body whip, it ceases to be nature, as does the oil in a laptop computer or a maple tree that becomes a table. And the genre describes nature as a unitary force or kind of place that Man encounters, and where we'll find universal meanings—but seldom something you encounter from a specific social position and point of view.

But such a way of seeing can fully explain exactly no encounter with nature in 2006, whether in a wilderness area, on a farm, or at the Beverly Center mall. I love to go hiking on the vast trail network here in the Santa Monica Mountains. Sure, that's a typical nature story in which I seek refuge and simplicity and quiet in L.A.'s wilds as antidote to the stress and noise of my daily life. But to narrate all the encounters with nature that define my hike, I also have to ask where the natural resources in my Gore-tex shell and hiking boots come from—the oil, stone, metals, and animal skins in my twenty-first-century hiker gear, which keeps me warm and dry and makes my closet look like an REI outlet. How do they connect me to the global transformation of nature? And how do they shape my experience of hiking? The Simple Life out in nature is complex as hell. I'd also have to narrate how wealthier Angelenos are more likely to live near L.A.'s mountain parks—and to own cars to get to them. And how does the particular work I do at a desk all week make a strenuous weekend hike sound like a good idea in the first place? The hike has to be a story about how our connections to one another define our encounters with nature. And it's about how the National Park Service in the Santa Monica Mountains has chosen my favorite trail routes, and how they manage fire suppression, and how they draw up hundreds of rules and policies to keep both the visitors and the parklands happy.

A FIFTH WAY:
AS LANDSCAPE AND ECOLOGY
WE BUILD IN AND MANAGE

WHICH BRINGS ME TO ZU-ZU the murdered Chihuahua. As the Los Angeles Times reported, Zu-Zu's story begins, or ends, like this: In summer 2002, a coyote entered the yard of a casting director in the Silver Lake area west of Downtown and ate her Chihuahua, Zu-Zu. Coyotes, her husband warned bitterly, are "urban terrorists": the bereft owner said, "I have no liberty in my front yard." A letter to the Times, though, lionized the coyote as the real victim, an indigenous animal encroached on by evil yippy Chihuahuas (if, like me, you tend to agree, then try substituting a Labrador retriever puppy for Zu-Zu).

When you bring domestic dogs into a landscape of native animals, then the resident carnivores are likely to see the pets as prey. When you use and change a landscape, then the place will respond. Nature is never passive. Every place has an active, very particular ecology, climate, topography, geology, flora, fauna. Zu-Zu stories narrate how we change places and how they respond and how we respond back and so on and so on. They're about paving, building, planting, bulldozing, fires and fire suppression, polluting and cleaning up, pet keeping and coyote predations, earthquakes and seismic retrofitting, water supply and flood management, and sewers and gas lines and lawns and gardens and roads and trails and parks.

Nature writers have in fact told this kind of story—usually, however, with an evil Chihuahua moral, in which Man stomps into nature primeval and ravages and desacralizes it. But as guidance for how we can inhabit places, seeing people inevitably as invaders in these stories works about as well as branding coyotes as terrorists. An "evil Chihuahua" moral demands that we leave the nature we live in as it is (in which case we'll die), but a "terrorist coyote" moral urges us to eradicate nature (in which case we'll die). Neither approach helps us navigate how to keep pet animals in a landscape with native predators—or how to make a road or build a house or ensure a water supply or figure out how to keep the air and water clean. Ideally, Zu-Zu stories should help us ask how we can create livable and sustainable cities. They should be deeply informed by knowledge of the ecology, geology, and natural history of the place. They should help us walk the essential line between doing nothing in nature and doing whatever we want. Like mango body whip tales, they should seek to understand what our connections to nature actually are so that we can think about what our connections should look like.

These are a few topics the Los Angeles Times has reported on in recent months: water deals in the West, discarded American computers shipped to China, dog parks, an L.A. landfill in the Mojave desert, the hybrid Toyota Priuses, diesel pollution in industrial south L.A., battles against new developments in the outer suburbs, new parks on the L.A. River, high silicosis rates among Chinese trinket-factory workers, oil refineries in Venezuela, farmer's markets, the best restaurants for peach dishes, sustainable water-use practices in Santa Monica, toxic plastics residues in polar bears in the Arctic, neighborhood lawn regulations, the fight over removing the feral peacocks who scream every morning in the Palos Verdes neighborhoods, pesticides buildup in frog populations, battles for public beach access in Malibu.

These are nature topics all, about how we live in and fight about nature, and about how we use it more and less fairly and sustainably, and about the enormous consequences for our lives in L.A., as well as for places and people and wildlife everywhere. And such topics beg for a literature—for a poetry, for an aesthetics—because to clearly ponder our lives in and out of cities, we have to be able to imagine and reimagine these connections to nature.

A SIXTH WAY:
AS A PREMIER SOURCE
OF HUMAN MEANING

IMAGINE THE SITE OF LOS ANGELES COUNTY four thousand years ago. The people who lived here—the ancestors of the Tongva, the Chumash, the Tataviam—used birds and deer to make food and clothes, and turned trees into shelter, and turned water, rocks, and dirt into energy, tools, boats, medicine, religious objects, art. (And in 2006 B.C.E., connections to nature were not all that simple either.) The people used and changed nature in order to live. They told stories about nature to explain the world and to guide their actions within it.

What do we do in Los Angeles now? Essentially the same thing. We use nature and tell stories about it to live and explain our lives. To use nature is to be human: that's a pretty fair working definition. To tell stories is to be a human explaining how things work. The stories that any people tell about nature are some of the most basic stories they tell. Is there nature in L.A.? The fact that the major nature story we tell in L.A., as in all cities, is that there is no nature here does not make this tale any less basic, powerful, or telling.

How do we make nature meaningful? "What nature means" tales are one last category of story I'll suggest, and nature writing has shown great interest in this kind of story—in fact the quest for meaning has defined the genre's very soul. Of course, nature writers have attached various meanings to a great range of places, animals, and plants. Yosemite? Majesty. A sacred place. The desert? Peace. Harshness. Clarity. Songbirds? Beauty. Delicacy. Earthquakes? Fury and vengeance. Water? A metaphor for life. But nature? The ur-meaning that frames all others? Wildness. Not-us-ness. The anti-modern. A place apart. Salvation. Refuge. And this ur-meaning historically has reigned as an exceptionally powerful American cultural assumption. Nature writing has preached it tenaciously, but hardly invented this way of seeing and of refusing to see. The vision of wild nature as counterpoint to a corrupted modern civilization has always played a central role in American national myths and identity. (Think City on a Hill, the mythic frontier, a hundred years of Westerns, and landscape photography.) To define nature as the wild things apart from cities is one of the great fantastic American stories.

And it's one of the great fantastic American denials. On Mapleton Drive in Holmby Hills in the Bel Air area, in the Santa Monica Mountain foothills, the TV producer Aaron Spelling has built what's widely publicized as the starship of Hollywood homes—a 56,550-square-foot French limestone mansion with 123 rooms, with two rooms for wrapping gifts and a rose garden on top of one of four garages. Here are two generally ignored facts about Spelling's famous homestead. First, it is a house of nature: Spelling built it, has maintained it, and stocks it with fantastic quantities of oil, stone, metals, dirt, water, and wood (a likely forest's worth of wrapping paper, to begin with). And second, there are very few maples on Mapleton Drive. Maybe maples grew here in abundance once, and maybe not. Either way, the street enjoys the idea of maple trees, which conjures a bucolic refuge above the smog, noise, and torrential activity of the megalopolis below. Call it maple mojo. Smaller manses of nature line the rest of Mapleton Drive as well as the neighboring streets Parkwood, Greendale, Brooklawn, Beverly Glen. No parks, no woods, no dales, no brooks, no glens. Just the mojo of wild nature.

Mapleton Drive showcases the denial intrinsic to the great American nature story. To say there's no nature in cities is a convenient way of seeing if I like being a nature lover and environmentalist but don't want to give up any of my stuff. We cherish nature as an idea of wildness while losing track of the real nature in our very houses. We flee to wild nature as a haven from high-tech industrial urban life, but refuse to see that we madly use and transform wild nature to sustain the exact life from which we seek retreat. We make sacred our encounters with wild nature but thereby desacralize all other encounters. Or in other words, if we cannot clearly understand cities and our lives within them unless we keep track of our connections to nature, still there may be some basic things we prefer not to see and understand.

Ideally, if there's any one argument I could persuade you of, it's that our foundational nature stories should see and cherish our mundane, economic, utilitarian, daily encounters with nature—so that what car you drive and how you get your water and how you build a house should be transparent acts that are as sacred as hiking to the top of Point Mugu in the northern Santa Monica Mountains and gazing out over the Pacific Ocean to watch the dolphins leap, the ducks float, and the sun set. True, there's a lovely yearning in the American vision of nature as a wild place apart—for simplicity, for a slower life. There's great wonder about the natural world, and terrific love for wild places and things. There's legitimate bewilderment, in response to the mind-boggling complexity of modern connectedness (how could I possibly keep track of where the nature in my Toyota wagon comes from?). There's a large dose of real regret, for the wanton destructiveness of toxic industrialism and excessive consumerism. And there's powerful, overriding denial, in the service of powerful self-indulgence and material desire, that pushes us to imagine nature out of rather than into our lives.

RIVER TRIP #1

JUST HOW POWERFUL? Well, in L.A., enough to let us lose track of an entire river—not just the nature in the stuff in our houses. We can't find L.A.'s major waterway, which sustained L.A. for 150 years and now runs under ten gridlocked freeways through the heart of L.A. County. A fifty-one-mile river in plain sight: lost.

The L.A. River is one of the city's central natural facts. L.A. inhabits a river basin, and the major river drains large portions of three mountain ranges out to the Pacific. The L.A. Basin, while large enough for a megalopolis, is small for that much drainage, and the L.A. River consequently poses a greater flood danger than most urban U.S. rivers. (Mark Twain wrote that he'd fallen into a Southern California river and "come out all dusty"—but apparently hadn't seen one of the raging flash floods.) In the 1930s, when a last-straw series of floods made half of L.A. canoeable, the city signed up the U.S. Army Corps of Engineers, who heroically proceeded to dig a concrete straitjacket for the river and all its tributaries—a twenty-five-year project that required 3.5 million barrels of concrete and remains the Corps' largest public works project west of the Mississippi. The Corps and County Public Works rechristened the river the "flood control channel." They recategorized it as infrastructure, with the freeways and electrical grid. To the public, in any case, the channel no longer looked wild enough to be a river or to count as nature at all. And this is how L.A. lost its river—not lost as in no longer had one, since L.A. actually still had it, but lost as in could no longer see or find it.

If a city is built and sustained through using, managing, and imagining nature, then however you see and manage your central natural facts should have massive citywide consequences. What happens when you deny that your river is a river?

The saga of the concrete L.A. River plays out as every brand of nature story. First, a "what nature means" tale: Angelenos reimagined the river as nonexistent, and banished it from their collective imagination of history and place. Also, a tale of wild things. Many birds and frogs continued to use the river (they apparently hadn't received the memo that it was no longer a river), but other birds and most fish species did disappear, along with extensive wetlands and riparian habitat.

Also, a Zu-Zu story. As Los Angeles altered the Southern California landscape to control the river's floods, we largely ignored the basic hydrological processes. The jacketed river could no longer flow out into its basin, and therefore no longer replenished the aquifer with water, the soils with nutrients, and the beaches with sand. The county designed the storm sewers, however, to empty into the channel, which promptly turned the river into L.A.'s Grand Sewer, which gathers pesticides, motor oil, trash, dog feces, and many hundreds more pollutants from driveways, lawns, roads, and parking lots across the 834-square-mile watershed and rushes the toxins downstream into the Pacific Ocean. And yes, floodwaters have stayed safely within the concrete walls, but the extra water from the storm sewers has actually dramatically increased the volume of the river's floods.

The cement channel also constitutes L.A.'s strategy to move stormwater, that life-giving natural resource, through the city. Here is the river's mango body whip story: a city that inhabits a place on Earth with a semi-arid Mediterranean climate pours as much of the rainwater as possible, which we get from the sky for free, into the storm sewers, through the river, and into the Pacific—and then pays dearly to import water by aqueduct from up to four hundred miles away. Call it watering the ocean, by draining watersheds across the West. And finally, a social geography of air story. L.A. may have wild places, but as the American city that has so consistently privileged private property over public spaces, it also historically has set aside remarkably little public park space per capita—and L.A.'s poorest areas suffer the worst shortages of neighborhood park space, enjoy the least private green space, and lie farthest from the mountain parks. In this infamously fragmented city, the poorest neighborhoods also invariably have been the most cut up by freeways and industry. The concrete channel turned the basin's most logical site for green space, and the city's major natural connector, into an outsize open sewer that carved a no-man's-land through many of the city's most fragmented and park-starved areas.

In sum, L.A.'s errant treatment of a major natural feature has profoundly exacerbated nearly all of L.A.'s notorious troubles—environmental chaos, social inequities, community fragmentation, water shortages, water imperialism, and erasure of civic memory. The good news, on the other hand—and I'll get to the restoration efforts on the river presently—is that if you use and manage this nature more sustainably and fairly, you can make the city a healthier, more equitable, and all-around lovelier place to live in. First, though, you have to see the nature in the place. You have to find it.

IS THERE NATURE IN L.A.? Far more than our philosophies dream of, and much more than in Portland or Boulder—more, possibly, on Mapleton Drive alone than in some small towns in Iowa. One may as well ask if there is water in the ocean. To get on the bus—to imagine a more vital and comprehensive nature writing—is to deem the question plain dumb silly, along with "Where is nature?" and maybe even "What is nature?" and especially that nonsense about the end of nature, which makes only as much sense as declaring an end to rocks or air or water and bespeaks exactly the way of thinking by which L.A. lost its river. The powering question of this literature should become, rather, What nature is it?—and then, How do we use nature? How do we change nature? How does nature react? How do we react back? How do we imagine nature? Who uses and changes and imagines nature? And often the most vital questions of all: How sustainably? How fairly? How well?

Raised in St. Louis, Jenny Price earned a Ph.D. in history from Yale University. Today she is a writer, Los Angeles Urban Ranger, and Research Scholar at the UCLA Center for the Study of Women. Author of Flight Maps: Adventures with Nature in Modern America *(Basic Books, 1999), she's written for* GOOD, Sunset, Audubon, *the* New York Times, *and the* Los Angeles Times. *Her essay "Thirteen Ways of Looking at Nature in L.A." appeared in* Believer *magazine; an earlier version was included in* Land of Sunshine *(University of Pittsburgh Press, 2006). She gives frequent tours of the L.A. River, and she lives on Venice Beach.*

BIBLIOGRAPHY AND
REPRINT CREDITS

Adair, Virginia Hamilton. "Mojave Evening." *Ants on the Melon.* Copyright 1996 by Virginia Hamilton Adair. Used by permission of Random House, Inc.

Atherton, Gertrude. *Adventures of a Novelist.* Copyright 1932. Used by permission of Ayer Company Publishers.

Austin, Mary. *The Land of Little Rain.* Boston and New York: Houghton Mifflin Company, 1903.

Caen, Herb. *Only in San Francisco.* Copyright 1960 by Herb Caen. Used by permission of Doubleday, a division of Random House, Inc.

Chase, J. Smeaton. "The Malibu: No Trespassing." *California Coast Trails: A Horseback Ride from Mexico to Oregon.* Boston and New York: Houghton Mifflin Company, 1913.

Clapp, Louise Amelia Knapp Smith. "Letter Tenth, A Trip into the Mines." *The Shirley Letters: From the California Mines, 1851–1852.* San Francisco: Thomas C. Russell, 1922.

Coolbrith, Ina. "Copa de Oro," "From Russian Hill." Boston and New York: Houghton Mifflin Company, 1895.

Dana, Richard H. *Two Years Before the Mast.* Boston and New York: Houghton Mifflin Company, 1911.

Didion, Joan. "Notes from a Native Daughter." *Slouching Toward Bethlehem.* Copyright 1966, 1968, renewed 1996 by Joan Didion. Used by permission of North Point Press, a division of Farrar, Straus and Giroux, LLC.

Doerr, Harriet. "Low Tide at Four." *The Tiger in the Grass.* Copyright 1995 by Harriet Doerr. Used by permission of Viking Penguin, a division of Penguin Group (USA) Inc.

Duane, Daniel. *Caught Inside: A Surfer's Year on the California Coast.* New York: North Point Press, 1997. Used by permission of Daniel Duane.

Gioia, Dana. "Cruising with the Beach Boys." Copyright 1986 by Dana Gioia. Reprinted from *Daily Horoscope.* Used by permission of Graywolf Press, Saint Paul, Minnesota.

Griswold, Mary Edith. "Three Days Adrift." *Sunset,* June/July 1906.

Hansen, Ron. "My Communist." *Harper's Magazine,* November 2001. Used by permission of Ron Hansen.

Harte, Bret. "San Francisco (From the Sea)." Boston and New York: Houghton Mifflin Company, 1870.

Hass, Robert. "After the Winds." *Time and Materials.* Copyright 2007 by Robert Hass. Used by permission of HarperCollins Publishers.

Jackson, Helen Hunt. *Ramona.* Boston: Little, Brown, and Company, 1884.

Jeffers, Robinson. "November Surf" and "Point Joe." *The Selected Poetry of Robinson Jeffers.* Copyright 1927, 1928, 1938 by Robinson Jeffers, renewed 1955, 1956, 1966. Used by permission of Stanford University Press.

King, Clarence. "Mount Whitney 1871." *Mountaineering in the Sierra Nevada.* New York: Charles Scribner's Sons, 1902.

Lamott, Anne. *Hard Laughter.* Copyright 1979, 1980 by Anne Lamott. Used by permission of North Point Press, a division of Farrar, Straus and Giroux, LLC.

London, Jack. *The Sea Wolf.* New York: Macmillan, 1904.

Manly, William Lewis. *Death Valley in '49.* San Jose: The Pacific Tree and Vine Company, 1894.

McDaniel, Wilma. "Valley Fog," reprinted from *Sister Vayda's Song,* copyright 1982 by Wilma Elizabeth McDaniel. "The Long Wait," reprinted from *A Primer for Buford,* copyright 1990 by Wilma Elizabeth McDaniel. "1939 in California," reprinted from *The Last Dust Storm,* copyright 1995 by Wilma Elizabeth McDaniel. "Watching Truck Drivers at Pancake House," reprinted from *A Primer for Buford,* copyright 1990 by Wilma Elizabeth McDaniel. All used by permission of Hanging Loose Press.

McNeal, Tom. "Winter in Los Angeles." *The Gettysburg Review,* Winter 1995, Vol. 8, Number 1. Used by permission of Tom McNeal.

Miller, Joaquin. "The Gold that Grew by Shasta Town." *The Complete Poetical Works of Joaquin Miller.* San Francisco: The Whitaker and Ray Company, 1902.

Miller, Max. *I Cover the Waterfront.* Copyright 1932 by E. P. Dutton and Company, Inc. Used by permission of Dutton, a division of Penguin Group (USA) Inc.

Mosley, Walter. *Devil in a Blue Dress.* Copyright 1990 by Walter Mosley. Used by permission of W. W. Norton and Company, Inc.

Muir, John. "The Sequoia and General Grant National Parks." *Our National Parks.* Boston and New York: Houghton Mifflin Company, 1901.

Nordhoff, Charles. *California: For Health, Pleasure, and Residence—A Book for Travellers and Settlers.* New York: Harper and Brothers, 1872.

Norris, Frank. *The Octopus.* New York: Doubleday, Page and Company, 1901.

Price, Jenny. "Thirteen Way of Seeing Nature." *Believer,* 2006. *Land of Sunshine: An Environmental History of Metropolitan Los Angeles.* Pittsburgh: University of Pittsburgh Press, 2005. Used by permission of Jenny Price.

Snyder, Gary. "John Muir on Mt. Ritter," "Hay for the Horses, " and "Mid-August at Sourdough Mountain Lookout." *The Gary Snyder Reader.* Copyright 2000 by Gary Snyder. Used by Permission of Counterpoint.

Soto, Gary. "The Elements of San Joaquin." *Gary Soto: New and Selected Poems.* Copyright 1995 by Gary Soto. Used by permission of Chronicle Books LLC, San Francisco. Visit ChronicleBooks.com.

Stegner, Wallace. *Angle of Repose.* Copyright 1971 by Wallace Stegner. Used by permission of Doubleday, a division of Random House, Inc.

Steinbeck, John. *The Grapes of Wrath.* Copyright 1939, renewed 1967 by John Steinbeck. Used by permission of Viking Penguin, a division of Penguin Group (USA) Inc.

Sterling, George. "The Cool, Grey City of Love." Copyright 1920 by George Sterling.

Stevenson, Robert Louis. *The Silverado Squatters.* New York: Charles Scribner's Sons, 1883.

Tan, Amy. *The Joy Luck Club.* Copyright 1989 by Amy Tan. Used by permission of G. P. Putnam's Sons, a division of Penguin Group (USA) Inc.

Twain, Mark. "Early Rising, As Regards Excursions to the Cliff House." *The Golden Era,* July 3, 1864.

Van der Veer, Judy. Selection from *November Grass.* Copyright 1940 by Judy Van der Veer. Estate of Judy Van der Veer.

Wolff, Tobias. "Desert Breakdown, 1968." *Our Story Begins: New and Selected Stories.* Copyright 2008 by Tobias Wolff. Used by permission of Alfred A. Knopf, a division of Random House. Inc.